PHILODEMUS
ON FRANK CRITICISM

SBL

Society of Biblical Literature

TEXTS AND TRANSLATIONS
GRAECO-ROMAN SERIES

edited by
John T. Fitzgerald

Texts and Translations 43
Graeco-Roman 13

PHILODEMUS
ON FRANK CRITICISM

PHILODEMUS

ON FRANK CRITICISM

Introduction, Translation, and Notes

by

David Konstan, Diskin Clay, Clarence E. Glad,
Johan C. Thom, and James Ware

Society of Biblical Literature
Texts and Translations

Scholars Press
Atlanta, Georgia

PHILODEMUS
ON FRANK CRITICISM

Introduction, Translation, and Notes by
David Konstan, Diskin Clay, Clarence E. Glad,
Johan C. Thom, and James Ware

Copyright © 1998 by the Society of Biblical Literature
Published in paperback 2007

Library of Congress Cataloging-in-Publication Data
Philodemus, ca. 110–ca. 40 B. C.
 [De libertate dicendi. English & Greek (Ancient Greek)]
 On frank criticism / Philodemus ; introduction, translation, and notes by
David Konsstan . . . [et al.]
  p. cm.—(Texts and translations ; 43. Graeco-Roman series ; 13)
 Includes bibliographical references (p.) and indexes.
 ISBN 0-7885-0434-7(cloth ; alk. paper)—ISBN 978-1-58983-292-3 (paperback ;
alk. paper)
 1. Parrhesia (The Greek word) 2. Epicureans (Greek philosophy)
I. Konstan, David. II. Title. III. Series: Texts and translations ; no. 43.
IV. Series: Texts and translations. Graeco-Roman religion series ; 13.
B598. P43D413   1998
187—dc21   97-52602
                    CIP

11 10 09 08 07   5 4 3 2

Printed in the United States of America
on acid-free paper

CONTENTS

PREFACE AND ACKNOWLEDGMENTS

The genesis of this book would have pleased Philodemus and his philosophical circle of friends, for it emerged out of the efforts of a group of scholars working in common. In 1993, the Hellenistic Moral Philosophy and Early Christianity Group, which meets annually at the conference of the Society of Biblical Literature, undertook to investigate over a period of three years Philodemus' *On Frank Criticism*, or Περὶ παρρησίας. No published translation of that work existed in English or any other modern language; the last edition of the text was by Alexander Olivieri, published in 1914. Yet Philodemus' essay was of vast importance to an understanding of the relationship between classical culture and early Christianity: it treats techniques of pedagogy and moral improvement within the philosophical community that were to be central concerns of Christian teachers, whether in a congregational or a monastic context. The need for a reliable translation, together with brief commentary and as good a text as possible (short of a new edition based on an autopsy of the papyrus, which for various reasons was not feasible), was apparent to everyone.

It was agreed, then, that a body of some two dozen scholars would prepare an initial translation, dividing the treatise into as many discrete segments. Participants included David L. Balch, Kate Cooper, Troels Engberg-Pedersen, Benjamin Fiore, S.J., John T. Fitzgerald, David E. Fredrickson, Pamela Gordon, Glenn S. Holland, Robert Lamberton, Abraham J. Malherbe, Alan C. Mitchell, Edward N. O'Neil, Frederic M. Schroeder, Alan Scott, David Sider, Gregory E. Sterling, Stanley K. Stowers, Fika J. van Rensburg, L. Michael White, and Richard A. Wright, as well as the present translators. To guide us, we had, in addition to Olivieri's apparatus and a handful of technical articles, a preliminary version composed by James Ware while he was a doctoral candidate at Yale University's Department of Religious Studies. When we reconvened a year later, the several partial translations had been circulated among the entire group, and in the course of a long meeting we discussed and debated many problems that had arisen. In the end, a committee of five, consisting of the present translators, was selected to prepare a full and final version, making use of both Ware's and the collective rendition.

The five translators then made a crucial decision: the text they would present and render would be based essentially on that of Olivieri. Some changes would be introduced, deriving primarily from a detailed review of

Olivieri's edition by R. Philippson, who exploited hand-drawn copies of the papyrus, called *disegni*, made under the supervision of the original excavators of Herculaneum in the 18th century, and from emendations proposed by Marcello Gigante, who re-examined parts of the papyrus that is now housed in the National Library in Naples. On rare occasions, the translators might adopt readings of their own, if they seemed necessary in order to make sense of a given passage. Their text, however, would make no pretense of being a new edition of Philodemus' *On Frank Criticism*. Such an edition would require a completely new inspection of the papyrus that took advantage of modern technological aids such as the binocular microscope. It was understood that Marcello Gigante was planning an edition on this basis. In the interest, however, of making Philodemus' treatise quickly accessible to a wider public, it seemed best to proceed on the basis of the available text.

The translators again divided Philodemus' text into parts, each taking a fifth as his share; they then circulated among themselves the portions on which they had worked, emending and correcting one another's versions. The complete translation was reviewed and revised by David Konstan, who must take final responsibility for what is printed here (he also prepared the indices); James Ware then went over the entire version yet again. Johan Thom set the Greek text, making certain that it agreed with what had been translated, and prepared the whole work—text, notes, translation, and indices—as camera-ready copy, making numerous improvements along the way. In the meantime, Clarence E. Glad was writing the introduction to the book. When the work was in its final stages, the translators benefited from a careful reading of the manuscript by Elizabeth Asmis. Every stage was marked by mutual cooperation and assistance.

John Fitzgerald presided over the colloquium during the period in which the translation was in progress. His goodwill, encouragement, and editorial assistance were invaluable to the enterprise. Many others provided help as the work proceeded; they are hereby acknowledged, albeit anonymously, for their contributions to the joint endeavor. But we must thank Pieter Janse van Rensburg and Annemaré Kotzé by name for their assistance in preparing the final, camera-ready copy.

The several universities at which we worked were generous in supporting our scholarly endeavors, and we hereby render our thanks to them. Some of us benefited as well from grants that were awarded while we were at work on the project: among these institutions, we are pleased to acknowledge the Icelandic Council of Science and the Institute of Theology at the University of Iceland, the Fulbright Foundation, the Guggenheim Foundation, and the National Humanities Center in North Carolina. We are also grateful to the editors of the

Society of Biblical Literature Texts and Translations (Graeco-Roman) Series, for accepting the work for publication.

We commit this work, conscious of the imperfections that must inevitably mark the translation of so fragmentary and difficult a text, to the hands of fellow investigators, in the hope that it will prove useful to their researches, and in the expectation that they will, in turn, correct our errors and contribute to a better understanding of Philodemus' extraordinary treatise.

The translators

ABBREVIATIONS

The abbreviations used for the titles of modern publications follow, where possible, the guidelines of the Society of Biblical Literature as published in the *Journal of Biblical Literature* 107 (1988) 579–96. Abbreviations used for well-known classical texts not listed below are based on *The Oxford Classical Dictionary* (3d ed.; ed. Simon Hornblower and Antony Spawforth; Oxford: Oxford University Press, 1996) xxix–liv.

AJP	*Americal Journal of Philology*
ANRW	*Aufstieg und Niedergang der römischen Welt*
BT	Bibliotheca Teubneriana
CErc	*Cronache ercolanesi*
CP	*Classical Philology*
Epicurus	
SV	*Sententiae Vaticanae*
JECS	*Journal of Early Christian Studies*
LCL	Loeb Classical Library
LSJ	Liddell-Scott-Jones, *Greek-English Lexicon*
LSJSup	Revised Supplement to LSJ (1996)
NovTSup	Supplements to *Novum Testamentum*
Philo	
De agric.	*De agricultura* (*On Husbandry*)
De migr.	*De migratione Abrahami* (*On the Migration of Abraham*)
Quis heres	*Quis rerum divinarum heres* (*Who Is the Heir*)
Philodemus	
Ir.	*De ira* (*On Anger*)
Lib.	*De libertate dicendi* = Περὶ παρρησίας (*On Frank Criticism*)
Mort.	*De morte* (*On Death*)
Oec.	*De oeconomia* (*On Household Management*)
Rh.	*Volumina rhetorica* (ed. S. Sudhaus; 2 vols.; Leipzig: Teubner, 1892–96); cited by volume and page number
Vit.	*De vitiarum* (*On Vices*)
Plutarch	
De liber. educ.	*De liberis educandis* (*On the Education of Children*)
De vit. pudor.	*De vitioso pudore* (*On Compliancy*)
Quomodo adulator	*Quomodo adulator ab amico internoscatur* (*How to Distinguish a Flatterer from a Friend*)
PW	Pauly-Wissowa, *Real-Encyclopädie der classischen Altertumswissenschaft*

INTRODUCTION

I. Philodemus' Life and Works

In the first century BCE, an Epicurean community existed at Naples under the leadership of the Greek teacher Siro. At nearby Herculaneum, the Syrian Epicurean Philodemus, who was associated with the influential patron Calpurnius Piso, the father-in-law of Julius Caesar, was also attracting students from different walks of life. Philodemus was a former pupil of Zeno of Sidon, the scholarch of the Epicurean school in Athens, and of Demetrius the Laconian. What is more, he cultivated interests in literary and philosophical studies, thus escaping the charge traditionally levelled at Epicureans that they entertained a deliberate disregard for general learning; Cicero refers to both Siro and Philodemus as the "excellent and learned friends" of Torquatus.[1]

Philodemus was born in Gadara in Syria c. 110 BCE and died c. 40/35 BCE. He was probably of Greek parentage and received a Greek education. The dates at which the Epicurean schools on the bay of Naples were founded are uncertain, but Philodemus may have arrived in Italy around the year 80 BCE. There is no secure evidence for the school's existence after 50 BCE, although the fact that the Epicurean library at Herculaneum was preserved until the eruption of Mt. Vesuvius in 79 CE strongly suggests that it did not disappear under the early Empire. The evidence shows that the Epicurean schools in Naples and Herculaneum were important intellectual and literary centers in the first century BCE.[2]

Philodemus' scholarly interests are evident from the quantity of charred papyri preserved in the house in Herculaneum that may indeed have been the residence of the Piso family. These consist both of Philodemus' transcripts of the lecture notes he took at Zeno's classes in Athens, for example, his notes *On Frank Criticism* (Περὶ παρρησίας, also known as *De libertate dicendi*),

---

[1] The Epicurean spokesman in Cicero's *De finibus* (*On Ends*) (see 2.119); see also Cic. *Fam.* 15.16.1; 15.19.2; *Acad.* 1.5; *Tusc.* 4.7. Cf. Clarence E. Glad, "Frank Speech, Flattery, and Friendship in Philodemus," in *Friendship, Flattery, and Frankness of Speech: Studies on Friendship in the New Testament World* (ed. John T. Fitzgerald; NovTSup 82; Leiden: Brill, 1996) 21–22.

[2] See E. A. De Lacy and P. H. De Lacy, *Philodemus: On Methods of Inference* (2d ed.; Naples: Bibliopolis, 1978) 145–52.

and of Philodemus' own compositions, including writings on historical matters, on scientific method, on rhetoric, music, and poetry, on theology, including *On Piety* and *On the Gods*, and, finally, on ethics.[3] Among the ethical writings are an introduction to ethics, a treatise in several books *On Death*, and a work in ten books *On Vices and the Opposing Virtues*, which includes one book *On Household Management*, one *On Arrogance*, and probably three books *On Flattery*.[4] Finally, Philodemus wrote an *Epitome on Conduct and Character, from the Lectures of Zeno*, which contains a work *On Anger* and the above-mentioned *On Frank Criticism*.[5]

The handbook Περὶ παρρησίας—the only known work in antiquity with this title—is translated here for the first time into a modern language. It is of great importance for the social history of Epicureanism, as it provides evidence for moral instruction in various Epicurean centers in Greece and Italy. The work offers hypothetical questions and answers on aspects of psychagogic theory as well as reflections on psychagogic practice. A complete description of the treatise is not possible, since the work is not extant in its entirety, but one may gain from the remaining fragments a fairly good picture of later Epicurean psychagogy and communal pedagogy.[6] The kinds of blame that are deployed in the service of moral improvement, and the frequency of terms signifying error and correction, are significant in a work entitled Περὶ παρρησίας, and indicate that παρρησία, when used in the context of moral

---

[3] See Elizabeth Asmis, "Philodemus' Epicureanism," *ANRW* 2.36.4 (1990) 2369–2406. Historical works: PHerc. 1018, *Index Stoicorum*; PHerc. 164 and 1021, *Index Academicorum*; PHerc. 155 and 339, *On the Stoics*; PHerc. 1232, PHerc. 1418 and 310, *On Epicurus*; *Works on the Records of Epicurus and Some Others*; PHerc. 1005, *To Friends of the School*. Work on scientific method: *On Phenomena and Inferences* = PHerc. 1065, on which see De Lacy and De Lacy, *Philodemus*. Works on rhetoric, music, and poetry: *On Rhetoric* and *On Poems* are preserved in numerous papyri; PHerc. 1497, *On Music*; PHerc. 1507, *On the Good King according to Homer*. Theological writings: PHerc. 1428, *On Piety*; PHerc. 26, *On the Gods*; PHerc. 152 and 157, *On the Way of Life of the Gods*.

[4] The untitled introduction to ethics (PHerc. 1251) is known as the *Comparetti Ethics* in honor of its first editor; PHerc. 1050, *On Death*; PHerc. 1424, *On Household Management*; PHerc. 1008, *On Arrogance*; PHerc. 222, 223, 1082, 1089, 1457, and 1675, *On Flattery*. See also PHerc. 346 (ed. M. Capasso, *Trattato etico epicureo (PHerc 346)* [Naples: Giannini, 1982]).

[5] PHerc. 182, *On Anger*; PHerc. 1471, *On Frank Criticism*. Philodemus' work *On Anger* was edited by C. Wilke (*Philodemi de ira liber* [BT; Leipzig: Teubner, 1914]), and has been re-edited, with a translation and commentary, by G. Indelli (*Filodemo, L'Ira* [La scuola di Epicuro 5; Naples: Bibliopolis, 1988]).

[6] See Clarence E. Glad, *Paul and Philodemus: Adaptability in Epicurean and Early Christian Psychagogy* (NovTSup 81; Leiden: Brill, 1995) 101–160; Marcello Gigante, *Ricerche filodemee* (Biblioteca della Parola del Passato 6; 2d ed.; Naples: Macchiaroli, 1983) 55–113.

reform, connotes the frank criticism of error. The most appropriate translation of Περὶ παρρησίας thus appears to be *On Frank Criticism*. Before discussing the treatise itself, however, it is well to situate the concept of frankness of speech in its larger cultural context.

II. The Idea of Frankness in its Cultural Context[7]

In the classical Athenian democracy, the word παρρησία was used in the political sphere to express the right of free speech of anyone who enjoyed full civic status in Athens. In the classical democracy, friendship had been embedded in a powerful ideology of equality and freedom from dependency. On the basis of this civic and democratic ideal, friends were imagined as constituting a network of social equals, bound by personal affection and committed to offering one another mutual assistance; their status was chosen and thus distinct from ascribed statuses, such as kinship and citizenship. In a context in which citizens derived their equality from their participation in a democratic city, the right of free speech pertained to anyone who enjoyed full civic status at Athens. The term παρρησία, accordingly, "represented democracy from the point of view of equality of rights."[8] Παρρησία seems to have had no special association with the idea of friendship at this time, although liberty of speech was naturally taken for granted as a principle obtaining among friends, just as it obtained among fellow-citizens in general, all of whom were equally entitled to express themselves without fear of neighbors or of those in power. From the time of Isocrates onward, however, frankness came increasingly to be perceived rather as a private virtue, and more particularly as an integral element in friendship. The conception of friendship itself, indeed, had undergone a subtle change.

With the rise of the Hellenistic kingdoms and the dependency of Athens upon foreign powers, there was a shift in the political discourse of free speech and, correspondingly, the focus of treatises on friendship underwent a palpable change: "Παρρησία as a private virtue replaced παρρησία as a political right."[9] As a private virtue, παρρησία denoted that personal candor which was

---

[7] For full discussion, see Giuseppe Scarpat, *Parrhesia: Storia del termine e delle sue traduzioni in latino* (Brescia: Paideia, 1964).

[8] Arnaldo Momigliano, "Freedom of Speech in Antiquity," in *Dictionary of the History of Ideas: Studies of Selected Pivotal Ideas* (ed. P. P. Wiener; New York: Charles Scribner's Sons, 1973–74) 2:259.

[9] Ibid, 2:260. For information in this and the following paragraphs, see David Konstan, "Patrons and Friends," *CP* 90 (1995) 333, 334, 336, 341; "Friendship, Frankness and Flattery," in *Friendship, Flattery, and Frankness of Speech: Studies on Friendship in the New Testament World* (ed. John T. Fitzgerald; NovTSup 82; Leiden: Brill, 1996) 9–14; "Greek Friendship," *AJP* 117 (1996) 75, 77–78, 86, 92; "Problems in the History of Christian

prized between true friends, as opposed to the political liberty to declare openly one's opinions in the civic space or assembly. The emphasis on social equality in the discourse of friendship that was characteristic of the popular democracy now gave way to a concern with relations between powerful figures, whether monarchs or wealthy aristocrats, and their retinues, who were conceived of as bound to their patrons by amicable ties. Attention shifted from the theme of equality to such issues as integrity and frankness, and the danger represented by self-seeking flatterers in the entourage of the rich and powerful. As the egalitarian assumptions behind the universal right to self-expression gave way to an ideology centered on rank and authority, it became necessary to insist on παρρησία as a duty incumbent upon friends without regard for rank or station rather than to prize it as a universal mark of citizen status.

The shift in the meaning of παρρησία from freedom of speech to personal candor is coordinate with the change from the egalitarian city-state to a regime of powerful rulers in a position to dispense patronage. With these changes, the figure of the flatterer became a key subject of ideological attention. Flattery was now seen as a corrupt form of participation in the entourage of grandees and emerged as the antithesis of the personal integrity and frankness expected of loyal associates. The central issue in discussions of friendship became trustworthiness among friends, especially on the part of the subordinate partner in the relationship, who was often suspected of employing flattery in the hope of personal gain. Since flatterers could simulate frankness, techniques were devised to detect such imposters and reveal them as false friends and adulators.

Essays by Plutarch and Maximus of Tyre on how to distinguish flatterers from friends reveal this set of concerns in the Roman period, as do treatises dealing with flattery and related vices. In the latter portion of his treatise on how one may distinguish a true friend from a flatterer, Plutarch discusses in detail the topic of frank speech; the reason is that παρρησία is the primary indicator of the candor characteristic of the true friend as opposed to the deceitfulness that marks the toady.

The term παρρησία, then, which in the classical democracy had signified the right of all citizens to express their views unhindered, designated under the Hellenistic monarchies the virtue of frank speech, not only as practiced by a subordinate in conversation with his superior but also as employed by a philosophical teacher seeking to heal the *psyche* of his disciples. In the latter context, where παρρησία was now part of the vocabulary of the Hellenistic philosophical schools, the concern was with frank criticism in relation to in-

---

Friendship," *JECS* 4 (1996) 90–91, 111; more generally, *Friendship in the Classical World* (Cambridge: Cambridge University Press, 1997).

struction, that is, the nurturing or therapeutic use of παρρησία. Disciples required honest and constructive correction: one needed to administer just criticism in a temperate way, avoiding both the excessive harshness that might discourage the moral improvement of the disciple and a lenient indulgence of the aspirant's lax ways.

Where the idea of friendship was adopted as a figure for the relationship among members of a philosophical school, the frankness encouraged between pupils was naturally associated with the language of friendship. On the basis of friendship, a disciple might have the courage to reproach other disciples boldly, being inspired by an unfeigned goodwill to use plain language without spitefulness. Not only is frank speech "akin to friendship," it is the "language of friendship" and the "most potent medicine in friendship,"[10] to be employed in mutual moral reform among friends.

The topic of frank speech is thus integral to the theme of moral education, or the correction of faults among friends to effect an improvement of character. Already in Isocrates, as we have seen, one finds the change in connotation of the word παρρησία from the right of free speech of citizens generally to that of candor between friends in particular, in relation to various other private virtues.[11] A high point in this development is *The Pedagogue* of Clement of Alexandria, who discusses the function of hortatory blame or παρρησία on the part of the Divine Word itself. The treatise *On Frank Criticism*, in which Philodemus discusses frank speech under the topic of how and when frankly to reprimand one's friends' failings, is a valuable instance of this tradition.[12]

III. The Nature of παρρησία in Philodemus' Περὶ παρρησίας

It is abundantly clear in Philodemus' treatise *On Frank Criticism* that the topic of frank criticism in moral reform (περὶ παρρησίας) is part of the topic of friendship (περὶ φιλίας). Members of the group admonish and censure each

---

[10] See Philo *Quis heres* 19, 21; *De migr.* 116–17; and Plutarch *Quomodo adulator* 74D.

[11] Related terms include ἐλέγχω, νουθετέω, ἐξουσία, ἐλευθεροστομέω, θαρρέω, εὐτολμία, and ἀλήθεια. The change in meaning of παρρησία is clear where Isocrates remarks that things which contribute to the education of men in private life include "παρρησία and the privilege which is openly granted to friends to rebuke and to enemies to attack each other's faults" (*Ad Nic.* 3; trans. by G. Norlin in the LCL). Παρρησία is a σημεῖον τῆς εὐνοίας τῆς πρὸς τοὺς φίλους: Isoc. *Antip.* 4; cf. *Demonic.* 1–6, 11–12, 20–31, 45–46; *Ad Nic.* 2, 12, 28, 42–49; *Antid.* 206–14, 289–90; *Nicocles* 55, 57; *De pace* 14–15, 70, 72; *Antip.* 3–4, 7, 9; *Philip.* 72. Note Plato *Prt.* 325AB; *Grg.* 525B; Aristotle *Eth. Nic.* 1155a12–16, 1171a21–1172a15, 1180a6–14; *Eth. Eud.* 1242b35–1243a14, 1243b15–40; *Mag. mor.* 1213b18–30; Xenophon *Oec.* 13.6–9.

[12] Glad, *Paul and Philodemus*, 51–53, 60–62, 106–7.

other in friendship,[13] "… < [for they think that it is the part of a friend to apply frank criticism and to] > admonish others…"; such tasks are expected of those who hold "the office of a friend" (col. XIXb). A forthright attitude toward others is part of this ideal;[14] or, as fr. 28 puts it: "Even if we demonstrate logically that, although many fine things result from friendship, there is nothing so grand as having one to whom one will say what is in one's heart and who will listen when one speaks. For our nature strongly desires to reveal to some people what it thinks."

The treatise *On Frank Criticism* appears together with *On Anger* in a larger work *On Conduct and Characters*.[15] *On Anger* reveals that the Epicurean community of friends had two aims: reform of character and theoretical inquiry. Anger thwarts the progress of people both because they do not share in the good of joint inquiry and because they cannot endure the rebukes or corrections of their teachers and fellow students. Reform of character is requisite for progress in wisdom and requires the correction of errors and passions.[16] The Epicurean ideal of fellowship and mutual aid demanded, accordingly, the active participation of friends in the evaluation and correction of one another, and *On Frank Criticism* is our prime evidence for the nature of that practice.

Frankness is conceived in the treatise as the opposite pole of the vice of flattery. The virtue that Philodemus contrasts with flattery, however, is not so much frank speech as such but rather friendship.[17] Philodemus' discussion of flattery and friendship draws on Aristotle's understanding of virtue as a mean between two vices: friendship, accordingly, is the mean between flattery and enmity.[18] Just as frank speech is a *sine qua non* of friendship, so ready assent,

---

[13] See Tab. V (App.): "[he] wishes [to admonish on] account of [friendship]…." Cf. Philodemus *Ir.* col. XXXV.19 Indelli.

[14] Glad, *Paul and Philodemus*, 107–8, 161–75.

[15] The subscript of PHerc. 1471 is: Φιλοδήμου τῶν κατ᾿ ἐπιτομὴν ἐξειργασμένων περὶ ἠθῶν καὶ βίων ἐκ τῶν Ζήνωνο[ς σχο]λῶν … ὅ ἐστι περὶ παρρησίας. Note the reference to ἐκ τῶν Ζήνωνος σχολῶν in PHerc. 1389 (cf. E. Kondo, "Per l'interpretazione del pensiero filodemeo sulla adulazione nel P. Herc. 1457," *CErc* 4 [1974] 45). *On Frank Criticism* is cited as the περὶ παρρησίας λόγος in *Ir.* col. XXXVI.24–25 Indelli. See the reference to περὶ παρρησίας πραγματεία in PHerc. 1082 col. I.1–7 (W. Crönert, *Kolotes und Menedemos* [Leipzig, 1906; reprint, Amsterdam: Hakkert, 1965] 127 n. 534) and τὸ τάγμα τῆς παρρησίας in *Lib.* col. XIIIb.4 and *Rh.* 2:1. Wilke proposed in his edition (*De ira*, vii) that *On Anger* belonged to the same epitome of Zeno's work as Περὶ παρρησίας.

[16] Philodemus *Ir.* col. XIX.14–27 Indelli; *Lib.* frs. 13.7–8; 22; col. XIVb.9–11.

[17] Contra R. Philippson ("Philodemos," PW 19.2 [1938] 2460, 2467–74) who maintained that frank speech was a virtue opposed to the vice of flattery. So Gigante, *Ricerche filodemee*, 59–62.

[18] Illustrated by PHerc. 1082 which deals with flattery (cf. col. II.1–4: φιλία … ἧς ἀντίπαλός ἐστιν ἡ κολακεία). Cf. Aristotle *Mag. mor.* 1193a20ff.; *Eth. Eud.* 1233b30ff.

speaking in order to please, and praise are characteristics of flattery. Whatever the relation between Philodemus' classification of frank speech in light of earlier discussions of friendship, however, it is clear that frankness, flattery, and friendship constituted a distinct triad in his thought,[19] as it did in Hellenistic discourse generally.[20] PHerc. 1082 is pertinent here:

> Let us make it clear to them that the goods of friendship are very durable and that flattery is the antagonist of friendship; let us also consider well the goods that arise from frank speech, both (the frank speech) directed towards one's intimate associates, and (the frank speech) directed towards all men, and let us avoid as vain the company of adulators, and still more let us not mix with them but seek cohabitation with those who speak candidly.[21]

The admonition encouraging readers to seek to live with those who speak freely and avoid those who flatter continues the contrast between flattery and honest conversation at the beginning of the section. For the Epicureans, conversation and reasoning together are indispensable.[22] Παρρησία is a type of ὁμιλία, intimately connected with friendship, though it is classified neither as an art nor as a virtue; rather, frank speech is an approximate or conjectural method used by friends in the therapeutic technique for the healing of souls, comparable to the methods employed by physicians in the art of healing and by pilots in the art of navigation.

In Philodemus' view, παρρησία has two aspects, one directed "toward all men" and the other "toward one's intimate associates" (PHerc. 1082 col. II.1–3). There is a good example of the former aspect in Lucian's essay, *Alexander the False Prophet*, in which Lucian assumes the role of a rational Epicurean who, together with Christians, attempts to deflate the false prophet Alexander of Abonouteichos and his claim to a special standing with the divine.[23] Frank speech was a weapon in the Epicureans' agitation against oracle-mongers and in their program of enlightening people generally concerning the workings of the universe, with a view to combatting the fear of death associated with certain kinds of beliefs concerning the gods. The latter, or more intimate, aspect of frank speech served more particularly to form character and to counter psychological disturbances and fears of other people. Such fears, like

---

[19] Glad, "Frank Speech."

[20] Konstan, "Friendship, Frankness and Flattery."

[21] PHerc. 1082 col. II.1–14. Cf. T. Gargiulo, "PHerc. 222: Filodemo Sull' adulazione," *CErc* 11 (1981) 104.

[22] I.e., ὁμιλία, κοινολογίαι, συλλογίζεσθαι, and συζήτησις. For συζητητικὸς τρόπος as a pedagogical technique, see Epicurus *SV* 74 and Philodemus *Ir.* col. XIX.25–26 Indelli; *Lib.* frs. 43, 53. Cf. F. Amoroso, "Filodemo Sulla conversazione," *CErc* 5 (1975) 63–76.

[23] Lucian *Alex.* 17, 25, 61. Cf. Epicurus *SV* 29.

the fear of the gods, of the unpredictability of the universe, and of death, were counted among the anxieties that destroy human happiness.

Philodemus' *On Frank Criticism* discloses a form of psychagogy that depends upon the active participation of all members of the community in the correction of one another. Thus, frankness is not only a pedagogical strategy on the part of the teacher, but also involves openness and the revelation of personal faults among both fellow-students and leaders for the sake of the moral development of the disciples. The teacher himself may also stand in need of criticism on occasion. Frankness, then, includes both the practice of balanced criticism as undertaken by the sage and the disclosure of private sentiments for the purpose of correction.

The Epicurean friends are encouraged not to conceal their faults but to confess them and bring them out into the open for criticism and mutual correction. "Confessional practice" is a somewhat anachronistic expression but it describes this activity well. Some of the fragments refer to the reporting of errors and indeed of spying, as well as the reluctance of some members to be forthcoming about themselves. Problems connected with communal living and the conditions of collective life, together with the focus on moral therapy through mutual criticism, may in part explain the preoccupation with openness or self-disclosure and the contrary danger of concealment. But the frankness and candor clearly served, in the first instance, a therapeutic purpose: self-disclosure was a means towards correction and improvement, as well as a barrier to dissension within the group.

IV. Form and Structure of *On Frank Criticism*

The treatise *On Frank Criticism* is "an epitome from the lectures of Zeno" in Athens which Philodemus attended.[24] The treatise survives in 93 fragments and 24 columns, labelled a and b for top and bottom of the papyrus sheet (the roll is broken in the middle), and an appendix which includes those dissociated scraps of papyrus that Olivieri did not manage to integrate into his Teubner edition of 1914. Olivieri associated these scraps with some of the 21 Tabulae into which the papyrus was divided when it was first opened in 1808. They are often so unyielding that we have not translated every possible word. Fifteen fragments or parts of fragments and columns are underlined in the papyrus, twelve of which are italicized in the translation. These twelve are section head-

---

[24] Cf. col. VIIb, "It is hard work for those who are handling {a topic} by way of an epitome to be precise about every kind, in the manner of those who dispose of each {kind} exhaustively, < [for example in what] > way a wise man will be disposed when some are practicing frankness..."

ings,[25] and indicate a change of subject matter. The following subtitles occur in the treatise as we have it, or as the text may plausibly be supplemented:

1) Fr. 53: "Whether they will declare things of their own and of one another to their fellow-students."
2) Fr. 56: "[Whether it seems to us that one will slip up in accord with] the [perfection] of reason [by means of what is preconceived.]"
3) Fr. 67: "Whether he will also speak frankly to those who do not endure frank criticism, and to one who is [irascible]..."
4) Fr. 70: "How will he handle those who have become angry toward him because of his frank criticism?"
5) Fr. 74: "Whether he is well-disposed toward us; whether he is intense in his goodwill; whether he has jettisoned some of the things charged against him, even if not perfected in everything; whether toward us and toward [others] [he will be] thankful..."
6) Fr. 81 (=83 N): "Whether a wise man will communicate his own {errors} to his friends with frankness."
7) Fr. 88 (=94 N): "How will we recognize the one who has endured frank criticism graciously and the one who is pretending {to do so}?"
8) Col. Ia: "...[to distinguish] one who is frank from a polite disposition and one who is so from a vulgar one."
9) Col. XXa: "...how, [when they recognize] that some of their number are more intelligent, and in particular that some of them are teachers, do they not abide frank criticism?"
10) Col. XXIb: "[Why does womankind not accept frank criticism with pleasure?]"
11) Col. XXIIb: "Why is it that, when other things are equal, those who are illustrious both in resources and reputations abide {frank criticism} less well {than others}?"
12) Col. XXIVa: "Why is it that old men are more annoyed {by frankness}?"

These headings highlight some of the main topics discussed in the work. Other fragments also appear to allude to topics for discussion, for example, the statement in fr. 3, "Both about never giving up nor treating everything [when] applying frank criticism we have pretty much spoken, as well as about ill repute in the eyes of the public and about separation from one's family." The themes of ill repute in the eyes of the public and that of separation from one's family members, which doubtless were issues of concern to Epicureans in Italy, are not dealt with explicitly anywhere in the extant treatise but were evidently discussed in Zeno's lectures as well as among the Epicureans in Naples. The issues of not giving up or of not dealing with everything when applying frank criticism occur throughout the fragments, especially in frs. 62–67, 78 (=80 N), 79 (=81 N), and 85 (=89 N) (cf. fr. 11). Fr. 5 also appears to allude to a

---

[25] The remaining three underlined fragments (fr. 5.6; cols. IIIa.3–5, XIXa.6–8) do not appear to indicate section headings, and are not treated as such in the translation.

topic heading: "And from what has been said it is possible to [take up] also {the question of} how one who [vehemently] resists frankness must behave with respect to frankness." This subject is dealt with intermittently in frs. 6–33 as well as in frs. 67–73. Although the first section heading does not occur until fr. 53, the first fifty-two fragments are clearly related thematically to the rest of the treatise.

Upper and lower parts of columns (distinguished as a and b) do not always show an immediate thematic connection, nor is there always an obvious relation between successive columns. The same is true of the fragments. Some of the fragments are so obscure that it is not clear how they relate thematically to surrounding fragments. All of this may suggest that the present order of fragments and columns is at least in part incorrect, and creates problems for any attempt to gain an overview of the treatise as a whole. Important themes, however, seem to be dispersed throughout the treatise, for example, the appropriate use of frankness in view of different types of students. In general, it is safe to say that there are four major foci of the epitome: first, the teachers' disposition and character; second, the teachers' methods and execution of the task at hand; third, the different types of students and the best way to deal with each; and, fourth, the relationship between the students themselves and their teachers as well as relations among the teachers.

Thus, even though the whole work is not extant, a fairly full picture may be gained of communal practices as evidenced in the surviving fragments by focusing on questions which the treatise itself raises, questions that are faced by any practitioner in the "art of moral guidance."[26] Also, we may better understand the type of psychagogy exemplified in the treatise by attending to the analogy between the conjectural art of frank criticism and medical practice, which illuminates certain features in the methods and procedures of the "moral physician," and reveals presuppositions concerning the nature of the pupils' sickness. Finally, we may acquire a better sense of Epicurean moral guidance through a topical analysis of the fragments, and by concentrating on how the friends within the community collaborate in the project of moral development.

V. A Thematic Overview

Throughout the epitome, the focus is on the teachers and their methods, and on different types of students and their reactions to frank criticism. Particular emphasis falls on the participation of all in a process of mutual evaluation and correction. Four aspects of Epicurean correctional practice are evident: first,

---

[26] Cf. De Lacy and De Lacy, *Philodemus*, 201 n. 64.

self-correction; second, correction administered by others; third, members reporting errors to teachers to be corrected; and finally, the wise correcting one another. Self-disclosure between fellow-students and the wise is consistently encouraged.

The treatise also examines the different types of teachers and their personal dispositions, as well as the methods or ways of applying frank criticism appropriately in view of the various types of students. The teachers, for example, must learn to recognize the different types, never to give up, and not to treat everything. The teacher's own intellectual acumen and moral disposition come under inspection, as in the distinction between those who have a polite or a coarse character, those who are envious toward others, those who can not abide frank criticism, gentle teachers, those who err, and how teachers fail or succeed in applying frank criticism appropriately.

Similarly, there are different types of students, with their several dispositions, for example, those who accept frank criticism graciously, those who cannot tolerate it, those who pretend to endure it, those who vehemently resist it, and those who respond with bitterness or become alienated intellectually when criticized. There are references to strong students, weak ones, tender ones, confused ones, those who are either too shy or too intense, sociable ones, the recalcitrant, the passionate, the obdurate, those who are puffed up or disobedient, the irascible, the incurable, those difficult to cure, pretentious ones, and those of a lesser intellectual ability. We also find reference to students who are well-disposed towards the instructors, earnest in their goodwill, and thankful, those who are improving, and those who have received different kinds of upbringing.

The epitome *On Frank Criticism* further reveals a dispute among Epicureans over methods of correcting disciples in the process of moral reform within the school. This debate centered on the appropriateness of harsh treatment in the cure of moral ills and the adaptation of frank speech to different recipients.[27] Philodemus has a positive view of the human condition and the possibility of improvement. All make progress, but some have matured more than others. He rejects an inconsiderate and abusive approach to moral ills, advocating rather a gentle kind of treatment. One should not revile, scorn, or treat those who err spitefully, but should rather sympathize with them; their natural weakness should be pitied and forgiven, and the teacher should apply frank speech opportunely and cheerfully in order to increase the goodwill

---

[27] Cf. fr. 8, "...<[therefore]> the person to whom he has become devoted is sociable [and he] touches upon this one in accord with his character"; col. XIIb, "...he will make it clear to them that he is bearing with them in an accommodating way." Cf. frs. 20, 25, 31, 37, 46, 79; cols. XIIa, XXIIb.2-4.

between him and those who are being prepared. If the young are ridiculed or inopportunely reproved, they become downcast, accept criticism badly, and cannot endure to listen to the teacher with goodwill. Excessive harshness may cause students to disassociate themselves, psychologically or physically, from the community.

In the context of this debate, students of two distinct general dispositions are mentioned, the "weak," obedient ones and those who are "strong" or disobedient.[28] The former are also referred to as those who are insecure in their new philosophic way of life or those who shun philosophy, whereas the latter are the stubborn or recalcitrant pupils, who cannot tolerate frank criticism on the part of others or violently resist frank speech; they are also called irascible, incurable, and difficult to cure. Philodemus also refers to members of the community as "those in preparation" or the "young," though the "young" are beginning students of philosophy generally, irrespective of their age.[29] He refers to the same group as students[30] or fellow-students,[31] neighbors,[32] disciples,[33] laymen,[34] children,[35] companions[36] or friends.[37] Sometimes, the pupils are simply referred to as "some" (sc., of the friends).[38] Each of these types needs a specific kind of treatment. The ability of the young, whatever their disposition, to bear the frank speech of the sage is a major concern of the handbook.

Besides discussing different types of pupils and the effect frank criticism has on them, Philodemus considers in the last three section headings negative reactions towards frank criticism on the part of persons of different social standing, gender, and age. Those particularly resentful of frank criticism include illustrious people (cols. XXIIb.10–XXIVa.7),[39] women (cols. XXIb.12–

---

[28] Philodemus refers to the former as ἀπαλοί and the latter as ἰσχυροί. See frs. 5.4–8; 7.2–3, 6; 10.9; 31.1–8; 36.4–9; 45.7–11; 65.9–11; 67.9–12; 70.7–9; cols. XIIb.5–6, XIIIa.12–13, XXa.1–5.

[29] Frs. 31.2, 36.5, 52.4–5, 71.8, 83.8; cols. VIa.6–7, XVIa.10.

[30] Οr κατασκευαζόμενοι. See fr. 55.3–4; also frs. 2.3, 25.6–7, 71.7–8, 76.3–4; col. XIIb.7.

[31] Συσχολάζοντες (frs. 75.4–5, 79.3) or συγκατασκευαζόμενοι (fr. 53.4, 7–8).

[32] Οr οἱ πέλας. Cf. fr. 61.3; Epicurus *SV* 67; PHerc. 1457 col. X.

[33] Μαθηταί (fr. 87.4).

[34] Οr ἰδιῶται. Cf. col. XIb.1–2. See also PHerc. 222, col. IV.6–7; Philodemus *Oec.* col. IX.14–16; *Mort.* cols. XXIII.9, XXXI.12, XXXV.28.

[35] *Lib.* fr. 18.1; col. XXIVb.10; *Vit.* col. VIII.15 Jensen.

[36] Οr οἱ συνήθεις. Cf. *Lib.* frs. 42.7, 52.12, 54.11.

[37] Ibid, frs. 8.10; 41.7; 50.8; 55.7; 70.5; 81.3, 8; 84.2; col. XIIIa.10.

[38] Frs. 61, 70.8; cols. XIIIa.10, XIXa.11, XIXb.11–12.

[39] Col. XXIIb, "Why is it that, when other things are equal, those who are illustrious both in resources and reputations abide {frank criticism} less well {than others}?" Cf. cols. VIIa, XIVa, and the reference to "great people" in fr. 22. In col. VIIa.8–12, Philodemus

XXIIb.9),[40] and old men (cols. XXIVa.7–XXIVb.12).[41] In the case of women, part of the problem is their greater psychological insecurity. Women believe that the "weakness of their [nature]" should be pitied and impute impure motives to those who admonish them, believing that they are being reproved out of contempt. They also feel disgraced by reproach, since they are "too impulsive and too vain and too fond of their [reputation]..." (cols. XXIIa–b). The illustrious too believe that they are criticized out of impure motives, or out of envy or hate, because of their good fortune. They have become accustomed "to being conversed with graciously by everyone" (cols. XXIIb–XXIVa). In the case of old men, it is noted that they tend to think they are more intelligent because of their age, and that they should be honored on account of it; they also think that some people criticize them "out of contempt for their weakness" (cols. XXIVa–b).

Philodemus is, however, primarily concerned with the effect frank speech has on pupils of different characters or dispositions. The first nine topic headings and the first fifty-two fragments all deal with this issue in one form or another. Thus, the opening fragments deal with the instruction of neophytes and their disposition, with the instructor's way of approaching them, and with the relationship between the two. The emphasis falls immediately on the method of criticism and its use in relation to different types of students, a topic that will recur throughout the treatise.[42] The question raised in fr. 5 of how to behave toward one who vehemently resists frankness receives extensive treatment from fr. 6 onward.

The teacher will indeed be frank with the one who has erred "and even with him who responds with [bitter]ness," but he reproaches "in moderation" (fr. 6). In view of the different types of students, he is careful and flexible, treating each appropriately by utilizing whatever means are at his disposal.

---

explains that both those who are prominent and the common people must be admonished as the individual case demands.

[40] Col. XXIb, "[Why does womankind not accept frank criticism with pleasure?]" Philodemus emphasizes that as the teachers in the community differ, so do the students: "just as a lad differs from a woman and old men will differ from <[women]> and youngsters alike" (col. VIa.4–8).

[41] Col. XXIVa: "Why is it that old men are more annoyed {by frankness}?" Cf. also cols. VIIa.2–3, XXIVb.

[42] Fr. 1 refers to the wise man's and philosopher's method by comparing it to a conjectural art (cf. fr. 57). Fr. 2 continues to speak of the wise and the fact that their "{frank criticism} should be administered appropriately" but focuses also on his disposition and the fact that the wise man "is not [angrily disposed] toward those being instructed." Fr. 4 alludes to those "benefactors" who "have done a service for the wise man out of reverence" and, possibly, the sages' concern for the well-being of such benefactors.

The teacher "touches upon" a "sociable" person "in accord with his character" (fr. 8) and may ascribe errors to others and even to himself as a heuristic
device (fr. 9). He can use a mixed form of frankness involving praise and
blame, or a simple form using blame alone (frs. 7.9–11; 14–15), "believing
that it must be risked [if] otherwise they {the students} do not pay heed" (fr.
10). Towards those "stronger than the tender ones and those somewhat more
in need of treatment," the teacher intensifies his frankness and "will employ
the harsh form of frankness" (fr. 7). The teacher will criticize "exceedingly
strong" students "with all passion and <[blame]..." (fr. 10). He will not give
up on the recalcitrant students but will persevere, saying to them "again <and
again, 'you are doing [wrong]'... >" (fr. 11; cf. fr. 3).

If the teacher does not adapt his methods in view of different types of students, they may become disheartened and the teacher's labor will possibly be
in vain. "And surely he will always fashion his words without anger <[so as]
not [to wrong] [further?] those who are treated roughly [by him]>" (fr. 12;
cf. fr. 2); but if a recalcitrant person maligns someone, the teacher will
censure him, albeit carefully, since "the one [who talks back] does not say
[sound things]" and may become "alienated intellectually" (fr. 13).[43] A
"vehement person" thus needs appropriate treatment, "but it is not possible [to
see] the individual character even of the well disposed [if they are concealed]"
(fr. 14). This is the first reference to the issues of openness and concealment,
which will be discussed in detail in frs. 39–42, 47–49, and 53–55.

Frs. 16–18 allude to the problem of putting up with harsher forms of
frankness and to instances in which the wise are slandered, a theme that is related to the issue of the negative response of students toward frank criticism
that has been in view from fr. 5 onwards. Frs. 19–22 further characterize the
recalcitrant and "base person" and refer as well to maledictions and insults,
and to the teacher's harsh response to the foolish student. We encounter also
the warning that one should admonish or treat disciples with "[moderate]
words" and advice, this in reference to a "pardon meted out for the things in
which they slipped up" (fr. 20). The mention of "individual traits" of "great
people" (fr. 22) indicates that sensitivity was required on the teacher's part in
respect to students of different social standing, along with the necessity of
adapting his method of instruction accordingly. These fragments, then, have
focused on the different types of students and the appropriate ways of addressing their specific needs and reactions.

Although some of the fragments that follow are particularly lacunose, they
seem still to focus on pedagogical method. Fr. 23 may refer to play-acting on

---

[43] Fr. 27 refers to a "spirit" which has "[not] been alienated in [the process of frank criticism]."

the part of the teacher; it is again noted that the teacher has to deal with different kinds of students, for example, evil people he chances to encounter. Fr. 25 focuses on negative responses, asking "how, through frankness, we shall heighten the good will towards ourselves of those who are being instructed by the very fact of speaking frankly" (cf. frs. 31, 74). Just as the students are to visualize their errors (frs. 42, 77 [=78 N]), so too the teachers are to form an image of which method may be most effective: "Let us set before our eyes also the difference that exists between a caring admonishment and an irony that pleases but pretty much stings everyone" (fr. 26).

Fr. 28 emphasizes the intimate relationship that exists among the Epicurean friends. Fr. 29 is obscure, but fr. 30 seems to focus on the student who is still dependent on "external things" and "pays less attention to his own injury"; such a person is "vexed at other things and in particular [suffers at the reproaches]...." Fr. 31 refers to "young men" who are "...very irritated] whenever [they are going to be reproached]..."; these "[accept] with annoyance what is said in frankness" and "cannot possibly endure [to listen] to [a teacher?] with goodwill" (frs. 25, 74). Fr. 32 appears to focus on some of the teachers, who "[proceed] {gradually} to admonishment ... just as others have seemed to heal suddenly, and contrary to [all expectation]." It also refers to the benefits received from frank criticism as a step in the students' progress (fr. 33).

Frs. 5-33 have collectively attended to the need on the part of teachers to administer their frank criticism appropriately in view of different types of students, particularly those who respond negatively to criticism. Frs. 34-52 give a more detailed account of the tension-filled social reality of a community of friends of inferior and superior station frankly criticizing each other in the reciprocal endeavor to be "saved by one another." Philodemus recognizes that differences in social status complicate the task of the teacher: a humble Greek instructing a powerful Roman aristocrat may pose ticklish problems in a hierarchical society. Although Philodemus contents himself with offering some practical advice on how to treat students of high station (e.g., cols. IVb, Xa, XIVa), the problem surfaces in various parts of the epitome (frs. 22, 36, 44-47; cols. VIIa, XXIIb.10-XXIVa.7). The superior disciples should "endure admonishment graciously" and should at times, although it is acknowledged to be difficult, obey those who are "too young in condition" (fr. 36). Despite the fact that students themselves, and possibly teachers and students alike, are made subject to one another in turns, "the encompassing and most important thing is" that they all "obey Epicurus, according to whom [they] have chosen to live..." (fr. 45).

Occasionally, Philodemus speaks of the wise as "perfect," in contrast to one who fails to understand, or who is senseless or ignorant. Nevertheless, the wise can still progress in their use of frankness and in their attitude toward others (fr. 2), and may themselves have to be corrected. The wise should thus not hate those who commit pardonable mistakes, "for how is he going to hate the one who errs, though not desperately, when he knows that he himself is not perfect and rem[inds {himself} that everyone is accustomed to err?]" (fr. 46). Goodwill and respect for others should govern the relationship between students and their leaders. One ought not to be "[frank in a haughty] and [contentious way], nor to [say any insolent] and contemptuous or disparaging things" (fr. 37), nor should one remind others of their errors in anger (fr. 38; cf. fr. 2).

In this tightly-knit social network of mutual correction, self-disclosure is paramount (frs. 14, 39-42, 47-49, 53-55); "to act in secret is necessarily most unfriendly" (fr. 41). The section heading in fr. 53, the first of twelve to occur henceforward in the fragments and columns, expands on the topic of self-disclosure: "Whether they will declare things of their own and of one another to their fellow-students?" This topic draws attention to an important dimension of Epicurean communal psychagogy. Apparently, not only was self-disclosure expected of the students but also the reporting of the errors of others to their fellow-students for correction (frs. 50-52, 76, 77 N). This should not only be done on a one-to-one basis but also in public, "in the presence of the students" (fr. 55; cf. also fr. 61).

A new section heading in fr. 56, "...[Whether it seems to us that one will slip up in accord with] the [perfection] of reason [by means of what is preconceived]" directs attention to the teachers, their intellectual acumen and moral disposition. Although it is questionable whether the wise can fail with regard to the perfection of reason and prudence, apparently they can become angry (fr. 58; cf. 2, 38, 87 [=92 N]) and fail in their application of frank criticism (frs. 57, 62-65). The possible failure of the wise in their use of frank speech is approached by way of an explication of how frank criticism is administered in various cases, and illustrated by medical imagery which becomes pronounced in this (frs. 56-66) and the following section (frs. 67-70).

As the epitome continues to explicate the way in which the wise may apply frank criticism appropriately, different types of students figure again into the discussion. Sometimes the students accuse the wise of being angry, and sometimes they shun philosophy and hate the wise and do not benefit from frank criticism, although they submit to it, because they are either weak or incurable (fr. 59; cf. fr. 70). Some are passionate or obdurate and disobedient and can deteriorate from a better to a worse condition (frs. 58, 65-67). This enumeration of various types of students who respond differently to frank criticism (cf. frs. 5-33) leads naturally to the third topic, introduced in fr. 67: "Whether he will also speak frankly to those who do not endure frank criticism, and to one who is [irascible]..." (cf. fr. 3). This question is indirectly answered in frs.

67-70 by describing the subtle nature of the artistry of moral guidance, with reference to the practice of doctors "who treat also one who is reasonably believed that he is not going to recover from his disease..." (fr. 69).

The forth topic is introduced in fr. 70—"How will he handle those who have become angry toward him because of his frank criticism?"—and develops further the reaction of students towards the teacher's frank criticism (frs. 71–73; cf. frs. 5, 67). In the face of the students' anger, the teacher "will endure what confronts {him} moderately and not as something groundless," knowing that they were previously ashamed when admonished (fr. 71; cf. fr. 20).

The fifth topic heading in fr. 74 presents a series of questions regarding the disciple: "whether he is well-disposed toward us; whether he is intense in his goodwill; whether he has jettisoned some of the things charged against him, even if not perfected in everything, whether toward us and toward [others] he will be [thankful]..." (cf. fr. 4). These questions are not fully dealt with in frs. 75–80 (=82 N) before the next topic is broached (fr. 81 [=83 N]). Some of the topics, though, are touched on in subsequent fragments; others, for example, the issue of goodwill and gratitude and that of the students' progress, have already been discussed in frs. 1–52. Teachers are not the only ones who administer reproaches; students are both to report the errors of their fellow-students and to present themselves for correction to other students.[44]

If fr. 76 has the teachers in view, it presents intriguing evidence for mutual psychagogy. The teachers hold up before the eyes of the students both their own errors and those of others. The practice is that of visualizing errors, of "putting mistakes in front of the eyes" of those at fault in order to facilitate their improvement (cf. frs. 26, 42). In addition to registering disapproval of excessive harshness and a caution against the desire to harm others, frs. 77 (=80 N), 78 (=80 N) and 79 (=81 N) contain some sharp warnings for the practitioners of moral guidance, whether teachers or fellow-students. People should not be reproached for everything, nor ought one to criticize "continually, nor against everyone, nor every chance error, nor {errors} of those whom one should not {criticize} when they are present, nor with merriment, but rather [to take up the errors] sympathetically [and not to] scorn [or insult] on..." (fr. 79 [=81 N]; cf. fr. 3).[45] Fr. 80 (=82 N) differentiates

---

[44] Cf. frs. 76, 77 N, and 79 (=81 N). Note fr. 75, "...that the reproaches occur, but not those {administered} by the teachers. Their fellow-students know the multitude of good things that we have and they too present themselves for correction < [humbly] > ..."; fr. 77 N, "...< [sometimes to report none] of the [incomparable] things..."; fr. 76, "to whom {i.e., their teachers} those who are being instructed will set forth their own errors with frankness, and will [propose for consideration] those of [others] as well...." Cf. frs. 41, 50-52.

[45] Fr. 77 (=78 N), "But to no one {of the students} is an equal error to be ascribed by those who are saving {them}, or at all events one of those that are < healable > through ad-

between those "favorably disposed" towards the teachers and those who are not. The fragment also advises that one honor those who "scrutinize one," presumably because one has profitted on account of the teachers' love and goodwill; the students are obliged to show their teachers goodwill.[46]

The sixth section heading focuses exclusively on the wise, asking "whether a wise man will communicate his own {errors} to his friends with frankness" (fr. 81 [=83 N]). The wise will disclose their errors but presumably only to those who are suited to know them.[47] Such forthrightness will benefit both the wise and others and should be practiced in an appropriate manner and not, for example, in a spirit of showing off (fr. 81 [=83 N]).[48] When the wise err like "young people," they should be "whipped," that is, reprimanded (fr. 83 [=86 N]). The next fragment picks up the issue of chastising the recalcitrant by drawing an analogy between the practice of the instructor and colt-tamers; "the [wise man], being a person-tamer, [probes] the disobedience of a young man who is [arrogant]" (fr. 87 N). A wise person will, "in the presence of many friends ... practice a [very tentative] frankness" (fr. 84 [=88 N]); it is not clear whether this statement is a response to the question raised in fr. 81 (=83 N) of whether the wise will disclose his errors to his friends. If so, the fragment indicates that when a wise man corrects the mistakes of another, he will be careful of the context.

References to students who have been "unexamined earlier," "disregarded as untreatable" and finally "recognized" and "restored fully," to "one who is ashamed" and addressed frankly again and again, to the "very shameful conditions" of some, and to "those who have no passion to be treated" (frs. 84 [=88 N], 84 [=89 N], 86 [=90 N]) all give evidence of the regular evaluation of a diverse body of individuals. The last fragments of this section contain reflections on the teachers' characters and the question of moral guidance. The

---

monishment < and [setting right], not of those to be [avoided] for their magnitude, but rather remit it in regard to peers [and] acquaintances>"; fr. 78 (=80 N), "...but {to reproach a student} for everything, without circumscribing {it}, is unfriendly to {his} security and a foolish harshness.... It is necessary, however, that this one {the student} be strongly guarded both from wishing to harm and from [seeming to be] stripped {of}>..."

[46] Fr. 80 (=82 N), "...{that they} differ from them, both in bearing a resemblance to the teachers, and further in being favorably disposed toward us, one must bear < [politely each time]> those who have scrutinized {one}. For these {the students} have profitted unhesitatingly on account of their {the teachers'} love, and practically on account of their [goodwill]."

[47] Fr. 84 N, "not to all, but to some"; fr. 82 (=85 N), "not in the presence of all."

[48] Fr. 84 N, "...< the wise man will [not consider that he is speaking] to [someone incurable]..."; fr. 82 (=85 N), "he is confident that he will do a service. < Therefore the one whom he [did not think worthy] of the attempt...>"

teachers who are "extremely cheerful and friendly [and] gentle" will "speak frankly again and again" regarding some things (fr. 85 [=89 N]); they try "persistently [to] tame people into love for themselves, [subt]ly helping [through] doctors even those who have no passion to be treated" (fr. 86 [=90 N]); when the teacher is "{...responding to an error or reproach that is} bearable and expected to cease, he will not be angry with an anger that hates, but rather with one that blames foolishness..." (87 [=92 N]; cf. frs. 2, 38, 58), and he approaches people with "moderate reminders" (fr. 93 N; cf. fr. 6).

The seventh section heading, "How will we recognize the one who has endured frank criticism graciously and the one who is pretending {to do so}?" (fr. 88 [=94 N]; cf. col. XVIIIa), signals some of the social pressures faced by the pupils and underscores the perceptiveness required of one who dispenses moral succor. The issue raised in the eighth section heading, "...[to distinguish] one who is frank from a polite disposition and one who is so from a vulgar one" (col. Ia), relates to an apparent problem involving the teacher's own nature in respect to the art of moral guidance. One who administers frank criticism should be morally advanced; he should be of a "polite disposition" and not of a base one. An analysis of character follows in cols. Ia–XXIb (cf. col. XXa). The initial columns examine in detail the disposition of the ideal psychagogue and its contrary (cols. Ib–IIb). Then the differences in the miens of the teachers are noted (cols. IIIa–b), as well as their approaches to different types of students, for example, the confused, one who is weakened or puffed up, or too shy or too intense, or those students who have had different kinds of upbringing (cols. IVa–b). The following fragments consider how various students employ frank criticism and progressively master the technique (cols. Va–b). Cols. VIa–VIIb again pick up the theme of different approaches on the part of the teachers toward different types of students.

With col. VIIa the focus shifts to mutual frankness among the wise, both in private and in public (cf. fr. 81 [=83 N]). Cols. VIIIa–XIa recognize that the wise may "reason falsely" and err and be themselves in need of correction (cf. frs. 56–58, col. IXb). In cols. XIb–XIVb, the relationship between those being instructed, whether laymen or more advanced individuals, and the wise comes to the fore; sometimes the wise man will not tolerate much frankness on the part of those who are to be instructed by him, and on other occasions he will (cf. cols. XIIb and XIIIb). Cols. XVa–XXb continue to focus on those being instructed and the relationship between them and their instructors. Two groups of people emerge in the discussion: those in need of advice and those whose role it is to give it. The former group is further divided into those capable of accepting advice and those who remain obdurate; the counselors, in turn, are discriminated into those who give advice effectively and those who

fail to do so. Cols. XVa–XVIIIb first address teachers who do not know how
to manage obdurate pupils, and then those pupils who give the impression of
being open to plain speaking but in fact are not (cf. fr. 88 [=94 N]): there is a
danger here of mistakes in judgment on the part of the mentors.

Cols. XVIa–XXIb in part address problems of moral and intellectual
acumen, and call attention to pretentious students or aspiring teachers who
have a desire for reputation, believing that they are faultless and that they are
"more suited to speaking frankly" because "they think that they are more intelligent than [others]..." (col. XIXa). When they recognize that others are
wiser than they, the situation becomes acute, as the ninth section heading indicates: "...how, [when they recognize] that some of their number are more intelligent, and in particular that some of them are teachers, do they not abide
frank criticism?" (col. XXa; cf. fr. 5). The answer given reveals differences of
opinion among Epicureans as to who has the right frankly to criticize others;
such a one must surpass others, not so much in "theoretical arguments" (col.
XXa) as in character, being able to perceive what is best in the affairs of real
life.

After addressing the tensions caused by variation in intellectual ability,
Philodemus turns his attention to persons of different social standing, gender,
and age. Here, as in the case of the different types of students, the major concern is the fact that different people respond differently to frank criticism. The
one who provides care is advised to keep this simple truth in mind, and indeed
the several themes that arise in the epitome are all bound up with this one
overarching issue.

VI. Medical Imagery

Although the application of the language of disease and cure to the philosophical enterprise was widespread in antiquity, the conception of philosophy as a
medical art assumed in Epicurean thought a foundational significance.[49] The
pervasiveness of this conception is reflected in the epitome as well, not only
through the frequent direct comparisons of philosophical activity to the healing

---

[49] See, e.g., Diogenes of Oenoanda's description of Epicurean philosophy as "drugs of
salvation" (τὰ τῆς σωτηρίας ... [φάρμα]κα, fr. 3, cols. V.14–VI.2 Smith) and the
"fourfold cure" (τετραφάρμακος) by which Philodemus epitomized the Epicurean
philosophy (PHerc. 1005 col. V.8–13 Angeli = Epicurus fr. 196 Arrighetti²): ἄφοβον ὁ
θεός, ἀν[ύ]ποπτον ὁ θάνατος καὶ τἀγαθὸν μὲν εὔκτητον, τὸ δὲ δεινὸν εὐεκκα[ρ]τέρητον,
"Nothing to fear in God, / Nothing expected in death, / Easily got is the good, / Easily
borne the bad" (trans. Dirk Obbink, *Philodemus: On Piety 1* [Oxford: Clarendon, 1996]
536); cf. Epicurus *SV* 54, 64.

arts, but also through the striking and repeated use of medical terms as more or less technical designations for the process of instruction within the Epicurean community of friends.[50]

The medical analogy arises in the comparison of moral instructors to doctors,[51] in references to diseases and medicines or to medical treatment and operations,[52] and in references to sick people who are either incurable,[53] un-

---

[50] See the Index Verborum, Greek-English, s.vv. ἀθεράπευτος (untreatable), ἀκεῖον (medicine), ἀκέομαι (heal), ἀκεστικός (healable), ἀκμάζω (be at its height), ἀναλθής (incurable), ἀναπλάττω (restore), ἀνεφόδευτος (unexamined), ἀνήκεστος (incurable), ἀπόθεσις (setting right), ἀσθενής (weak), ἀψίνθιον (wormwood), βοήθεια (assistance, assisting; fr. 67.8-9), βοηθέω (help; fr. 86.7 [=90 N]), διαίρεσις (operation), ἐλλέβορος (hellebore), εὐτύχημα (well-being), ζμίλιον (scalpel), θεραπεία (treatment), θεραπεύω (treat), θεράπευσις (treatment), ἰάομαι (heal), ἰατρός (doctor), κενόω (purge), κένωμα (purge), κλυστήρ (clyster), κουφίζω (relieve; fr. 66.9), νοσέω (be ill), νόσημα (disease), νόσος (disease), συνοίδησις (swelling), σῴζω (save), σωτήρ (savior), and σωτηρία (security, salvation).

[51] Fr. 39, "...it is completely shameful to help themselves to some *treatment* of the body although not [having] need of *doctors* in everything, but in the case of the soul not to try [the admonition of the wise man]..."; fr. 63, "It is like when a *doctor* assumes because of reasonable signs that a certain man is in need of a *purge*, and then, having made a mistake in the interpretation of the signs, never again *purges* this man when he is afflicted by another *disease*"; fr. 64, "For although a *doctor* in the case of the same *disease* had accomplished nothing through a *clyster*, he would again purge {the patient}. And for this reason he will again criticize frankly..."; fr. 69, "...toward those who are expected not to halt insofar as depends on reasonable {arguments}, imitating *doctors* who treat also one who is reasonably believed that he is not going to *recover from his disease*, and just as he also exhorts those who reasonably..."; fr. 86 (=90 N), "...{the teachers try} persistently [to] tame people into love for themselves, [subt]ly helping [through] *doctors* even those who have no passion to be treated"; col. XVIIa, "...but when they observe that their character is prone to error, they are stung. And just like those who call skilled *doctors* to an *operation* when they apply the *scalpel* to those who are ill, so too when what is stinging in frank criticism meets the eye of these people and they believe that they will commit no error, or that they will escape notice even if they have erred many times, they call upon {their teachers} to admonish..."; Tab. XII M, "...and failure occurs with the foremost *doctors*...."

[52] Fr. 8, "For some *are treated* more pleasantly and more easily..."; fr. 20, "...[treat]ing with [moderate] words"; fr. 23, "...[declaring failings] and other evils [with] laughter or with an evilly striding [swagger], he both *treats* those who are being admonished, and..."; fr. 30, "...but he pays less attention to his own injury who still is very much in need of external things and someone who, because of his condition, opposes one thing and obstructs another with *[medicine]*, since pain is present"; fr 32, "...just as others have seemed *to heal* suddenly, and contrary to [all expectation]"; fr. 40, "...whom he calls *the only savior*, and {to whom}, citing the phrase, 'with him accompanying {me},' he has given himself over *to be treated*, then how is he not going to show to him *those things in which he needs treatment*, and [accept admonishment]?"; fr. 44, "...and knows how *to treat* {them}"; fr. 79 (=81 N), "...{so that} he can be treated either by us or by another of his fellow-students..."; col. IIb "...but he endures the other {i.e., blaming} pleasurelessly and

diagnosed, or untreatable.[54] We also find references to symptoms of sickness,[55] to people being saved,[56] and to the restoration of well-being.[57]

Philodemus uses medical imagery to throw light on matters of moral exhortation, on the means and methods of correct diagnosis and prognosis, the need for perseverance in difficult cases, and for patient care on the doctor's part. In regard to medical imagery, therapy in Philodemus takes two forms, namely, medicinal and surgical, that is, cures by means of drugs or the scalpel, conforming in this to the Hippocratic norm. Pharmacy is of a mixed character in that it involves both agreeable and bitter medicines. Besides purgatives, such drugs as wormwood and hellebore are invoked.[58] These

---

as though {he were drinking} *wormwood*"; col. XXIb, "...by which they deflate {them} and *treat {them}* and apply some of the other fine things that derive from frank criticism..."; Tab. XII end of fr., "...that it happens that even those who [have drunk] *hellebore* are not ridiculous to *{[doctors]}*." Note the reference to *treatment* in fr. 39, the *purging of a disease* in frs. 63–64, and the reference to an *operation* and the *scalpel* in col. XVIIa, all indicated in previous note.

[53] Fr. 59, "For since they are either weak or *have become incurable* because of frankness..."; fr. 70, "...< [we see them for the sake of] external things often proceeding [toward what is *in]curable>* ..."; fr. 84 N, "....< the wise man will [not consider that he is speaking] to [someone *incurable*, and] he will [communicate] {his errors}..."

[54] Fr. 84 (=88 N), "And when some one of the others appears who was *unexamined* earlier or was disregarded as *untreatable*, after this, when he is recognized, since there was foresight, {he} reasonably..."

[55] Fr. 65, "And though he disobeyed then, when the passion *was at its height*, now, when it has relaxed, he will be called back..."; fr. 66, "...[and although he disobeyed earlier, disdaining the reproach as foreign {to himself}], later he will [give up] and obey the admonition. Then, he was *afflicted with passions* that puff one up or generally hinder one, but afterwards, when *he has been relieved*, he will pay heed"; fr. 67, "...when they {have recognized} at the same time that the *swelling* will be intensified to this extent, and have recognized the {*swelling*} deriving from other {passions}, and by the persistence, but that it will be reduced, if he quickly turns away from assisting the one who is slipping up."

[56] Fr. 34, "Perhaps for those who are *saving* {others} this is [very] difficult..."; fr. 36, "...and considering *being saved* by one another to be supplies toward contentment and great goodwill..."; fr. 43, " < For in fact if it is possible for you, having spoken frankly, to stay in the same {condition}—if you will withhold nothing—[you will] *save* a man [who is a friend]> ..."; fr. 77 (=78 N), "But to no one {of the students} is an equal error to be ascribed by those who are *saving* {them}, or at all events one of those that are < *healable*> through admonishment < and [setting right], not of those to be [avoided] for their magnitude, but rather remit it in regard to peers [and] acquaintances> "; fr. 78 (=80 N), "For when each person reasons, it will happen that he knows things that are [worth] nothing but that the one who *saves* {others} < *heals* everyone...> "; col. VIb, "And if one has needed frankness minimally, while another has been *saved* by means of this...." Note also the reference to the "only savior" in fr. 40.

[57] Fr. 61, "Sometimes when *well-being has been restored*..."

[58] Gigante, *Ricerche filodemee*, 75; Cf. Euripides fr. 403.6 Nauck; Plato *Plt.* 298C; *Resp.* 406D, 407D.

medicines, like the surgical method itself, suggest the sharpness which is a necessary aspect of frank speech.

The medical model, then, in suggesting the mixed nature of exhortation, gives evidence of the need for good judgment on the part of Epicurean spiritual directors and underscores the legitimate use of harshness in moral exhortation, especially in the case of recalcitrant students. The point is emphasized in the analogies with hellebore, wormwood, and surgery to describe the therapeutic task. The most sustained use of medical imagery occurs just when Philodemus focuses on recalcitrant students (frs. 56–70). Their "sickness" is of such a nature that it requires more drastic measures than obedient students need.

The comparison with physicians underlines the conjectural or approximate nature of moral instruction, both in the evaluation of the students' dilemmas and in the application of frankness in the treatment itself, and clearly indicates the need to adapt treatment to particular cases and the possibility that even a mature person may fail in the care of others. The method is conjectural in the same way as the art of the physician, the rhetor, or the pilot, that is, there are no general rules that are valid for all instances. Each situation creates a unique problem to which the pilot, rhetor or physician must adapt his skill. The art in question is thus subservient to the situation, for example, the weather at sea, the rhetor's particular audience, or the nature of the patient.

VII. Conclusion

What general social practices may be inferred from Philodemus' treatise *On Frank Criticism* as we have it, often depends on the tricky question of whether a particular fragment is alluding to teachers or students. In many cases, absolute certainty cannot be attained. But it seems clear that the care of souls among the Epicureans was communal and not restricted to a few members invested with preeminent authority. Philodemus is indeed concerned mainly with the candor that the teacher exhibits in relation to a student under his authority, but he also emphasizes the usefulness of frankness in general in advancing solidarity among the Epicurean friends and their mutual collaboration in moral development. Just as some members of the entourage of the rich and powerful were expected, on the basis of friendship, to advise and correct the errors of their superiors, so too those of an inferior character and social position within the philosophical community were allowed to admonish others and to correct the errors of their moral superiors. The fragments thus reveal the connection between frank speech and the ideal of friendship as a commitment to reciprocal honesty, and invoke as well the kind of sincerity expected of an inferior in relation to a patron.

In the Epicurean communities, where friends of unequal power and status joined in mutual psychagogy for moral improvement, both symmetrical and asymmetrical forms of social relationship had their place.[59] The system of psychagogy was rotational, and the one who provided care might next be the object of admonishment. The problems voiced in the epitome suggest that frank speech and openness among friends of unequal power and status were not a vague or abstract ideal but rather a tense social reality. Part of the purpose of the treatise is to address these tensions and present guidelines for their resolution. What is striking about this fluid system of rotational psychagogy is its collaborative nature: friends within the fellowship, whether teachers or fellow-students, are expected to participate in a process of mutual edification, admonition, and correction, all in a spirit of goodwill and moral solidarity.

---

[59] For an attempt to account for both the symmetrical and asymmetrical elements of Epicurean psychagogy and the participation of people of different social standing in such a practice, see Glad, *Paul and Philodemus*, 132, 152–160; "Frank Speech," 54–59.

SIGLA

I. Sigla Used in the Text

[ ]	conjectures for missing letters or words due to fragmentary state of text
< >	letters or words added by various editors
⟦ ⟧	unnecesary letter
( )	parentheses in Olivieri's text
*	indicates space of one letter left blank in papyrus
α̣	mutilated or uncertain letter
α̇	doubtful letter; underlined sentence indicates section title
5	line numbers in the left margin are our own, based on editors' supplements; those in the right, Olivieri's

II. Sigla Used in the Translation

< >	text based on the disegni as inspected by Philippson and others and compared with Olivieri's text
[ ]	Olivieri's supplements
<[ ]>	supplements suggested by Philippson or Gigante
{[ ]}	translators' supplements
{ }	translators' additions or clarifications
( )	parentheses in Olivieri's text
?	indicates grave doubt about a restoration
italics	indicates section heading in the text

III. Sigla Used in the Text and Translation

pap.	PHerc. 1471
N	original Naples edition (*Herculanensium voluminum quae supersunt*, vol. 5, pts. 1 and 2 [1835, 1843])
Neap. edd.	original Neapolitan editors
O.	Alexander Olivieri, *Philodemi* ΠΕΡΙ ΠΑΡΡΗΣΙΑΣ *Libellus* (Leipzig: Teubner, 1914)
Ph.	R. Philippson, review of O., *Berliner Philologische Wochenschrift* 22 (1916) 677–88
G.	Marcello Gigante, *Ricerche filodemee* (2d ed.; Biblioteca della Parola del passato 6; Naples: Macchiaroli, 1983)

ΦΙΛΟΔΗΜΟΥ ΠΕΡΙ ΠΑΡΡΗΣΙΑΣ

Fr. 1

        ὑποπῖπτον γὰρ
δὴ καὶ τό τινας μήτε cυν-
αιcθάνεcθαι τὰc ἁμαρτίαc,
μήθ' ὃ cυνφέρει διαγινώc-
5   κειν, ἀπ[ιcτ]εῖν ποεῖ. * καθόλου τ' ἐπιπαρρηcιά\ζεται
cοφὸc καὶ φιλόcοφοc ἀνήρ,
ὅτι μὲν cτοχα\ζόμενοc
εὐ[λ]ογίαιc ἔδε[ιξ]ε παγίωc
10 o[ὐδέν

---

5 ΑΠ[...]CIN pap.   9 εὐλογία[ι]c O.   10 o[ὐδέν
suppl. G. 63

Fr. 2

        ὀργίλωc]
οὐ [διατίθετα]ι cοφὸc πρὸc
τοὺc κ[ατ]αcκευα\ζομένουc·
ἂν δὲ μὴ πρ]ὸc τοῦτο χωρῇ <ι>,
5   πῶc δὴ τολ]μήcουcιν ἕκα-
cτ]οι μὴ π[ροcδ]έχεcθαι
τὴν παρρηcίαν; οἰκονο-
μηθήcεcθαι δὲ καὶ τὸ δεῖν
οἰ]κεῖον ἐπ[εὶ φ]ύντων

---

6 π[ροcδ]έχεcθαι Ph. π[άνυ ἀν]έχεcθαι O.   9 ἐπ[εὶ
φ]ύντων Ph.

26

PHILODEMUS *ON FRANK CRITICISM*

Fr. 1: For of course when it also happens that some neither perceive their own[1] errors nor discern what is advantageous, it causes (them) to dis[trust].[2] And, in general, a wise man and philosopher speaks frankly because on the one hand, conjecturing by reasonable arguments,[3] he has shown[4] <[in no way]> rigidly...[5]

Fr. 2: ...a wise man is not [angrily disposed] toward those being instructed. [But if he does not] give way to this {i.e., anger}, [how then] will they severally [dare] not <[to accept]> his frank criticism? And that {frank criticism} should be administered appropriately,[6] since being <[naturally inclined]>...[7]

---

[1] Or: "perceive in common"; so Gigante, *Ricerche filodemee*, 63; Glad, *Paul and Philodemus*, 164, 173; "Frank Speech," 58n. LSJ translate "be aware of in oneself."

[2] "Disobey" (ἀπειθεῖν) is also possible; or, retaining pap.'s C, e.g., "denial" (ἀπόφασιν).

[3] Reading εὐλογίαις with pap. and G., against O.; cf. C. J. Vooijs and D. A. van Krevelen, *Lexicon Philodemeum* (2 vols.; Murmerend: Muuses, 1934; and Amsterdam: Swets & Zeitlinger, 1941) s.v.

[4] Sc. either "that..." (relative clause) or perhaps a direct object, in which case translate "pointed out."

[5] Cf. translation in Marcello Gigante, "Philodème: Sur la liberté de parole," in *Actes du VIIIe Congrès, Association Guillaume Budé* (Paris: Les Belles Lettres, 1969) 202; on παρρησία as a "conjectural art" (τέχνη στοχαστική), cf. Gigante, *Ricerche filodemee*, 62–75; Glad, *Paul and Philodemus*, 133–37; for the comparison with medicine, cf. Marcello Gigante, "'Philosophia medicans' in Filodemo," *CErc* 5 (1975) 55; Asmis, "Philodemus' Epicureanism," 2393 n. 56: "Psychic healing is a stochastic art, which uses παρρησία as a method."

[6] οἰκεῖον taken adverbially; cf. Vooijs and Krevelen s.v.

[7] Ph. further conjectures "human beings" as those who are naturally inclined.

Fr. 3

[ἐὰν.....] ἢ παρ[ησίας
εἴδωλον [ε]ῦ προσφέρων-
ται. * καὶ [περὶ τ]οῦ μ[η-
δέποτ' ἀπογινώσ[κειν μηδ]ὲ
5   πάντα διαλαμβά[νειν ἐν τ]ῶι
π]ροσφέρειν τὴν παρρη[cί-   5
α]ν εἰρήκαμέν που, καὶ πε-
ρ]ὶ τῆς ἀδοξίας τῆς παρὰ
τοῖc] πο[λ]λοῖc κα[ὶ] περὶ τοῦ
10   τῶν οἰκείων ἀ[πο]cπαc-
μοῦ   10

_____

1 [ἐὰν.....] ἢ παρ[ρηcίαc Ph.

Fr. 4

         καὶ τὴν [μὲν διά-
πτωcιν ἐν μηδενὶ τιθέ-
μεν[ο]c, ἐν μεγά[λ]ω[ι] δὲ
τὴν ἐ[πιτυ]χίαν. * [οἱ] δ' εὐ-
5   εργετ[ή]cαντεc ἀπ[ὸ c]εβαc-
μοῦ τὸ[ν] cοφὸν εὐγεν[εί-
αc δ[.]..[...]νεc.[...] ὥcτε πῶc ἀποcτήc[ονται] τῆc
τούτων cωτηρ[ίαc....] μὴ
10   καὶ Ἐπίκουροc c[

Fr. 5

         ταῖ]c π[επαρρη-
cιαcμέναιc τῶν ἀνδ[ρ]ῶν
φωναῖc ἐνθουcιάζον-
τε[c]. ἔξεcτι δ' ἐκ τῶ[ν] εἰρη-
5   μ[έ]ν[ω]ν ἀν[αιρε]ῖcθα<ι> καὶ τὸ
πῶc ἔχει[ν] δεῖ πρὸc παρρηcίαν τὸ[ν cφοδρ]ῶc ἀντέ-
χο[ν]τα παρρηcίαι. *

Fr. 3: ... <[if]> they present [well]⁸ ... <or> an image of <[frankness]>.⁹ Both [about] never giving up [nor] treating¹⁰ everything [when] applying frank criticism we have pretty much spoken, as well as about ill repute in the eyes of the public and about separation from one's family.¹¹

Fr. 4: ...while he also regards {their} failure as of no account, but {their} [success] as great. [Those] who have done a service for the wise man out of reverence¹² ... nobility ... so that how will [they] shun the security of these¹³ ... not even Epicurus...

Fr. 5: ...being inspired by the [frank] sayings of men. And from what has been said it is possible to [take up] also {the question of} how one who [vehemently] resists frankness must behave with respect to frankness.¹⁴

---

⁸ Or perhaps "again" (αὖ).

⁹ Punctuating with a full stop in place of O.'s comma.

¹⁰ Gigante, "'Philosophia medicans,'" 55 n. 41, interprets διαλαμβάνειν as "memorize."

¹¹ Or "from one's own affairs."

¹² Cf. Philodemus *Oec.* col. XXIII.22–30, where "reverence" is juxtaposed to paying for "philosophical discourse"; there, payment received for sharing philosophical discourses is considered the best source of income for philosophers. See Asmis, "Philodemus' Epicureanism," 2388.

¹³ Ware suggests the singular, ἀποστήσεται: "how will he {the wise man} be aloof to the well-being of these {sc. benefactors}."

¹⁴ Despite the fact that the last part of the sentence is underlined in the Greek, this does not appear to be a section heading; see Introduction, pp. 8–9, esp. n. 25. Cf. for the topic Plutarch *Quomodo adulator* 72E.

Fr. 6

[τῶι
μὲν ἁμαρτή[σαντι παρρη-
cιάc[ε]ται, τῶι δὲ καὶ [πικρ]ό-
τητας ἀποδιδόντι. διὸ
5   καὶ Ἐπίκουρος, Λε[οντ]έωc
διὰ Πυθοκλέα πίc[τιν] θε-
ῶ[ν] οὐ παρέντο[c,] Πυθοκλεῖ
μὲν [ἐ]πιτιμᾶι μετρίωc,
πρὸc δὲ τὸν γράφει [τ]ὴν
10   λαμπρὰν καλουμένην
ἐπιc[τολ]ήν, λαβῶ[ν ἀρχὴν
ἀπὸ τοῦ] Πυθ[οκλ...

—————————
9 τὸν pap. Sedley, *CErc* 6 (1976) 46 n. 78 <αὐ>τὸν O.

Fr. 7

πρὸc δὲ τοὺc μᾶλ-
λον τῶν ἀπαλῶν ἰcχυ-
ροὺc καὶ τοὺc πλεῖόν τι
τ]ῆc ἐπιcτάcεωc δεομέ-
5   νουc ἐπιτίνει, πρὸc δὲ
τοὺc ἰcχυροὺc καὶ μόλιc,
ἂν ἐγκραυγαcθῶc[ι], με-
ταθηcομένουc καὶ τῶι
cκληρῶι χρήcεται τῆc
10   παρρηcίαc εἴδει· * καὶ γὰρ

Fr. 8

δι[ὸ] κοινὸν τὸ π[ρό]cωπ[ο]ν
ὧι προcπέπονθ[ε καὶ] τού-
του παρεφάπ[τ]ε[ται πρ]οcχα-
ρακτηρικῶc· τ[ι]ν[ὲc γὰ]ρ ἥδι-
5   ον καὶ ῥᾶ<ι>ον ἁγνο<ο>ύντων
θεραπεύονται [τ]ῶν καθη-
γουμέν[ων ἐφ᾿ ο]ῖc cυνεν-
πίπτουcιν εἰc ἃ ποιοῦcι[ν.
ἔcτιν δ᾿ ὅτε φήcε[ι] λέγειν
10   τ[ι]νὰc τῶν φίλων καὶ δι[α-
κελεύεται φυλ[

—————————
1 διό Ph. διά O. κοινόν pap. Ph. καινόν O.

Fr. 6: ...he will be [frank] with [the one who has] erred and even with him who responds with [bitter]ness. Therefore, Epicurus too, when Le[ont]eus because of Pythocles did not admit [belief][15] in gods, reproached Pythocles in moderation, and wrote to him {sc. Leonteus} the so-called "famous letter," [taking his point of departure from] Pyth[ocles']...

Fr. 7: ...and toward those stronger than the tender ones and those somewhat more in need of treatment, he intensifies[16] {frankness}, and toward the strong who will scarcely change {even} if they are shouted at, he will also employ the harsh form of frankness.[17] And in fact...

Fr. 8: ... < [therefore] >[18] the person to whom he has become devoted is sociable[19] [and he] touches upon this one in accord with his character.[20] For some are treated more pleasantly and more easily when their teachers are ignorant [of the conditions on which][21] they {the students} come together for what they do. There are times when he {the teacher} will say that some of the friends are speaking[22] {about him?} and he encourages {him?} {[to guard?}[23]...

---

[15] David Sedley, "Epicurus and the Mathematicians of Cyzicus," *CErc* 6 (1976) 46, emends to πύστιν, and suggests that Leonteus rejected "inquiry" about the gods.

[16] ἐπιτίνει = ἐπιτείνει.

[17] On weak vs. strong students, cf. Glad, *Paul and Philodemus*, 137-52; "Frank Speech," 33-34; Marcello Gigante, "Motivi paideutici nell'opera filodemea *Sulla libertà di parola*," *CErc* 4 (1973) 41; also fr. 10.8-11 and col. XXIIb.5 for "the strong."

[18] Reading διό with Ph. (O. neglects to note that the last letter is missing in the papyrus).

[19] Reading κοινόν with pap. (for the sense, see LSJ s.v. IV.3.b); O. emends to καινόν, "new."

[20] προσχαρακτηρικῶς only here; LSJ translate "as extension of character."

[21] Or "the circumstances in which."

[22] Or "will tell some of the friends to speak {sc. frankly}"; so, apparently, Gigante, *Ricerche filodemee*, 78: "si afferma sicuramente che i giovani sono sono curati con maggiore mitezza e facilità, quando i maestri ignorano gli errori e fanno parlare liberamente." For the sense of φῆμι as "tell," see LSJ s.v. IV; LSJSup gives an example with the accusative of the person.

[23] Supplying φυλ[άττειν.

Fr. 9

καθ]όλου [δ' ἁμαρτημάτων ἐκείνων τ[ά]δε καὶ τάδ[ε] καὶ ἅ-
πε[ρ ὁ] Ἐπίκουρος Λεοντίου
πυνθά[ν]εται πρ[οcυ]ποc-
5 τήcεται πρὸc Κολώτην.
ἐπεὶ καὶ μετάξει ποτ' ἐ-
φ' ἑαυτὸν ὁ cοφόc θ' ἁμαρ-
τημ' ἄνετον ἐν τ[ῆι] νεότη-
τι γε[γ]ονέ[ν]αι

Fr. 10

τὰ πολλὰ μὲν
διαφι[λ]οτεχν[ή]cει τοιούτω[ι
τρόπω[ι. οὐ μ]ὴν ἀλλά πο-
τε καὶ ἁ[πλ]ῶc ποήcεται
5 τὴν παρ[ρη]cίαν, παρακιν-
δυνευτέ[ον ε]ἶναι νομίζων, <ἐὰν>
ἄλλωc μὴ ὑπ[α]κούωcι[ν. καὶ
μέντοι [γ]ε τοὺc [ὑπε]ρβαλλόν-
τωc ἰcχυροὺc καὶ φύcει κ[αὶ
10 διὰ προκοπὴν πα[ν]τὶ θυ-
μῶι [κ]αὶ [κα]κι[cμῶι] καὶ

7 [καὶ: [οὐ suppl. O.   11 [κα]κι[cμῶι] καὶ suppl. Ph.

Fr. 11

μᾶ[λ-
λ[ο]ν εὐφραίνειν κ[αὶ] τ[ῆι
ἐπ[ιζ]ητηcομένηι [π]ερὶ αὐτοὺc ἐπαγρυπνήcει· * [μ]ε-
5 τὰ δὲ ταῦτα καὶ τὰ πα[ρ]α-
κολουθοῦντα καὶ cυναν[α-
φθηcόμενα δύcκολα τοι-
ούτοιc οὖcιν ἐκθήcει πά-
λιν [καὶ πάλιν "κα]κῶc ποεῖc"
10 κα[ὶ.........] λέγων

9–10 suppl. Ph.

Fr. 9: ...[in general] such and such of [their (sc. the students') errors] and what Epicurus learns from Leontion he will {hypothetically} ascribe[24] to Colotes. Since the wise man will also sometimes transfer to himself an intemperate error, {saying} that it occurred in his youth...

Fr. 10: ...in most instances he {the teacher} will practise the art[25] in such a way. But at times he will also practise frankness [simp]ly, believing that it must be risked [if] otherwise they {the students} do not pay heed.[26] {[And]} those who are exceedingly strong, both by nature [and] because of their progress, {he will criticize} with all passion and < [blame] and > ...

Fr. 11: ...rather to rejoice even in the watchfulness that will inquire further concerning them {the students}. And after these things he will also set forth the difficulties that accompany and will be attached to those who are such, <saying> again <and again, "You are doing [wrong]," and>...

---

[24] For this sense, see Vooijs and Krevelen s.v.; the interpretation depends in part on taking the next clause closely with this one.

[25] διαφιλοτεχνέω not in LSJ; Gigante, *Ricerche filodemee*, 73, notes a connection with ποικίλη φιλοτεχνία.

[26] Cf. Glad, *Paul and Philodemus*, 143-46 (following Norman W. De Witt, "Organization and Procedure in Epicurean Groups," *CP* 31 [1936] 209), for the distinction between a mixed form of frankness involving praise and blame and a simple form using only blame (= "harsh frankness," fr. 7.9-11). Cf. also Asmis, "Philodemus' Epicureanism," 2393; different view in Gigante, *Ricerche filodemee*, 72-74.

Fr. 12

> κα[ὶ οὕτω φανε-
> ρὸν ποιήσει τοῦτο τῶι τυγ-
> χάν]οντι τῆc παρρηcίαc·
> ἂν δ]ὲ μή, τὸ πο[νεῖ]ν οὐδὲν
> 5 ἀνύcει πλέον, ἔτι δ᾽ ἀθυ-
> μώcει, καὶ μὴ < ν > διὰ π[α]ντὸc
> ἀοργήτωc ποήcεται τοὺ[c
> λόγου[c ὥcτε] μὴ βιαζο-
> μένο[υc ὑπ᾽ αὐ]τοῦ πλ[έ]ον
> 10 ἀδικεῖν.]

8-10 suppl. Ph.

Fr. 13

> καθόλου] δ᾽ ἐπὶ τούτ[ωι
> βλα< c >φ[ημοῦντ]οc ἐκείνου μέμ-
> ψεται, [τοὐναν]τίον δ᾽ ἐπὶ
> ταῖc ἐ[ρεθιζούcαιc τ]ὸν νουθε-
> 5 τούμενον λύμαιc καὶ
> φανερὸν κἀκείνωι π[ο-
> ήcει τ[ο]ῦτο· cυνβαίνει
> γὰρ τὴν διάνοιαν ἀπο-
> cτρέφεcθαι μέν, ὡc οὐχ ὑ-
> 10 γιᾶ] λέγοντοc [το]ῦ ἀντ[ι-
> λέγοντοc

9-10 ὑ | [πο]λέγοντοc Neap. edd.

Fr. 14

> ὥcτε τῆι πρὸc τ[ὸ cφοδρ]ὸ[ν
> ποιότη[τ]ι κεχρῆcθαι, [ἐν ἧι
> δ᾽ οὐκ ἔcτι τὴν ἰδιότη[τ]α
> καὶ τῶν φιλοφρόνων [ἀ]φα-
> 5 νῶν. ὅταν μὴ παρελπίζη < ι >
> τινὰc ἢ cφόδρα μεγάλωc τὸν
> ἴδιον ἐμφαίνη < ι > δυcχεραc-
> μόν, οὐκ ἐπιλήcεται τοῦ
> φιλτάτου λέγω< ν > καὶ γλυκυ-
> 10 τ]ά[του] καὶ τῶν ὁμοίων καὶ

2 [ἐν ἧι O. [ἰδεῖν Neap. edd.   4-5 [ἀ]φα | νῶν Neap.
edd.   5 μὴ< ν > O.

Fr. 12: ...and [in this way] he will make this [clear] to him who en-
counters frankness. [If] not, his [labor] will accomplish nothing further, and
furthermore will dishearten {the student}. And surely[27] he will always fashion
his words without anger < [so as] not [to wrong] [further?] those who are
treated roughly [by him] >.

Fr. 13: and [in general][28] in this case he will censure him when he
[maligns], and [on the contrary] in the case of offenses that [irritate] the one
who is being admonished he {the teacher} will also make this clear to him as
well. For it happens, on the one hand, that one is alienated[29] intellectually,
since the one [who talks back] does not say [sound things][30]...

Fr. 14: ...so as to employ the quality against [what is vehement],[31] but it is
not possible [to see][32] the individual character even of the well disposed [if
they are concealed]. When he is not disappointed in some people, or very
vehemently indicating his own annoyance,[33] he will not, as he speaks, forget
"dearest" and "sweetest" and similar things and...

---

[27] O.'s μὴ is awkward with indicative ποήσεται; Ph. suggests μὰ Δία <διὰ> παντός,
"by Zeus he will always...," which is attractive but involves a greater change.
[28] O.'s supplement, although not indicated as such in his text; cf. Ph. col. 682.
[29] For this sense of ἀποστρέφομαι, see LSJ s.v. B.II.1.
[30] The Neapolitan editors conjectured "does not take into acccount."
[31] Or perhaps, reading τὸν σφοδρόν, "a vehement person"; cf. fr. 5.7-8.
[32] O. reads "in which (it is not possible, etc.)."
[33] See LSJSup s.v. δυσχερασμός.

Fr. 15

καὶ δ[ιὰ
τί παυσαμένων ἐπὶ το[ὺ]ς
ὕμν[ου]ς μετ[α]βήσεται καὶ
τού[τοις] δὲ πῶς αὐτοῦ
5　τὴν ἀ[νακ]άκχεσιν ἐνηνο-
χότ[ας] ἐπιδείξει; cυνελ[όν-
τι δ᾽ εἰπεῖν οὕτω παρρησί-
αι <χρήσεται> coφὸς ἀνὴρ πρὸς τοὺς φίλους ὡς Ἐπίκουρος καὶ Μη-
10　τρόδω[ρος

---

3 ὕμν[ου]ς cf. O. in app. crit.

Fr. 16

μηδὲ
τότε δακνώμεθα μό-
νον, ἀλλὰ μέχρι ἂν καθα-
ρεύοντας ἐπιδείξωμεν
5　αὐτο[ύς]· * πείθειν δὲ καὶ δι-
ὰ τῶν [ἔργ]ων, ἀλλὰ μὴ μόνον δ[ιὰ το]ῦ λέ[γει]ν, ὅτι τὴν
παρρ[ηcίαν cπα]νίως ἐνη-
νόχαcι

Fr. 17

[μὴ
χρωμένου καὶ [παρας]ει-
τικῆι καθόλου πάντων.
κἂν δι᾽ ἄλλων [ἔτι μ]ᾶλλο[ν
5　ἡ παρρηcία γένηται, μὴ νο-
ε[ῖν τι]ν᾽ οὕτω ἠ[ιρ]ῆcθαι　　　　5
χάριν δι[α]βολῆc [ἡ]μῶν,
ἀλλὰ............
...κἂν διὰ [τῆς] γεγονυ-
10　ίας π[αρρ]ηcίας κ[έντ]ρον τι

---

1 [μὴ suppl. Ph.　2–3 [παρας]ει|τικῆι suppl. Ph.
7 [ἡ]μῶν: ἄλλων Ph.　8–9 ἀλλὰ: ὑφ᾽ ἡμῶν
προcλαμβαν]όμε|νον suppl. Ph.　9–10 suppl. Ph.

Fr. 15: ...and why, when they[34] have stopped, will he {the teacher} move on to {[accolades]},[35] and how will he exhibit [to these] [those] who have endured his ridicule? In short, a wise man will employ frankness toward his friends in the way that Epicurus and Metrodo[rus]...

Fr. 16: ...and let us {the teachers} not only be stung[36] then, but {continue to be so} until we can show that [they][37] are pure. To persuade also through [deeds], and not just [through speaking], because they have [seldom] endured frankness...

Fr. 17: ... < not? > employing also a {form of frankness that is} <[agitating] >[38] of all in general. Even if the frankness {used} by others should be [still greater], do not [think] that [someone] has chosen thus for the sake of slandering [us],[39] but...[40] And < if through [the frankness] that has arisen some [goad] >...

---

[34] The subject of "stopped" may be masculine, i.e., "the students," or neuter, sc. (e.g.) "the criticisms."

[35] Cf. fr. 74.1.

[36] On "stinging" frankness, cf. Gigante, "'Philosophia medicans,'" 59–60.

[37] Or, reading αὐτούς instead of αὐτούς, "that we are pure"; cf. fr. 44.6 where καθαρεύων refers to the teachers. Gigante, "'Philosophia medicans,'" 57, retains O.'s text.

[38] Ph.'s conjecture, evidently derived from παρασείω, "shake from side to side," presumably means something like "stirring up."

[39] Ph. proposes "others" instead of "us."

[40] Ph.'s restoration "because he is accepted by us" is pure speculation.

Fr. 18

     ὦ παῖ, καθάπερ τρο[φ]ὴν
     ἀλλοτριοῦσαν ἔ[κ]πτ[υε
     ἀταράχως. * ἐὰν δὲ μηδ᾿ ἀ-
     γαπῶσι, πάσης τετευχότες
5   τροφ[ῆς ἰδί]ας καὶ βοηθείας,
     ἕως δυνατὸν ἦν, ἀλλ[ὰ] καὶ
     βλασφημεῖν καὶ λυμαίνε-
     σθαι τὸν c[ο]φὸν [τὸν] ὑφ᾿ αὑ-
     τοῖς π[ει]ρῶνται [καὶ κ]ωμω<ι>-
10   δοῦντ[ες σκώπτειν

Fr. 19

     τοῦτ᾿ ἐστιν, λέγεσθαι]
     πα[ρ᾿] ἡμῶν δεῖ, μ[ονίμου
     καὶ ἀκινήτου καὶ τ[ὴν
     φύc[ι]ν ὥσπερ κυνιδ[ίου
5   τοῖς εἴκουσιν ἀγνώ[μονος·
     εἰ μὴ καὶ πονηροῦ π[οτε φαν-
     ταcίαν, ἐ[ὰ]ν εὐτυχῆ[ι, δεί-
     ξοντος, * ἔτι δ᾿ εὐεπί[φο]ρον
     αὐτὸν παρασχήσοντος
10   ἄλλοις τὸ τὸν πολεμοῦν-
     τα μ[ὲν ἀμύ]νεσθαι, * καὶ

---

4 κυνιδ[ίου Konstan κυνίδ[ιον O. κυνιδ[ίοις G. 107

Fr. 20

     φωναῖ[c μετρίαις
     θεραπ]εύων, διὰ δὲ τὴ[ν προ-
     θυμία]ν αὐτῶν καὶ τήν, [εἴ γ᾿ ἐ-
     δυνήθησαν, ὠφελίαν ἡ-
5   μῶν, ἔτι δὲ τὴ[ν] μεριζο-
     μένην cυνγ[ν]ώ[μ]ην ἐν οἷς
     διέπεσον, ὡς ἔν τε τοῖς
     πρὸς Δημόκριτον ἵστα-
     ται διὰ τέλους ὁ Ἐπίκουρος
10   κ[αὶ πρὸς] Ἡρακλείδην ἐν

---

2 θεραπ]εύων vel νουθετ]εύων O.

Fr. 18: O child, calmly spit {it}[41] out just like food that repels. If they are not content, although they have obtained every [suitable] food and assistance, so long as it was possible, but try to malign and abuse the wise man at their service and to ridicule and [mock] him...

Fr. 19: [This is characteristic], it must [be said] on our part, of one who is [fixed] and unmovable and [senseless] by nature like a little dog[42] to those who back off, if not of one who will also [at times] show the [image] of a base person, if he should fare well, and who will furthermore present himself to others as inclined [on the one hand to warding off] one who makes war on him, and...

Fr. 20: ...[treat]ing[43] with [moderate] words, because of their [eagerness] and their benefit to us, [if] they were able, and further because of the pardon meted out for the things in which they slipped up, as Epicurus consistently maintains both in his books against Democritus [and against] Heraclides[44] in...

---

[41] Sc. other teachings; De Witt, "Organization and Procedure," 207, sees a reference to "all other knowledge," Gigante to the "non-Epicurean method" of frankness or to everything foreign to Epicureanism (*Ricerche filodemee*, 74; "'Philosophia medicans,'" 59).

[42] Gigante, *Ricerche filodemee*, 107nn, restores "like little dogs," taking the "immovable" person to be a teacher (for ἀκίνητος used of the Stoic sage or σπουδαῖος, Gigante compares Philodemus *Ir.* col. XXXV.21-24), while the puppies are students; the sentence thus contrasts "an immovable and insensible teacher with young people who back off like little dogs."

[43] O. also suggests "admonishing" as a possible supplement.

[44] We have no knowledge of either work. The book against Democritus may according to Usener have been part of the work listed by Diogenes Laertius (10.27) as "Epitome of Objections to the Physicists"; see Michael Erler, "Epikur," in *Die Philosophie der Antike 4: Die Hellenistiche Philosophie* (ed. Hellmut Flashar; Basel: Schwabe, 1994) 86. Heraclides of Pontus proposed a theory of elementary particles which differed from the atomism of Democritus and Epicurus.

Fr. 21

ἕνεκα τῆς [εἰς
τοὐναντίον μεταγ[ωγῆς,
ὡς τοῦτ᾽ αὐτὸ μόνον [ἀπ-
εργαζομένου. τὸ δὲ πῶς
5   ἐκεῖνος ἕξ[ει] ζωῆς, οὐδὲν
πονε[ῖ,] κἀφ[ρο]νοῦντος
τῆιδε [τῆι] ὁ[δηγί]αι σπανίως
τε πάνυ χρ[ῆτ]αι· καὶ πά-
σης ἀποστρ[ο]φῆς περιγε-
10   γραμμένης καὶ κατάρα<ς κα>ὶ
λοιδορίας ἀπάσ[ης] καὶ δ[ι᾽
ἀπο[ν]οίας

6-7 κἀφ[ρο]νοῦντος | τῆιδε [τῆι] ὁ[δηγί]αι suppl. Ph.

Fr. 22

με[ταθ]ήσ[ει το]σού-
τους, [τῆς] τῶν ἰδιωμάτων
αὐτ[ῶν ε]ὐθηνήσεως οἰκο-
νομουμένης πρὸς ταῖς
5   ἄλλαις, ἃς ὅ τε καιρὸς [κ]αὶ τὰ
πα]ραπ[λήσια] δίδωσιν α[ὐτοῖς, τι-
μαῖς. ἀγάγοι δ᾽ ἂν ἴσως πο-
τ[ὲ] ὁ σο[φ]ός, ἂν ἦ[ι] σπανιωτά-
τη], πα[ρρ]ησίαν

5 τὰ <ἕτερα> O., omit. Ph.

Fr. 23

[σφάλματα προφέρων με-
τ]ὰ γέλωτος ἢ τῆς κάκ[ι-
ο]ν περιπατούσης σο[βαρό-
τ]ητος καὶ κακὰ [ἄ]λλα, τοὺς
5   νουθετουμένο[υς] κα[ὶ] θερ]α-
πεύει καὶ τὰς.................
....
....
....καὶ
10   πρὸς ὃν ἔτ[υ]χε γινώ[σκων καὶ

Fr. 21: ...for the sake of a transfer [to] the opposite, since he is accomplishing this very thing only. He does not at all labor over how that one will fare in life, and if he {the student} <[is foolish?]> he {the teacher} employs this approach very sparingly. And when every recourse has been determined and every malediction [and] insult,[45] both through madness...

Fr. 22: ...[he will change] such great people, if the richness[46] of their individual traits is managed along with the other [honors] which opportunity and the [like] give [them].[47] The wise man might sometimes practice frankness, if it is very occasional...

Fr. 23: ...[declaring failings] and other evils [with] laughter or with an evilly striding [swagger],[48] he both treats those who are being admonished, and...

....
....
....

both toward someone he chances to know, [and] in the case of those he has chanced upon, and he does not conjecture about [evil people]...

---

[45] It is also possible to translate, "when every recourse to all malediction and insult has been limited."

[46] [ε]ὐθήνησις, elsewhere unattested, is apparently proximate in sense to εὐθηνία. Perhaps read εὐθύνσεως, "straightening."

[47] Gigante, *Ricerche filodemee*, 68, and Martha Nussbaum, "Therapeutic Arguments: Epicurus and Aristotle," in *The Norms of Nature: Studies in Hellenistic Ethics* (ed. Malcolm Schofield and Gisela Striker; Cambridge: Cambridge University Press, 1986) 42, take καιρός as an opportunity to be recognized and exploited by the teacher; this seems more difficult to extract from the text.

[48] σοβαρότης, conjectured by O., is not in LSJ, and the meaning of the clause is obscure; Philodemus perhaps refers here to play-acting on the part of the teacher.

ἐφ' ὧν ἔτυχεν, καὶ τῷ[ν πονη-
ρῶν οὐ στοχάζεται.

---

1 suppl. O., cf. Ph.   5-6 κα[ὶ] θερ]α | πεύει sic O.

Fr. 24

καί ποτε μετ]ὰ τῶν ἄλλων
.......]ος ὁμιλήςας, ἀπέφε-
ρε πολι]ὰν τὴν κεφαλήν, φή-
ςας ὡς] "οὐδ' ἂν αὐτὸς εἶπεν
5   πρὸς] ἄλλον".................
....
....
.................'Αλεξάνδρου
π]υνθανόμενοι πότε-
10   ρο]ν ἑλληνικῶς αὐτὸν ἢ
βαρ]βαρικῶς προςαγορευ-
τέον, κα]ὶ μυρί[ο]ις ἄλλοις

Fr. 25

οὐδ' εἰς καιρὸν ἐνχρονί-
ζειν ἐπιζη[τ]οῦμεν οὐδὲ
κατ' ἄλλον τρόπον, καὶ τοῦ
πῶς διὰ παρρηςίας ἐπιτε-
5   νοῦμεν τὴν πρὸς αὐτοὺς
εὔνοιαν τῶν κατ[αςκε]υα-
ζομ[έ]νων παρ' αὐτὸ τὸ πε-
παρρηςιάςθαι. * [χα]λεπὸν
μὲν εἶναι το[ῦτο] διε[ςά-
10   φ[η]ςεν εἰ γε[..]αιτο

---

10 γε[ρ]αίτε[ρον suppl. Ph.

Fr. 26

ὡςπερε[ὶ
θεωρῶν παιδεύοντα, τοὺς
ἐν τῶι κόςμωι πάντας ςτυ-
γήςει. τιθῶμεν δὲ πρὸ ὀμ-
5   μάτων καὶ τὴν διαφο-
ρὰν ἣν ἔχει κηδεμονι-
κὴ νουθέτηςις [ἀρ] ἀρες-
κούςη]ς μέν, ἐπιει[κ]ῶς δὲ

Fr. 24: ...[and sometimes], ... having conversed [with] the others, he turned away his [grey] head, saying that "he {sc. Epicurus} would not have said [to] another..."

....

....

when they inquired of Alexander whether they should address him in Greek or a barbarian language, [and] to ten thousand others...

Fr. 25: ...nor do we seek to dawdle up to the critical moment, nor in some other way, and of how, through frankness, we shall heighten the goodwill towards ourselves[49] of those who are being instructed by[50] the very fact of speaking frankly. He[51] has made it [clear] that this is difficult, if...

Fr. 26: ...as if, observing him teaching, he will hate all of them in the world. Let us set before our eyes also the difference that exists between a caring admonishment and an irony that pleases but pretty much stings everyone.[52] For in fact some who are enticed by this...[53]

---

[49] So De Witt, "Organization and Procedure," 207, Glad, *Paul and Philodemus*, 130, 142. Gigante, *Ricerche filodemee*, 68, understands "towards them," i.e., the students.

[50] So too Gigante, *Ricerche filodemee*, 68; contra De Witt, "Organization and Procedure," 207, who translates "in spite of" (cf. LSJ s.v. παρά C.III.7).

[51] O. suggests this is Zeno.

[52] Contra Gigante, *Ricerche filodemee*, 81, who sees in this fragment "a consciously positive evaluation of Socratic irony ... as an excellent requirement of caring admonishment"; for the Epicurean criticism of Socratic dissimulation, cf. Mark T. Riley, "The Epicurean Criticism of Socrates," *Phoenix* 34 (1980) 55–68; Glad, *Paul and Philodemus*, 121–22, 127.

[53] O.'s conjecture for line 12 ("gladly receive admonishment") is pure speculation.

δ]ακνούσης ἄπαντας <ε>ιρω-
10 νείας· καὶ δὴ γὰρ ὑπὸ ταύ-
της ἔ[ν]ιοι δελεα[ζό]μενοι

---

12 [τὴν νουθέτησιν ἡδέως ἀναδέ|χονται] suppl. O.

Fr. 27   [τὸν θυμὸν
ἐν [τῆι παρ]ρησί[αι μὲν οὐκ
ἀπες[τρα]μμένον ἐμφαί-
νους[ι]ν. πολλάκις δὲ τι-
5 μ[ῶςί] σε καὶ οὐ [τ]ὴν ἐ[π]ί σοι
διαλέ[γουσ]ιν τ[ε]θαρρηκό-
τως ἐπιφών[η]σιν· "εἶτ' οἶ-
μαι κατὰ λόγον". * ὡς παρὰ
τοιούτων, ὁπόταν ἀκού-
10 σ]ωσιν, [ἤ]κουσιν ἄτεροι καὶ
διατι[θ]έντ[ες π]ως πρὸς
τ]οιο[ύτους

4-5 τι|μ[ῶςί] σε Ph. τὸ | μ[...]σε O.   11-
12 διατι[θ]έντ[ες π]ως πρὸς | τ]οιο[ύτους Ph.

Fr. 28   [κα-
λ]ῶς ὁ Φιλο[ν]ε[ίδ]ου θηρευτής·
κἂν π[ε]ριδεικνύωμεν
ἐπιλογιστικῶς, ὅτι πολ-
5 λῶν καὶ καλῶν ἐκ φιλίας
περιγινομένων οὐδέν
ἐστι τηλικοῦτον ὡς τὸ ἔ-   5
χει<ν>, ὧι τὰ[γ]κάρδ[ι]ά τις ἐ-
ρεῖ καὶ λ[έγ]οντος ἀκούσε-
10 ται. σφόδ[ρ]α γὰρ ἡ φύσις ὀρέ-
γεται πρ[ό]ς τινας ἐκκαλύ-
πτειν ἃ [ν]οεῖ. λοιπὸν δὲ   10

1-2 [κα|λ]ῶς ὁ Φιλο[ν]ε[ίδ]ου θηρευτής· Ph.

Fr. 27: ...they indicate that [their spirit] has [not] been alienated in [the process of frank criticism]. Often they <[honor]> you and they do not boldly examine the charge against you: "I think, then, with reason." Since, from such people, whenever they are listening, others come and <being rather disposed toward [such people]>...

Fr. 28: ... <[nicely] the hunter of [Philonides?].> Even if we demonstrate logically that, although many fine things result from friendship, there is nothing so grand as having one to whom one will say what is in one's heart and who will listen when one speaks.[54] For our nature strongly desires to reveal to some people what it thinks. And furthermore...

---

[54] See Asmis, "Philodemus' Epicureanism," 2395 n. 60: "It is not clear whether Philodemus (or Zeno) endorses this view. If so, he values the intimacy of friendship more than the security that results from it."

Fr. 29

καταρχώμεθα cή[με]ρόν
που καὶ α[ὐ]τὰc τ[ιθῶμ]εν
εἰc ἐκε[ί]νου τὴν [αἴcθ]η-
cιν· ὃ κα[ὶ] τῶν κω[μω<ι>δ]ογρ[άφων
5   ἐμιμή[c]αντό τινεc εἰc-
αγα[γ]όντεc πρεσβύτ[αc], μ[ὴ
καλῶc μὲν ἀποθ[νή]<ι>cκον-
ταc, ἐλεοῦνταc δὲ τοὺc υἱ-
οὺc [αὐτῶ]ν γηράc[κονταc.

2–4 καὶ λ[ι]τὰc τ[ιθῶμ]εν | εἰc ἐκε[ί]νου τὴν [cτέρ]η|cιν·
suppl. Ph.

Fr. 30

      ἀλλ᾽ ἧττον ἐ-
πιcτρέφε[ται] τῆc ἑαυτοῦ
βλ]άβηc ὅ τε προcδεόμε-
νοc ἔτι πάνυ τῶν ἔξω-
5   θεν καὶ τιc ἀπὸ τῆc δια-
θέ[c]εωc, ἀ[κε]ίοιc, τῶι μὲν
ἀν[τ]ιταττόμενοc, τὸ δὲ
καταποδ[ί]ζων, ἅτε προc-
ὸν ὀδυ[ν]ηρόν. ἄχθεται
10 δὲ τά τε ἄλλα καὶ ἐπὶ ταῖc
[ἐπιτιμήcεcιν ἀλγεῖ.

5 καὶ <πᾶc> τιc O.

Fr. 31

      [τῶν
νέων ο[ἱ μὲν διερεθίζονται,
ὅταν μέ[λ]λω[cιν ἐπιτιμᾶcθαι,
κἂν] ἀχα[ι]ῶι περι[βλη]θῶ-
5   cι. τούτου μὲν οὖ[ν] ἐπι-
cτ]ρεφόμενοι, τὸ λεγόμε-
νον διὰ [τῆc] παρ[ρηcία]c
δυcχερῶ[c προcδέχονται,
καὶ ἐπὶ τ[ού]τωι διαγε[νό-
10 μ]ε[νοί τιν]εc οὐκ ἔcθ᾽ ὅ-

Fr. 29: Let us begin today perhaps and [let us place] them before his [awareness].[55] Which some of the [comic playwrights] also portrayed when they brought on stage old men who did not die nobly but pitied [their] sons growing old...

Fr. 30: ...but he pays less attention to his own injury who still is very much in need of external things and someone who,[56] because of his condition, opposes one thing and obstructs another with [medicines], since pain is present. And he is vexed at other things and in particular [suffers at the reproaches]...

Fr. 31: ...of [the] young men, [some are very irritated] whenever [they are going to be reproached], [even if] they are clothed in Greek style.[57] Paying attention to this,[58] accordingly, [they accept] with annoyance what is said in frankness, and for this reason[59] [some] [who have been through it] cannot possibly endure [to listen] to [a teacher?][60] with goodwill.

---

[55] It is not clear to what "them" or to whom "his" (literally: "of that one") refers. Ph.'s restorations may be translated: "and let us make entreaties for the loss of that [i.e., life]."

[56] Omitting O.'s addition πᾶς, "all."

[57] Punctuating with Marcello Gigante, "Per l'interpretazione dell'opera filodemea 'Sulla libertà di parola,'" *CErc* 2 (1972) 64 n. 59. Ph. col. 683 suggests that "Greek" refers to the philosopher's dress; cf. texts cited in Gigante, "Interpretazione," 64 n. 60.

[58] Their annoyance (so Gigante, "Interpretazione," 64 n. 61), or perhaps the fact of being dressed as philosophers.

[59] Or, adopting G.'s reading διαγελώμενοι, we may construe: "when laughed at for this" (sc., wearing a philosopher's dress); cf. De Witt, "Organization and Procedure," 209.

[60] O.'s restoration is hesitantly accepted by Gigante ("Interpretazione," 64). The disegni reading suggests ἰδιώτου, "a layman"; in this case, the reference is to students who adopt a philosopher's dress and therefore refuse to listen to what a non-philosopher may say to them.

πως [καθηγη]τοῦ ἀκ[ούειν
κατ᾽ εὔνοιαν τολ[μῶσιν.

---

5 μὲν οὐ[κ] Ph.   9–10 διαγε[λώ|μ]ε[νοί G.
98 11 ...ΙΩΤΟΥ disegni

Fr. 32   τινὲς δὲ λ]αβόντες
τὴν ἀρχὴν πάνυ] πόρρωθεν,
ἔδο[ξαν ἐλθεῖ]ν ἐπὶ τήν, εἴ
ποτε γένοιτο, [ν]ουθέτησιν,
5   ὡς ἄλλοι [αἰ]φνίδιοι, καὶ π[α-
ρὰ] προς[δοκία]ν π[άν]τα ἰᾶ[c-
θαι δ]εδ[οκήκ]αϲι. τὸ δ᾽ ἄπ[α-
ϲι δε]δοκ[ημέ]νον, ὡς ὠφε-
λήϲ]ετα[ι τὸ] κνίϲμα δ᾽ ἔ[ϲτι-
10   ν ὅ τε θ[εραπε]ύεται καὶ κα-
θίϲτηϲι [τὴ]ν προκατ[α-
ϲκευὴν δραστικήν.]

9–12 suppl. Ph.

Fr. 33   καὶ μηδὲ τὴν ἐ-
λ]αχί[ϲτ]ην ε[ἰπ]εῖν αὐτοῦ
παρὰ [τ]οῦτο [π]ρο[c]κοπὴν
καὶ καταγν[ο]εῖν, μηδὲ
5   καθ᾽ ἕκ[αϲτον] τῶν [ψ]εγό[ν-
των [δι]καίων· ἀλλ᾽ ἔφη, κ[όϲ-
μον ἐπ᾽ ἄλ[λω]ν καὶ cὺν αὐ-
τῷ]ι [δὲ τ]ὸ καλὸν ἔξει[c

---

2 ε[ὐρ]εῖν Ph.   4 καταγω[γ]ὴν Ph.   5–6 [ψ]εγό[ν]-
των Ph.   8 ἔξει[c disegni, cf. etiam Ph.

Fr. 34   τὸ δὲ
ἄλ]λοις ὑπ[οτάτ]τεϲθαι
δεϲ]ποτικ[ῶϲ] καὶ ἔξουϲι
ϲφοδρ]ῶϲ δ᾽ [ἔ]χουϲιν ἀφό-
5   ρητ]ον. ἴϲωϲ <δὲ> τόδε ϲώ<ι>ζουϲι
πάνυ χ]αλεπόν, εἰ μὴ καὶ
τὸ δ]εῖϲθαι πρὸς πολλῶν   5

Fr. 32: ...[some], taking [their point of departure] from [very] far {back}, seemed to [proceed] {gradually} to admonishment, if it should ever occur, just as others have seemed to heal suddenly, and contrary to [all expectation].[61] But it has seemed [to all] that there will be benefit and that it is the irritation that both < [is treated] > and establishes an < [effective] preparation > ...

Fr. 33: ...and to mention neither his minimal [progress]—by this much[62]— and to ignore[63] {it}, nor {mention} each of those who < [blame] > {him} justly. But, he[64] said, < you will have > orderliness amid others and, with him, a fine...

Fr. 34: ... < [to be subjected to others] > who will also behave < [tyrannically] > they [vehemently] hold to be un[endura]ble. Perhaps for those who are saving {others} this is [very][65] difficult,[66] unless the need to be [ingratiating] with many and to [have honors] from many also [prevent]...

---

[61] Different interpretation in Glad, *Paul and Philodemus*, 136–37.

[62] For παρὰ τοῦτο in this sense, cf. LSJ s.v. παρά C.III.5.a.

[63] Ph. suggests καταγωγήν, "return."

[64] The reference is perhaps to Zeno.

[65] O. reads "in no way."

[66] Or, "for those who are saving this, it is [very] difficult."

χαριε]ντίζεϲθαι καὶ τὰϲ
τιμὰϲ ἔχ]ειν παρὰ πολλῶν
10 κωλύουϲιν]

1-3 τὸ δὲ | ἄλ]λοιϲ ὑπ[οτάτ]τεϲθαι | δεϲ]ποτικ[ῶϲ]
suppl. Ph.   6 πάνυ χ]αλεπόν Ph. οὔτι χ]αλεπόν O.
10 κωλύουϲιν Ph. κωλύωϲιν O.

Fr. 35

μ[άλιϲτα δὲ ζητή]ϲομεν
νο[υ]θετεῖν, εἰ καὶ μὴ τῶι
ϲοφῶι καὶ τῶι φ[ιλ]οϲόφωι
παραπλήϲιον· * εἶτα πα-
5 ραμεληθέντο[ϲ] τινὸϲ τῶν
τοιούτων οὐ κωλύομεν
ἐπιμέμφεϲθαι, [τ]ὸ δὲ διὰ
τὴν ποτε παράπτωϲιν ἁ-
πλῶϲ διαβεβλῆϲθαι πρὸϲ
10 τὸ ϲύνολον ο[ὐ]κ [ὀ]ρθῶϲ
ἡγούμεθα. * [πᾶ]ϲι δ᾽ ἡμῖν
μηδὲ τὸ

Fr. 36

καὶ τὸ δ[ι᾽ ἀλ]λήλων ϲώ<ι>-
ζεϲθαι πρὸϲ εὐφορ<ί>αν καὶ
μεγάλην εὔνοιαν ἐφόδι-
ον ἡγουμένουϲ, * ἐπεὶ καὶ
5 τὸ νεωτέροιϲ κατὰ τὴν
δ[ι]άθεϲιν πειθαρχῆϲαί
π[οτε, ἔτι δὲ] τὴν νουθέτη-
ϲιν ἐνε[γ]κε<ῖ> ν δεξιῶϲ ἀγα-
θὸ]ν καὶ πρόϲφ[ορον

Fr. 37

μηδ᾽ ἀ[π]ὸ
τῆϲ ἰδίαϲ κ[ατ]άρχεϲθαι βλά-
βηϲ, ὧ[ι]περ [το]ὺϲ πλείϲτουϲ
ὁρῶμεν] τῶν φιλολόγων,
5 μ]ηδὲ ϲοβ[αρῶ]ϲ καὶ [δι]ατε-
ταμένωϲ παρρηϲιάζε]ϲθαι,
μηδ᾽ ὑβριϲτικὰ] καὶ κα-
ταβλ[ητικά τινα μη]δὲ δια-

Fr. 35: ...but we shall [most of all seek] to admonish, even if not like the wise man and the philosopher. Then, if someone from among such men has been slighted, we do not prevent {him} from casting blame, and we do not rightly consider that he has simply been discredited toward the whole {group} because of a former slip. To [all] of us, neither the...

Fr. 36: ...and considering being saved by one another to be supplies toward contentment and great goodwill, since even to obey [at times] those who are too young in condition, [and further] to endure admonishment graciously, are good and [fitting]...

Fr. 37: ...nor to begin with one's own injury, < as [we see] >[67] that the majority of scholars {do}, nor to be [frank in a haughty] and [contentious way], nor to [say any insolent] and contemptuous or disparaging things[68] or even anything...

---

[67] Adopting Ph.'s readings; O.'s reading translates "by which it happens that the majority of scholars are tripped up."
[68] Cf. Plutarch *Quomodo adulator* 67EF.

συρτικὰ [λέγειν] ἤ τι καὶ

---

3 ὥ[c]περ Ph. ὥ[ι]περ O.   4 ὁρῶμεν] τῶν φιλολόγων
Ph. γίνεται] τῶν φιλολόγων <cφάλλεcθαι> O.

Fr. 38   μηδέπο[τέ
τι κ[α]τ[αβ]λητικὸν ὅλω[c
μηδ᾿ ἐ[πιτ]εταμένωι κ[α-
θόλου τόνωι, * μηδ᾿ ὀργι-
5   ζομένους ὑπομιμνή<ι>c-
κοντ[ά]c τε, διότι καὶ αὐτο<ὶ>
π]ολλάκις ἐπιτιμώμε-
νοι φέ]ρουcι, καὶ ὑ[π᾿ α]ὐτῶν
τοιο]ύτων οἴcουcιν νο[υ-
10   θετούμ]ενοι. * προcηκόν-
τωc δὲ] παρακαλοῦντα[c

5-6 ΥΠΟΜΙΜΝΗC|ΚΟΝΤ.C ΤΕ pap.
ὑπομιμνή<ι>c|κοντ[ά]c τε Ph. ὑπομιμνή<ι>c|κειν
ποτέ O. 6 αὐτο<ὶ> Ph.   8 φέ]ρουcι Ph. οἴc]ουcι O.

Fr. 39   μεμνῆcθαι δὲ τοῦ ἀ-]
πρεπὲc εἶναι μὴ τοῖc] κα-
θη]γουμένοιc [τὰ ἑαυτῶν
ο[ἷ]ον ἐπι<ρ>ρίπτειν καὶ μό-
5   νοιc ἐκείνοιc ἐπέ[χει]ν,
ὡc οὐδ᾿ ἐπὶ τῆc παραcκευ-
ῆc τῶν ἀγαθῶν, καὶ τοῦ
τελέωc αἰcχρὸν εἶναι,
τῆc μὲν τοῦ cώματος
10   θεραπ[ε]ίαc ἑαυτοῖc τι cυν-
αντιλαμβάνεcθαι κα[ὶ
μὴ τῶν ἰατρῶν ἐν ἅ-
παcιν <ἔχοντας> χρείαν, ἐπὶ δὲ τῆc
ψυ[χ]ῆc μὴ πειρᾶcθαι
15   [τῆc τοῦ cοφοῦ νουθετήcεωc

---

4 ο[ἷ]ον Ph. ὅ[λ]ον O.   13 <ἔχοντας> Thom
<ἔχειν> O.

Fr. 38: ...never {to say} anything contemptuous at all nor in general in a strained tone, nor reminding {them} when angry, because they themselves often [endure][69] being reproached and will endure [being admonished] by such men. But by suitably exhorting...

Fr. 39: ...[and to remember that it is improper not] to cast < [so to speak]> [their own affairs] upon the teachers and to present {them} to them only, as {if it were} not for the provision of good things, and that it is completely shameful to help themselves to some treatment of the body although not {[having]} need of doctors in everything, but in the case of the soul not to try [the admonition of the wise man]...

---

[69] O. reads "will endure."

Fr. 40

[χρὴ

γὰρ αὐτῶι δεικνύειν ἀν-]

υ]ποστόλως τὰς διαμαρ-

τί]ας καὶ κοινῶς εἰπ[εῖ]ν

5 ἐ]λαττώςεις. * εἰ γὰρ [ἦ]γη-

c]άμενος ἔνα τοῦτ[ο]ν [ὁ-

δηγὸν ὀρθοῦ καὶ λ[ό]γου

κα[ὶ] <ἔργου>, [ὅ]ν φ[ης]ι cωτῆρ[α] μό-

νο[ν, κ]αὶ ἐπιφωνή[c]ας τὸ "τού-

10 του [γ' ἐ]cπομένοιο," παρέδω-

κεν [ἑαυ]τὸν θεραπε[ύ]ειν,

πῶς οὐχὶ μέλλει ταῦτ', ἐν

οἷ]c δεῖται θεραπεύcε-

ως, δει]κνύειν αὐτῶι κα[ὶ νουθέτηςιν

15 προςδέχεςθαι;]

Fr. 41

ἀλ-

λ' ἀναγκαίως τό τε λαθραι-

οπραγεῖν ἀ[φ]ιλώτατον

δήπουθεν· ὁ δὲ μὴ προς-

5 α[ν]αφέρων φανερός ἐς-

τιν περιςτέλλων καὶ ταῦ-

τα τῶν φίλων τὸ[ν ἐ]ξο-

χώτατ[ον·] καὶ π[λ]εῖον ο[ὐ-

δὲν ἔςται κρύπτοντος·

10 οὐ γὰρ ἕν ἔλαθεν. * ὄν[τως

Fr. 42

τιθένα[ι πρὸ ὀμμάτων τὰ

τῶν "εἰ μὴ φιλ[άρ]γυρον ἢ

ἐρῶντα [ποεῖ]c παρακα-

θαρεῦcα[ι]" λόγον ἐξελεγ-

5 χόντων· ἔ[τι δὲ] τἄλλα πά-

ρακολουθοῦντα· καὶ τῶν

cυνήθων δὲ [π]ολλοὶ μη-

νύcουςιν ἐθελονταί πως,

οὐδ' ἀνακρίνοντος τοῦ

10 καθηγουμένο[υ δ]ιὰ τὴν

κηδεμ[ονία]ν καὶ καθό-

5

Fr. 40: ...for it is necesssary to show him his errors forthrightly and speak of his failings publicly. For if he has considered this man to be the one guide of right speech and [action], whom he calls the only savior, and {to whom}, citing the phrase, "with him accompanying {me},"[70] he has given himself over to be treated, then how is he not going to show to him those things in which he needs treatment, and [accept admonishment]?

Fr. 41: ...but to act in secret is necessarily most unfriendly, no doubt. For he who does not report {errors} is clearly covering up these things too from the most outstanding of his friends,[71] and there will be no advantage for the one who hides {things}; for not one thing escaped notice. [Truly]...

Fr. 42: ... < to put [before {his} eyes[72] the] {words} of those who test the argument, "unless you [make] an avaricious man or one who is in love be cleansed...," [and, further], the other things that follow {this} > .[73] And many of the companions will somehow voluntarily disclose {their secrets}, even without the teacher interrogating {them}, because of their concern and, in general, < complete choice as > ...

---

[70] Homer *Il*. 10.246-47, of Diomedes choosing Odysseus as his companion.

[71] I.e., the wise man.

[72] On visualization in Epicurean therapy, cf. Philodemus *Ir*. cols. I.21-27, III.13, IV.15-16 Indelli.

[73] I.e., the consequences of such vices.

λο]υ τέλ[ειαν] αἵρ[ες]ιν ὡς

1–6a suppl. Ph.   12 τέλ[ειαν] αἵρ[ες]ιν ὡς Ph.

Fr. 43

[τῶν γὰρ
ἀγαθῶ[ν ἕνεκα μεταποι-
ήσομεν [τὸν] ὁμ[ιλί]α<ι> γε-
νησό[μενον] φίλ[ων] τρόπον·
5   εἰ δὲ [ἀγαθ]ῶν, πῶς οὐχὶ καὶ
τῶν κακῶν; ὡς γὰρ ἕνε-
κεν εὐφροσύνη[ς] ἐκείνων,   5
οὕτω καὶ τούτων προσήκει
συνπαθίας χάριν, δι᾽ ἣν βο-
10 ηθούμεθα. * καὶ γὰρ εἰ μὲν
ἔς[τι παρ]ρης[ι]άσαντα μεῖ-
ναι ἐπὶ τῶν αὐτῶν, εἰ μη-
θὲν ἔξε[ις], σώς[εις] ἄνδ[ρα
φίλον·]

1–3 suppl. Ph.   4 ΦΙΛΟ.ΤΡΟΠΟΝ pap. φίλ[ων]
τρόπον Ph. φιλότροπον O.   10b–14 suppl. Ph.

Fr. 44

προσεκκάουσι[ν,
ὅταν ἐνέχωνται τοῖς α[ὐ-
τοῖς, κα[ὶ] μὴ φιλοῦσι μη-
δ᾽ εἰδόσι διορθοῦν μηδὲ
5   πείσουσι τοὺς πολὺ κρείτ-
τους, ἀντὶ τοῦ καθαρεύον-
τι καὶ στέργοντι καὶ κρείτ-
τονι καὶ γινώσκοντι θε-
ραπεύ[ε]ιν. ἄν τε μετὰ δ[ε-
10 ξ[ι]ῶν, [χ]ωρὶς τοῦ τἀπίχει-
ρα κάλλιστα κομίζεσθαι,

Fr. 45

[με-
τὰ πολλῆς πεπ[ο]ιθήσεως
ἄλλους νουθετήσομεν
καὶ νῦν καὶ διαπρέψαν-
5   τες οἱ καθ[ηγη]τῶν οὕτως
ἀπότομοι γενηθέντες·

Fr. 43: ... <[for, on account] of {our} good {qualities},[74] we shall [reform the] character of [friends]>[75] as it will come to be <by means of {our} conversation>. But if {on account} of [{our} good {qualities}], how not also of {our} bad ones? For, just as it is suitable on account of the good cheer of the former, so too thanks to sympathy for the latter,[76] through which we are helped. <For in fact if it is possible for you, having spoken frankly, to stay in the same {condition}—if you will withhold nothing—[you will] save a man [who is a friend]>...

Fr. 44: ...they further inflame {them} whenever they are involved with those same men, who do not like {them} nor know how to correct {them} nor will persuade those who are much better, instead of {being involved} with one who is pure and loves {them} and is better and knows how to treat {them}. And if he, with [handshakes], without obtaining the finest wages...

Fr. 45: ...we shall admonish others with great confidence, both now and when those {of us} who have become offshoots of our teachers have become eminent. And the encompassing and most important thing is, we shall obey Epicurus, according to whom we have chosen to live, as even...[77]

---

[74] So O., taking the reference to be to students who admire the traits of their teachers; Glad, *Paul and Philodemus*, 85-87, 109-110, 141-42, understands "the good students," and that the fragment refers to the teacher's approach to students of good or bad character.

[75] Following Ph.'s reading. O. reads "one who is attached to {our} character."

[76] Ph. understands "to endure frank criticism," to which the following clause then refers.

[77] O. reads $\pi\alpha\rho|\rho\eta\sigma$... at the end of the line.

καὶ τὸ cυνέχον καὶ κυρι-
ώτ[α]τον, 'Επικούρωι, κα-
θ' ὃν ζῆν ἡ<ι>ρήμεθα, πει-
10   θαρχήcομεν, ὡc καὶ παρ-
ρηc....]

Fr. 46   εἰ τὰ ὑπ]ο-
πτευόμενα π[ε]ρὶ το[ῦ c]ο-
φοῦ, καὶ κοινῶc τ[ο]ῦ κ[α-
θηγουμένου, καθάρcε-
5   ωc δεῖται. πῶc γὰρ μιcεῖν
τὸν ἁμαρτάνοντα μὴ
ἀπογνώ[c]ιμα μέλλει, γι-
νώcκω[ν] αὐτον οὐκ ὄν-
τα τέλε[ι]ον καὶ μιμνή<ι>[cκων,
10   ὅτι πάντεc ἁμαρτάνειν εἰώ-]
θαcιν;]

Fr. 47   καὶ
διαπ[ράξομεν οὐδὲν ταῖ]c
παρ[ρηcίαιc, εἴ γ' ὡc βαcι]λεῖc
ἐκελεύο[μεν] εἰ[πεῖν ἐξ ἀρ]χῆc,
5   ἀλλὰ δέοc, μ[ὴ βλάπτωμε]ν
τοιαῦτα λ[αλοῦντεc] ἡμᾶc.
διὸ cυνφέρ[ο]ν [τ]ὰ διcταζό-
μενα μεταδιδόνα[ι·] τὰ
τοίνυν [πρ]ὸc [παρρηc]ία[ν
10   οὕ]τωc διατιθέν[τεc τ]ά τε   5

1-5 suppl. Ph.   6 λ[αλοῦντεc] Ph. λα[λεῖ πρὸc] O.

Fr. 48   πα[ρρηc]ιάζεcθαι δ' ἡ<ι>[ρήμε-
θ' ἀ[παθῶc], οὔτ[ε διὰ] φι-
λήcεωc τοῦ λαλεῖν ὑπὲρ
τοῦ πάθου[c], ὥcπερ ἔ[ν]ιοι π[οι-
5   οῦcι τῶ[ν ἐρ]ώντων, ὅτ[αν κα-
ταλέγε[ιν] τ[ὴ]ν μοῖράν τι-
νοc ὅμοιόν [τ'] εἰπεῖν ὑποcπά-
cωcι cυνδειπνοῦντεc. ἄλ[λα

Fr. 46: ...[if the] things that are suspected concerning the wise man, and the teacher generally, need purification. For how is he going to hate the one who errs, though not desperately, when he knows that he himself is not perfect and rem[inds {himself} that everyone is accustomed to err?]

Fr. 47: ... < and we [shall accomplish nothing by {exercises of} frank speech, if we, indeed, like kings], kept ordering {them} [to speak from the beginning], but {we have} fear lest [we harm ourselves]> when we <[utter]> such things.[78] Therefore, it is advantageous to share things that are doubted. Setting forth the things relating to [frankness] in this way, then, and [the]...

Fr. 48: ...and we have [chosen] to be frank [dispassionately], and not [through] fondness for speaking in behalf of passion as some men do when in love, when their fellow diners shy away from recounting someone's lot and from saying that kind of thing. Other things are worthy of discussion in respect to {one's} disposition. But if one examines and...

---

[78] O. restores "[he] speak[s] such things [to] us."

δὲ τἀξιό[λ]ογα κατ[ὰ τῆ]c δια-
10 θέcεωc· ἐὰν δ' ἐξετάζῃ<ι> καὶ

Fr. 49   ἐπαι]νεῖc-
θαι τὸν Ἡρακλείδην, ὅτι τὰc
ἐκ τῶ[ν] ἐνφαν[η]cομένων
μέμψειc ἥττο[υ]c τιθέμε-
5 νοc τῆ[c] ὠφελία[c] αὐτῶν,
ἐμήνυεν Ἐπικούρωι τὰc
ἀμαρτίαc· καὶ Πολύαινοc
δὲ τοιοῦτοc ἦν, ὅc γε καὶ Ἀ-
πολλωνί]δου ῥα<ι>θυμοῦν-
10 τ]ο[c, ἐφοίτ]α πρὸc Ἐπ[ί]κουρον.

Fr. 50   ἀλ[λὰ
καὶ τὴν δυcωπίαν ἡμᾶc πε-
ριcτῆναι· * διά[β]ολόν τε
γὰρ ο[ὐ]χ ἡγήcετ[α]ι τὸν ἐπι-
5 θυμοῦντα τὸν φίλον τυ-
χεῖν διορθώcεωc, ὅταν
μὴ τοιοῦτοc ᾖ<ι> τιc, ἀλλὰ
φιλόφιλον· τὴν γὰρ διαφο-
ρὰν ἀκριβῶc ἐπίcταται
10 τὴν ἐν τούτοιc, ἐὰν δὲ μὴ
μεταδιδῷ<ι> κ[ακό]φιλον
καὶ φιλόκακον [κ]α[ὶ] τοῦ τε

Fr. 51   ἀκ[ού]cει μᾶλλον, [ἄ-
μα καὶ θεωρῶν ἡμᾶc κα[ὶ
ἑαυτῶν γινομένουc κα-
τηγόρουc, ὅταν [τ]ι διαμα[ρ-
5 τάνωμεν. * τὸ δὲ τοὺc
πλείοναc ὑποφείδεcθαι
ποιοῦν, μὴ καὶ αὐτοὶ δια-
βληθῶcιν, οὓc χρὴ καθά-
πτεcθαι τοῦ φρονοῦντ[οc
10 κακῶc

Fr. 49: ...that Heraclides is [praised] because, deeming the censures for the things that would be revealed to be less {important} than their benefit, he disclosed to Epicurus his errors. Polyaenus too was such a man, who indeed, when A[polloni]des was remiss, [would go] to Epicurus...

Fr. 50: ...but that we also avoid false modesty.[79] For he will not consider a slanderer one who desires that his friend obtain correction, when he is not such {i.e., a slanderer}, but rather one who is a friend to his friend. For he understands exactly the difference between these, and if he does not give away[80] a bad friend and a friend of the bad, and of the...

Fr. 51: ...he {the teacher} will rather listen, at the same time as he observes us becoming accusers even of ourselves, whenever we err. That which makes most people, who must upbraid the one who is thinking badly, be sparing, lest they themselves be slandered...

---

[79] Cf. Plutarch De vit. pudor. 528C–536E.
[80] I.e., report such people to the teacher.

Fr. 52

μ[ᾶ]λλον, ἀλλὰ [μὴ τὴν ἴϲην
μετροῦντες, ἵνα θ[η]ριωθ[ῶ-
μεν πρὸς αὐτούϲ (οὐ γὰρ
πε[ρὶ] φ[ι]λίουϲ οὐδὲ περὶ ν[ε-
5   ωτέρουϲ γίνεται ταῦ-
τα), * μηδὲ τοῖϲ καθηγη-
ταῖϲ προστροχάζοντεϲ,
ἵνα δ[ο]κῶμεν αὐτοῖϲ εὐ-
νοεῖ[ν], ἅ τιϲ εἴρηκεν κα-
10   τ᾽ αὐτῶν ἢ πε[πο]ίηκεν ἀπα[γ-
γέλλοντεϲ, καὶ ταῦτα κα-
τὰ c[υ]νήθων, μηδὲ κατ[α

Fr. 53

                                εἰ
ἄρα κατὰ τρόπ[ον] ϲυλλογι-
ζόμεθα. * εἰ καὶ πρὸς τοὺς
ϲυνκαταϲκευαζομένουϲ
5   τὰ ἑαυτῶν καὶ τὰ ἀλλήλων προοίϲονται. πρὸς
τοίνυν τοὺϲ ϲυνκαταϲκευ-
αζομένουϲ λέγειν τὰϲ
ἰδίας ἀγνοίαϲ εὐλαβῶϲ
10   ἐκτέον. ἔνιοι γὰρ οὔτ᾽ ὠ-
φελήϲουϲι βάθουϲ ἐϲτε-
ρημένοι ϲυ[ν]έϲεωϲ τάχα

Fr. 54

                        καὶ ϲτορ-
γὴν πρὸς ἡμᾶϲ τήνδ᾽, οἵηϲ
ἰδεῖν βίαν οὐ προϲφερο-
μένουϲ· * ἐνίοτε γὰ[ρ οὗ-
5   τοι μᾶλλον ὠφελοῦ[ϲι
τῶν ἐν τῶι λόγω<ι> ῥυ[θμι-
κῶν, καὶ θᾶττον ἂν δ[ιαρ-
ραγείηϲαν ἤ τι προϲ[θεῖ]ναι
τῶν οὐ δεόντων ἐκ [πο-
10   λυχαρο[ῦ]ϲ ὁμοιώ[ϲεωϲ· καὶ
περὶ τῶν ϲυνή[θων

---

3 ΕΙΑΝ pap. βίαν O. app. crit.

Fr. 52: ...more, but [not] measuring out [an equal {portion}], so that we are bestial toward them (for these things are not done concerning friendly people or those who are too young), nor running up to the teachers so that we may seem to bear them goodwill by reporting what he {a student} has said or done against them, and {doing} these things against their companions, nor against...

Fr. 53: ...if, then, we infer properly. *Whether they will declare things of their own and of one another to their fellow-students.* One must, then, be cautious in speaking of one's own ignorance to fellow-students. For some, who are bereft of depth of understanding, will neither benefit perhaps...

Fr. 54: ...and not applying to us this love, which is of such a kind that one may see its [force]. For sometimes they will no more benefit {others} than experts on rhythms in a speech, and they would sooner burst than add something that is not wanting from a graceful simile. [And] about their companions...

Fr. 55

κα[ὶ δι-
δ]όναι παρρησίαι τὰ πε-
ρὶ αὐτοὺς ἐπὶ τῶν κατα-
σκευαζομένων, τίθε-
5   σθ[α]ι παρ᾽ Ἐπικούρωι καὶ χάριν διορθώσεως. * οὐ μὴν
ἀλλ᾽ εἴ τω<ι> φίλον, λεγέσθω[ι]·
"διὰ τί τῶν μὲν ἐξ ἀφρο-
σύνης ἁμαρτημάτων
10   χάριν διορθώσεως ὁ
παντὸς ἀγνεύων [οὐδ᾽ ἂν]
οὐδ᾽ ἐν ἂν προσενέγκ[αιτο;"

Fr. 56

εἰ ἡμῖν δοκεῖ διαπεσεῖ-]
σθαι κατὰ] τὴν [τελειότητα
τοῦ] λογισμοῦ π[ροειλημμένοις.
ν[ῦ]ν οὐχ ἡμ[ῖν] δοκεῖ δια-
5   πεσεῖσθαι προειλημμέ-
νο[ι]ς τε κατὰ λογισμοῦ τε-
λειότητα καὶ φρονήσε-
ως· * καθὸ δὲ καὶ τὸ μὴ
τυχεῖν τοῦ τέλους καὶ τὸ
10   παρελθεῖν [ἐκ] τῶν οὐ δυ-
ναμένων διὰ παντὸς
ἀνθρώπωι φ[υ]λαχθῆναι,
διαπεσεῖσθαι καὶ ἐν παρ-
ρησίαι οὐκ ἀδύνατον.]

Fr. 57

[κἂν μὴ
κατειλήφηι ἐρ[ῶν]τας
ἢ κατασ[χ]έτους κακίαις
τισίν, ἀλλὰ σημειωσά-
5   μενον. εὐλόγιστα δὲ στο-
χαστὰ μὴ διὰ παντ<ὸς> ἀ-
ποβαίνειν οἷα κατηλπίσ-
θη, κἂν ἄκρως ἐκ τῶν [ε]ἰκό-
των συντίθηται τὰ τῆς
10   εὐλογία[ς, δεῖ γ]ε κἂν θές[ει

Fr. 55: ...and they [present] for frank criticism what concerns themselves in the presence of the students, to be put before Epicurus and for the sake of correction. Nevertheless, if it is pleasing to someone, let it be said: "Why is it that the purifier of everyone {i.e., Epicurus}, for the sake of correction of the errors arising from foolishness, would not present even one..."[81]

Fr. 56: *[Whether it seems to us that one will slip up in accord with] the [perfection] of reason [by means of what is preconceived.]*[82] Now, it does not seem to us that we will slip up, having been outstripped in accord with the perfection of reason and prudence. But in respect both to not attaining perfection[83] and to passing [from] things that can not be permanently defended[84] by a human being,[85] one will slip and [it is not impossible] both in [frank criticism]...

Fr. 57: ...[even if] {it is the case that} he has [not] caught them in love or possessed by some vices, but has inferred {it} from signs. But that reasonable conjectures do not always turn out as expected, even if one concludes strictly from what is likely things {that come} of reasonable argument, [one must, at least,] agree, even if by hypothesis, because reason induces {one} to treat fully and...

---

[81] Sc., perhaps, "of his own errors as an example."

[82] For προειλημμένα, cf. the role of "preconception" or πρόληψις in Epicurean epistemology.

[83] Or "not attaining one's end."

[84] Or, restoring τι in place of O.'s suggestion ἐκ, "and to something eluding [us from] the things that can not be in every case guarded."

[85] I.e., ideas not grounded in προλήψεις.

ὁμολογῆcαι, διότι λόγοc
αἱρεῖ κατενχειρεῖν * καὶ

Fr. 58   [ὅ-
θεν ὡ[c] ὀργίζε[τ]αι δι' αὐτὸ τ[ὸ αἰτ]ιᾶcθαι πρόc τινων
ὀργιcθῆναι, καὶ παρρηcιά-
5   cεται δ[ι]ὰ τὸ ποῆcαι παρρη-
cιάcαcθαι πρὸc αὐτούc, οὐ-
κ ὀλι< γ >άκιc δὲ κατὰ μεικτὸν
τρόπον διαπτ[ώ]cεωc γε-
νομέ[ν]ηc. * ἐπιcτήcειε
10   δ' ἄν τιc, εἰ δυναμένου βελ-
τίονο[c] μειωθῆ[ν]αι διὰ [μα-
κρότητα χρόνου, φοβού-
μενο[c μ]ή τι μέγα cυνβῆ< ι >

Fr. 59   ἔ]cτι δ' ὅτε καὶ φιλοc[ο-
φίαc ἀποcτήcεται, τάχα
δέ που καὶ μιcήcει τὸν
cοφόν, ἐνίοτε δ' ὑποίcε[ι
5   μέν, ο[ὐ]δὲν δ' ὠφεληθήcε-
ται, διαλαβόντοc ὠφελη-
θήcεcθαι. * καὶ ταῦτα cυν-
πεcεῖται, φημί, διὰ πολ-
λὰc α[ἰ]τίαc· ἢ γὰρ ἀcθενε[ῖ]c
10   ὄντεc ἢ γενόμενοι [δ'] ἀ-
ν]αλθεῖc ὑπὸ τῆc παρρηcίαc

Fr. 60   καὶ κατηξίωc[άν τινεc
παρρηcιάζεcθα[ι πρὸc
τοὺc τοιούτ[ουc, εἰκῆ]ι δέ,
τῆc πικρᾶc πα[ρρηcίαc] ὁ-
5   μοιότητα πρὸc τὴν [λοι]δο-
ρίαν ἐχούcηc, ὡc λοιδορού-
μενοι καὶ ἀπὸ δυcνοίαc·
πολλοὺc δὲ καὶ γόητεc ἄν-
θρωποι μετὰ τὴν ἀνάτα-
10   cιν ἐγλαβόντεc ἀποδια-

Fr. 58: ...hence, just as he is angry because of the very [accusation] on the part of some people that he was angry, he also speaks frankly because they made him speak frankly toward them, a failure occurring not infrequently in a mixed way. One might understand if, given that a better person can deteriorate over a long stretch of time, {and} fearing lest something serious happen...

Fr. 59: ...but there are times when he will shun even philosophy, and perhaps will even hate the wise man, and sometimes he will submit, but will not be benefitted, although he {the teacher} has supposed that he will be benefitted. And these things will occur, I say, for many reasons. For since they are either weak[86] or have become incurable because of frankness...

Fr. 60: ...and [some] have judged it right to speak frankly [to] such people, but [moderately],[87] given that sharp frankness bears a similarity to insult, as if insulting indeed out of ill will. Men who are charlatans, too, divert many, seizing them after some stress and enchanting them with their subtle kindnesses.

---

[86] Or "sick" (Glad).
[87] O. supplies "others."

στρέφουσι ποικίλαις φιλο-
φροσύναις κατ[ε]πάισα[ντες.

---

3 εἰκῆ]ι δέ Ph. ἄλλο]ι δέ O.

Fr. 61   ἐλύ[π]ηce
τὸν νουθετούμενον ἀ-
γνώcτωc τοῖc πέλαc διὰ
π]ᾶ[ν] καὶ μηδ᾽ ἂν ἱλαρῶc εὐ-
5   θὺc ἕνεκα τῆc φάcεωc ὀδυ-
νᾶcθαι· * ἐνίοτε δ᾽ ἀνα-
πλαcθὲν εὐτύχημα, πολ-
λάκιc δὲ καὶ φανερὸν [ἄ]λ-
λοιc γενόμενον, ἔλα-
10   θ[ε]ν καθηγούμενον, * εἰ
μή [τ]ι οὐκ ἀπρόcωπον δι-
αλήcεται cυνπαραληφθὲν

4–5 ἐνί|οιc G. 82

Fr. 62   ἐπιτιμώ]μενος
ἢ φθον[εῖν] ἢ χλευάζειν
ἤ τι πάcχειν τῶν τοι[ο]ύ-
των· [φά]ναι δὲ κ[α]ὶ τὸ δ[ο-
5   κεῖν ἄλ[γι]ο[ν] δι᾽ αὐτῶν ὥcπερ εὐκαταφρονήτων δι-
ορθοῦcθαι· εἰ μὴ καὶ τὸ παρ-
ρηcιάcαcθαί ποτε τὸν co-
φόν, οὐδ[ὲ]ν αὐτῶν ἡμαρ-
10   τηκότων, παραλογιcθέν-
τα καὶ παρρ[ηc]ίαν ἴcωc
ἀτ]όπ[ωc διὰ πολλὰc] αἰτίαc
προcφέροντα].

Fr. 61: ...he {the teacher} hurt the one who was being admonished [wholly] unbeknownst[88] to those nearby,[89] and {they said?} that, {admonished} cheerfully, he would not even have been pained straightaway on account of the statement. Sometimes when well-being has been restored,[90] and often even when it has become clear to others, it has escaped the notice of a teacher. If something not impersonal that has been brought in will not escape notice...

Fr. 62: ...that [the one being reproached] {thinks that they} envy or scorn {him} or are experiencing some such thing; and that {he} says that it is more painful even to seem to be corrected by them, as they are contemptible, except for the fact that even the wise man has at times spoken frankly when they have not erred, because he has reasoned falsely and perhaps [applies] frankness [wrongly for many] reasons.

---

[88] LSJ s.v. ἀγνώστως, "inconsiderately"; Vooijs and Krevelen s.v., "imprudenter"; but these renderings fail to account for the dative τοῖς πέλας.

[89] I.e., his fellow-students; see Gigante, *Ricerche filodemee*, 82.

[90] Gigante renders "feigned" (ibid.).

Fr. 63   [οὐ-
χ ἡμαρτηκὼc [εὑρεθήcεται.
παραπλήcιον γάρ ἐcτιν ὥc-
περ εἴ τιc ἰατρὸc ὑπολαβὼν
5   διὰ cημείων εὐλόγων
προcδεῖcθαι τουτονί τινα
κενώματοc, εἶτα διαπε-
cὼν ἐν τῆι cημειώcει, μη-
δέποτε πάλι κενῶcαι τοῦ-
10   τον ἄλλη<ι> νόcωι cυνεχόμε-
νον. * ὥcτε νο[ῶ]ν καὶ δι᾽ αὐτὸ τοῦτο πάλι π[αρ]ρηc[ιά-
cεται].

Fr. 64   καὶ μηδὲν π[εράνα]c πάλι χρή-
c]εται πρὸc [τ]ὸν α[ὐ]τόν. * εἰ δ᾽ ἡ-
μαρτηκὼc οὐχ ὑπήκουcε
τῆc παρρηcίαc, πάλι παρρη-
5   cιάcεται· * καὶ γὰρ ἰατρὸc ἐ-
π[ὶ] τῆc αὐτῆc νόcου διὰ κλυc-
τῆ]ροc οὐδὲν περάναc, πάλ[ι
κε]νοῖ. * καὶ διὰ τοῦτο πάλ[ι
π]αρρηcιάcεται, διότι πρό-
10   τερον οὐδὲν ἤνυcε, καὶ
πάλι ποήcει τοῦτο καὶ πά-
λιν, ἵν᾽ εἰ μὴ νῦν ἀλλὰ νῦν
τελεcφορήcηι.]

Fr. 65   [εἰ δὲ
παρρηcί]αι χρήcεται π[άλιν,
φανε[ῖται] οὕτωc ἐφικέcθαι.
πολλάκι δ᾽ ἀντιcτρόφωc,
5   ποτὲ δὲ καὶ ποήcαc, ἢ ἐξ-
ῆc πρότερον ἢ δευτέρ[α,
τάχα δ᾽ ἡ τρίτη τελεcφορή-
cει· * καὶ τότε, τοῦ πάθουc
ἀκμάζοντοc, ἀπειθήcαc,
10   νῦν, ἀνέντοc, μετακληθή-
cεται· καὶ διὰ τοῦτ᾽ ἀπειθή-

Fr. 63: ...[he will be discovered not] to have erred. For it is like when a doctor assumes because of reasonable signs that a certain man is in need of a purge, and then, having made a mistake in the interpretation of the signs, never again purges this man when he is afflicted by another disease. Thus, [judging] by this very thing {i.e., the analogy}, he will again [speak frankly].

Fr. 64: ...and [having accomplished] nothing he will again employ {frankness} toward the same man. If, although he has erred, he {the student} did not heed the frank criticism, he {the teacher} will criticize frankly again. For although a doctor in the case of the same disease had accomplished nothing through a clyster, he would again purge {the patient}. And for this reason he will again criticize frankly, because before he accomplished nothing, and he will do this again and again, so that if not this time then another time...[91]

Fr. 65: ...[if] he will employ [frankness again], he will be seen to succeed thus. And often conversely, at times even when he has done it, either the second one in turn, or perhaps the third {application of frankness} will first succeed.[92] And though he disobeyed then, when the passion was at its height, now, when it has relaxed, he will be called back; also having disobeyed for this reason, {namely,} that he attacks since he pretended that the opposite things [would escape notice], [he will now be called back].

---

[91] O. suggests the supplement "he will succeed," or the like.

[92] Ph.'s suggestion may be translated "though the earlier does not, the second and third will succeed"; G.'s "at times even when he has done it either earlier, beginning on the same (day), or on the second (day), he will in fact, perhaps, succeed on the third (day)."

cac, ὅτι προcβάλλει δι[αλ]ή-
c]εcθαι τἀνα[ντ]ία ψ[ε]υcθείc,
νῦν μετακληθήcεται.]

5-6 ποηcάcηc μ[ὴ | τῆc πρότερον (sc. παρρηcίαc) Ph.
5-7 ποηcαc ἢ ἐξ [αὐ]|τῆc πρότερον ἢ
δευτέρ[αι], | τάχα δὴ τρίτη<ι> G. 104

Fr. 66   [καὶ
πρότερον ἀπειθήcαc, ὡc ἀλλο-]
τρίαν ὑπερ[ορῶν ἐπι-
φοράν, ὕcτερ[ο]ν δ᾽ [ἀπαγο]ρεύ-
5   cαc, πειθαρχήcει τῆ[ι νο]υθε-
τείαι· * καὶ [τ]ότε cυν[ε]χόμε-
νοc τοῖc ἐκχαυνο[ῦ]cι πά-
θεcιν ἢ κοινῶc ἀντικρού-
ουcιν, εἶτα κουφιcθείc, ὑπα-
10   κούcεται· * καὶ τότε τυχὼν
τῶν διαcτρεφόντων, νῦν
οὐ τεύξετα[ι]· καὶ πρότερον
ἀν[τ]ιδοκε[ύ]ων, κα[ὶ] το[ῦ]-
το πλανω[δ]ῶc οὐ πεπόη-
15   κεν, ὕcτερο[ν] φωραθεὶc κα[ὶ
εὐφρονῶν ποήcει.]

3-4 ὑπερ[ορῶν ἐπι]|φοράν G. 79-80 ὑπερ[βάλλων
cυμ]|φοράν O.

Fr. 67   ἅμα [καὶ] τὴν cυνοίδ[η]cι[ν
ἐπιταθηcομένην οὕτω[c,
τήν τ᾽ ἐκ τῶν ἄλλων καὶ
αὐτῶν τῆι προcκαρτερή-
5   cει cυνειδηcάντων, ἐλατ-
τωθηcομένην δ᾽, ἐὰν τα-
χέωc ἀποτρέπ[η]ται τῆc
τοῦ διαπίπτοντοc βοη-
θείαc. * εἰ καὶ πρὸc τοὺc μὴ
10   φέρονταc παρρηcίαν π[α]ρ-
ρηc[ι]άcεται, καὶ πρὸc τὸν
ὀργίλον.]

Fr. 66: ...[and although he disobeyed earlier, disdaining the reproach[93] as foreign {to himself}], later he will [give up] and obey the admonition. Then, he was afflicted with passions that puff one up or generally hinder one, but afterwards, when he has been relieved, he will pay heed. Then, he encountered {passions} that distort {one}, but now he will not encounter them. Earlier, he was on the look-out,[94] and in wandering about[95] he has not done this; later, when he has been detected, he will indeed [do it cheerfully].

Fr. 67: ...when they have recognized at the same time that the swelling will be intensified to this extent, and {have recognized} the {swelling} deriving from other {passions}, and by their persistence, but that it will be reduced, if he quickly turns away from assisting the one who is slipping up. *Whether he will also speak frankly to those who do not endure frank criticism, and to one who is [irascible]...*

---

[93] O.'s supplements may be translated: "surmounting the mishap."

[94] ἀν[τ]ιδοκε[ύ]ων. The verb is unattested elsewhere. The meaning "oppose one opinion to another" is proposed by Gigante, *Ricerche filodemee*, 79–80; and Vooijs and Krevelen.

[95] Gigante, *Ricerche filodemee*, 80, "in an erroneous way."

Fr. 68

    ποικίλης τε φ[ιλοτ]εχνί-
ας οὔσης, οἵαν ἐπεσημη-
νάμεθα, καὶ τῆς κεραν-
νυμένης δαψιλέσι τοῖς ἐ-
5 παίνοις καὶ προτρεπομέ-
νης τἀκόλουθα τοῖς ἀ-
γαθοῖς πράττειν, οἷς ἔχουσι,
πῶς οὐκ ἂν τῶν τοιού-
των ποιοῖτο τὰς ὑπομνή-
10 σεις; καὶ κατὰ τὰς δ[ι]δομέ-
νας δὲ [τῆς] πρὸς παρρησί[αν
ἀφορμὰς]

Fr. 69

    πρὸς τοὺς ὅσον ἐ-
πὶ τοῖς εὐλόγοις προσδο-
κωμένους οὐ[χ]ὶ σταθή-
cεcθαι, μιμούμενός τε
5 τοὺς καὶ τὸν εὐλόγως
νομιζόμενον οὐκ ἀπαλ-
λαγήcεcθαι τοῦ νοσήμα-
τος θεραπεύοντας ἰατρούς,
καὶ κ[α]θάπε[ρ] καὶ π[ροτρέ-
10 πεται τοὺς εὐλόγω[ς

Fr. 70

    ὁρῶμεν αὐτοὺς ἕνεκα τῶν]
ἔ]ξω πολλάκις [εἰς τὰ ἀν-
η]κεστὰ προβάντ[ας, εἰ ἐπέρ-
χεταί τι καὶ μέχρις ἀρτίως
5 εἰς τοὺς φίλους καὶ μάλι-
στα τοὺς καθηγουμένους.
πῶς χρήcεται τοῖς διὰ   5
τὴν παρρησίαν ὀργίλως
πρὸς αὐτὸν ἐσχηκόσιν;
10 ἐπεὶ δ᾿ ἐνίους cυνβαίνει,
πα[ρ]ρηcιαcαμένου τοῦ
c[ο]φοῦ, [δι]ατίθεcθαι πρὸς   10
αὐτὸν ὀργίλως, ἐὰν μ[ὲ]ν
ἔνμονον ἔχωcι τὴν [πα]ρ-

Fr. 68: ...since the artistry is subtle,[96] being such as we have indicated, and that which is combined with plentiful praises also exhorting {them} to do things that are consequent upon the good {qualities} that they possess, how would he not make mention of such things? And in accord with the given [capacities] for frank criticism...

Fr. 69: ...toward those who are expected not to halt[97] insofar as depends on reasonable {arguments},[98] imitating doctors who treat also one who is reasonably believed that he is not going to recover from his disease, and just as he also exhorts those who reasonably...

Fr. 70: ... < [we see them for the sake of] external things often proceeding [toward what is in]curable > , [if] something, even until recently, [goes against] the friends and especially the teachers. *How will he handle those who have become angry toward him because of his frank criticism?* Since it happens that some, when the wise man has spoken frankly, are angrily disposed toward him, if they have continual [frank criticism]...

---

[96] For the contrast between this "subtle" or multi-faceted ($\pi o\iota\kappa\iota\lambda\eta\varsigma$) form of frankness and the "simple" or severe form which uses only blame, cf. frs. 7, 10, 58.7-8, 60.3-10; Plutarch *Quomodo adulator* 73C-74C; and see n. 26 above.

[97] Sc. in their error.

[98] On the psychagogic enterprise as one which proceeds on the basis of probable inferences, cf. frs. 1.5-9, 56, 57, 63.3-5; and see n. 5 above.

15 ρησίαν]

1–3a suppl. Ph.

Fr. 71

ἐκ παρ]αλλήλου θεω-
ρήσας ὅτ[ι κα]τασκευαζό-
μενός τ᾽ ἀπαισχυνθείη,
μετρίως τε τὸ συναντή-
5 σαν οἴσει καὶ οὐχ ὡς ἀγέ-
νητον. προειδὼς τε πολ-
λοὺς εἰκὸς ἀπαυχενίζειν
τῶν νέων καὶ τοῖς ἄλλοις,
οἷς περι[λύ]πως ὀ[ργιζο-
10 μένους [δη]λοῦσι, [βοηθοῖς
χ[ρήσε]σθ[αι] προσαναπαυό-
μ[ενό]ς [τε] πρὸς ἀδεῶς [ἀντέχοντας

1 ἐκ παρ]αλλήλου suppl. Ph.   9–12 suppl. Ph.

Fr. 72

(διὸ
καὶ Ἐπίκουρος πρὸς Ἰδο-
μενέα γράφει μέχρι τού-
του ζῆν εὔ[χ]εσθαι)· * καὶ
5 παραδείξει πόσοι κακῶς
ἀ[π]ώλοντο παντὸς στερό-
μενοι διὰ τὴν τοιαύτην
διάθεσιν τοῦ μετὰ παρρη-
σία[ς] ὁμιλῆ[σαί τισι] καὶ πάν-
10 τ]α δ᾽ ὅσα προ[σενεγκό]ντες
με]τ[ά]γομεν, [κατ]α[φή]σει

8 τοῦ Ph. τῶι O.   11 suppl. Ph.

Fr. 73

[νουθε-
τεῖν, ἐπειδὴ [προσηκόν]τω[ς δια-
τίθεται, καθάπερ ὁ Ἐπίκουρος ἐπ[ιφο]ρὰς τ[ι]ν[ας] πρὸς
5 Ἀπο[λλ]ωνίδην ἐπόησεν,
ὥστε καὶ τοι[αῦτ᾽] α[ἰ]τι-
ώμε[νος, ἐ]άν [γ᾽ ἀλη]θινὸς

Fr. 71: ...analogously, having observed that he was ashamed when he was being instructed, he {the teacher} will endure what confronts {him}[99] moderately and not as something groundless. And knowing beforehand that it is likely that many of the young ones will rear their necks {against the yoke}[100] and <[will employ]> others, <to whom they [reveal] that they are painfully [angered], as [helpers], he, relying, before those who resist fearlessly, {on}>...

Fr. 72: ...(therefore even Epicurus writes to Idomeneus[101] that he prays to live up to this point). And he will point out how many came to ruin badly, bereft of everything because of such a disposition to converse with frankness [with certain people], and <[he will assent]> to all that we, having applied, <[transfer]>...

Fr. 73: ...to [admonish] {him}, since he is [suitably] disposed, just as Epicurus made certain reproaches against Apollonides, in such a way that, even in accusing him of these things, <provided he was [truth]ful, he [persuaded others] to acknowledge {them} as their own,[102] and many things, even if, being great men, they impugned[103] as having suffered {them} undeservedly and, [citing a rather Cynic-like rejoinder]>[104]...

[99] Or "the incident."

[100] For the metaphor, see Gigante, "Motivi paideutici," 39–41.

[101] This letter is not extant. For Epicurus' correspondence with Idomeneus, see G. Arrighetti, *Epicuro: Opere* (2d ed.; Turin: Einaudi, 1973) 427–32.

[102] Or "provided he is [truth]ful, he [persuades], and [others] acknowledge {them} as their own."

[103] Or "impugn besides."

[104] The subject of "citing" is still the "great men"; "many things" is the object of some lost verb in the singular, the subject of which was Epicurus (or perhaps the teacher).

ἦι, π[είθειν ἄλλους] δ' οἰκει-
ῶσαι * πολλά [τε, κἄ]ν ὄν-
10   τες μεγάλοι προς[επέ]λθω-
cι[ν, ὥ]cπερ ἀν[α]ξιοπαθή-
cαντες καὶ [ἀπάντηcιν κυ-
νι[κω]τέραν ἐπ[ιφωνοῦν-
τες]

7-14 ἐ]άν κτλ. suppl. Ph.

Fr. 74   ἠνείχετο [c]εμ[νό]τα-
τ' εἰς θυμουμένους π[ρ]αέ-
α παρέ[χ]ων, εἰ τοῖς ὕμνοις
ἐπαιρόμενος· ὕστερο[ν
5   δ' εἰ φιλόφρων ἐcτὶν πρὸς
ἡμᾶς, εἰ κατὰ τὴν εὔνοι-
αν ἐπιτεταμένος, εἰ   5
τῶν ἐνκαλουμένων
ἀπηντληκώς [τ]ι, κἂν
10   μήτε δὲ ἄ[παν]τα τε[λ]ει[ού-
μενος, εἰ καὶ πρὸς ἡμᾶς
καὶ πρὸς [ἑτέρ]ους εὐχα-   10
ριcτήcει;]

1-3 ἠνείχετο - εἰ suppl. Ph.

Fr. 75   γίν[ε-
cθαι τὰς [ἐ]πιτιμ[ή]cεις, ἀ[λ-
λ' οὐδὲ τὰς ὑπὸ τῶν καθ[η-
γουμένων. οἱ δὲ cυcχ[ο-
5   λάζοντες οἴδαcι τὸ[ι] πλῆ-
θος ὧν ἔχομεν ἀγαθῶν
καὶ παρέχουcιν αὐτοὺς
κἀκε[ῖ]νοι διορθοῦcθαι
ταπ[ει]ν[ῶc] οὐδ' ἐπὶ τού-
10   των ἡ παρρηcία γίνεται

---

9 ταπ[ει]ν[ῶc] Ph. ταῦτ', ἀλ[λ'] O.

Fr. 74: ...<he {the student} tolerated it most [solemnly], exhibiting [mildness] toward those who were maddened, if> he was lifted up by accolades. Later: *whether he is well-disposed toward us; whether he is intense in his goodwill; whether he has jettisoned some of the things charged against him, and even if not perfected in everything, whether toward us and toward [others] [he will be] thankful*[105]...

Fr. 75: ...that the reproaches occur, but not those {administered} by the teachers. Their fellow-students know the multitude of good things that we have and they too present themselves for correction <[humbly]>,[106] nor in the case of these does frank criticism occur...

---

[105] The italicized series of clauses are apparently topic headings. However, Ph. col. 685 takes them as the protasis of a conditional sentence.

[106] O.'s reading, which is difficult to construe, means "this {is so}, but."

Fr. 76

                [εἰ
μήτε πάντα [ποοῦcιν ἐκεῖ-
ν[ο]ι προcηκ[όντωc μ]ή[τε
τεύξετα[ι] νο[υθετήcεωc
5 τὰ τοιαῦτα [κ]αὶ τοῖc κ[αθη-
γουμένοιc ἀν[άπτ]ου[cιν,
οἷc ἐκθήcουcιν οἱ κατας[κευ-
αζόμενοι[c] μετὰ παρρη[cί-
αc τὰ ἑαυτῶν ἁμαρτή[μα-   5
10 τα καὶ [ἄλλω]ν δ᾽ ὑπο[θή-
cονται, "ἐπα]νέλθετε" λέ-
γοντεc].

1-5 εἰ - τοιαῦτα suppl. Ph.   7-8 ΕΧΘΗCΟΤ⊂ΙΝ ΟΙ
ΚΑΤΑC...|ΑΖΟΜΕΝΟΙC pap. ἐκθήcουcιν οἱ
κατας[κευ]|αζόμενοι[c] G. 102 n. 235   11-
12 "ἐπα]νέλθετε" λέ|[γοντεc] suppl. Ph.

Fr. 77 N

                [μηδὲν
ἐ[μφα]νίζειν [ἐνί]οτε τῶν
μὲν [ἀcυ]μβλήτ[ω]ν τ[ὸ] δ[ὲ πάντωc δεινὸν ὂν [ἢ] κεκα[κ]ι-
5 cμένον πολλ[άκι]c ἡcυχί-
αιc αὐταῖc καὶ τ[ῶ]ι μηδ[ὲ]ν
ποιε[ῖ]ν τῶν δει[ν]ῶc τῶ[ι] με-
γέθει [ἐχόντων κατορθοῦν.

1-8 suppl. Ph.   3 [ἀcυ]μβλήτ[ω]ν G. 101
[κα]ταβλητ[ῶ]ν Ph.

Fr. 77 (=78 N)

             ἔνια τῶν ἔν τιc[ι
τόποιc ἐπιδεικνυμ[ένων π]ρὸ
ὀ[μ]μάτων. * παρὰ δὲ τῶν cωζόν-
των οὐδενὶ τὸ ἴcον <πρ>οcα-
5 ναθετέον ἁμάρτημ᾽ ἢ τοῦ-
τό γε τῶν διὰ νουθετήcε-
ω]c ἀπ[ο]θ[έcεώ]c τε ἀκεcτι-
κ[ῶ]ν, οὐ τῶ[ν] τὸ μέγεθ[οc
φ[ευκ]τῶν, ἀλλ᾽ ἡλικιώ[ταιc

Fr. 76: ... <[if those men] neither [do] all things suitably nor will such things {as they do} meet with [admonition]>... and [they ascribe] to their teachers, to whom {i.e., their teachers} those who are being instructed will set forth[107] their own errors with frankness, and will [propose for consideration] those of [others] as well, <saying, "Return.">

Fr. 77 N: ... <[sometimes to report none] of the [incomparable][108] things, but it being in [every] way terrible [either] that one who has been blamed often [succeeds],[109] by these very silences and by doing none of those things that [are] terrible in magnitude>[110]...

Fr. 77: (=78 N): ...some of the things that in certain places are exhibited before their eyes. But to no one {of the students} is an equal error to be ascribed by those who are saving[111] {them}, or at all events one of those that are <healable> through admonishment <and [setting right],[112] not of those to be [avoided] for their magnitude, but rather remit it in regard to peers [and] acquaintances>.[113]

---

[107] In support of his emendation, Gigante, *Ricerche filodemee*, 102 n. 235, notes that in Philodemus κ is frequently aspirated before θ in the case of ἐκτίθημι and its cognates; cf. W. Crönert, *Memoria Graeca Herculanensi* (Leipzig: Teubner, 1903) 56.

[108] Ph. reads "contemptible" (?).

[109] Or "but [to correct] that which is in [every] way terrible [or] has been blamed often."

[110] The sense of lines 3–8 is difficult. Ph. col. 685 calls lines 3–4 "very corrupt"; Gigante, *Ricerche filodemee*, 101 n. 228, notes that Ph.'s reconstruction of lines 3–8 neither consistently respects the surviving traces in the disegni nor produces an entirely coherent text.

[111] O. has "the living."

[112] Literally, "bone-setting."

[113] Or "to peers [and] acquaintances."

10   καὶ] γνω[ρ]ίμοις τό γ᾿ ἔφες.

3-4 cωζόν|των fortasse Ph. ζῶν|των O.
7-10 ἀπ̲[ο]θ[έσεώ]ς κτλ. suppl. Ph.

Fr. 79 N   κα[ὶ δι]ὰ [παρρησίας
                  ἐπιτενοῦμ[ε]ν [τὴν εὔνοιαν
                  ....πρὸς ἐα[υ]το[ύς
                  ....
                  ....
                  ....
                  ....
                  ....κρύπ[τειν τ]ὰς ἁμαρ-
                  τίας κα[ὶ

79 N suppl. G. 101-2, omitt. O. et Ph.

Fr. 78 (=80 N)   τὸ δ᾿ ἐπὶ πᾶσι χωρὶς τοῦ
                  π]εριέχειν ἄφιλον ἀσφα[λ]εί-
                  ας] καὶ δριμὺ μωρόν ἐστιν·
                  ἐκ]άστο[υ] γὰρ λογιζομένου,
              5   το]ῦτο cυνβήσεται τὰ μη-
                  δε]νὸς <ἄξια> εἰδέναι τὸν cώ<ι> ζον-
                  τ]α δὲ τοῦτο πάντας
                  ἀκ]εῖςθαι. * δεῖ μέντοι πε-
                  φυλ]άχθαι cφόδρα [τό]νδ[ε
              10 καὶ το]ῦ β[λά]ψαι θέλειν κα[ὶ
                  δοκ]εῖν γυμνούμενον

7-11 suppl. Ph.

Fr. 79 (=81 N)   δύνηται [δ᾿] αὐτὸς ἢ
                  δι᾿ ἡμῶν ἢ δι᾿ ἄλλου τῶν
                  c[υ]cχολαζόντω[ν θ]ε[ρ]απευ-
                  θῆναι, * μηδὲ cυνεχῶς αὐ-
              5   τὸ ποιεῖν, μηδὲ κατὰ πάν-
                  των, * μηδὲ πᾶν ἁμάρτη-
                  μα καὶ τὸ τυχόν, μηδ᾿ ὧν
                  οὐ χρὴ παρόντων, μηδὲ
                  μετὰ διαχύσεως, ἀλλὰ cυν-

Fr. 79 N: ... < and [through frankness] we will intensify [the goodwill] ... toward themselves ...

....

....

....

....

...[to] hide the errors and > ...

Fr. 78 (=80 N): ...but {to reproach a student} for everything, without circumscribing {it}, is unfriendly to {his} security and a foolish harshness. For when each person reasons, it will happen that he knows things that are [worth] nothing[114] but that the one who saves {others} < heals everyone of this. It is necessary, however, that this one {the student} be strongly guarded both from wishing to harm and from [seeming to be] stripped {of} > ...

Fr. 79 (=81 N): ...{so that} he can be treated either by us or by another of his fellow-students, and not to do it {i.e., criticize frankly} continually,[115] nor against everyone, nor every chance error, nor {errors} of those whom one should not {criticize} when they are present,[116] nor with merriment,[117] but rather [to take up the errors] sympathetically [and not to] scorn [or insult] on...

---

[114] Pap. either "things of no account" (as O.) or perhaps "no one's affairs."

[115] Cf. Plutarch *Quomodo adulator* 73A–C.

[116] Cf. ibid., 70C–71E.

[117] On the necessity of avoiding ridicule when criticizing faults cf. frs. 37.4–8, 38.1–6, 60.3–10; col. Ib.10–12; Tab. IV J.

84 Philodemus *On Frank Criticism*

10 παθῶ[c] τ[ὰc ἁμαρ]τιαc ὑπο-
λαμβάνειν καὶ μὴ] καθυ-
βρίζειν μηδὲ λοιδορεῖ]ν ἐπὶ

Fr. 80 (=82 N)   διαφέρε[ιν] δὴ
αὐτῶν καὶ πρὸc καθ[ηγη-
τὰc ἀναλογίαν ἔχον[ταc,
ἔτι δ᾽ εὐνόωc πρὸc ἡ[μᾶc
5 διακειμένουc, ἀ[νε]νε-
κτέον ἀc[τ]ε[ί]ωc ἑκάc[τοτε
περιαθρήca[ντ]αc. * οὗτοι
γὰρ ὠνή[θηca]ν ἀπροφα-
cίcτωc μὲν διὰ τὴν ἀγά-
10 πηcιν, ἐνπράκτωc δὲ δι-
ὰ τὴ[ν εὔνοια]ν. οὐδὲ ἀπο-
κνητέο[ν

6 ἀc[τ]ε[ί]ωc ἑκάc[τοτε suppl. Ph.   11-12 οὐδὲ
ἀπο|κνητέο[ν suppl. Ph.

Fr. 81 (=83 N)   εἰ cοφὸc
τὰ περ[ὶ] αὐτὸν ἀναθήcε-
ται τοῖc φίλοιc μετὰ π[αρ-
ρηcίαc. * τὸ τοίνυν ὑπ᾽ ἐνί-
5 ων ἐν [τ]ῶι τόπωι τούτω[ι
ζητούμενον, εἰ cοφ[ὸc τὰ
π[ερ]ὶ αὐτὸν ἀναθήcετα[ι
το[ῖ]c φίλοιc μετὰ παρ[ρηcί-
αc, ἀ]νοικείωc μὲν [τοῦτο
10 ποεῖτ]αι διὰ τὸ περια[υτί-
ζεcθαι]

9-11 ἀ]νοικείωc κτλ. suppl. Ph.

Fr. 84 N   τ]ὸν cοφὸν μὲν [οὐ λέγειν
ἡγ]ήcεται τ[ῶι ἀν]αλθε[ῖ· καὶ
ἀναθ]ήcετα[ι
οὐ πᾶcιν, ἀλλ᾽ ἐν[ίοιc·
5 καὶ τὰ περὶ ἀπ[ει]ρ[ο]κα-
λί]αc εἰρημένα καὶ τα[ῦτα

Fr. 80 (=82 N): ...{that they}[118] differ from them, both in bearing a resemblance to the teachers, and further in being favorably disposed toward us, one must bear <[politely each time]> those who have scrutinized {one}. For these {the students} have profitted unhesitatingly on account of their {the teachers'} love, and practically on account of their [goodwill]. < Nor must one shrink from >...

Fr. 81 (=83 N): ...*Whether a wise man will communicate his own {errors} to his friends with frankness.*[119] As for the matter which is explored by some on this topic, {namely} whether the wise man will communicate his own {errors} to his friends with frankness, <[this is done] inappropriately {if} on account of [showing off], {but} >...

Fr. 84 N: ... < the wise man will [not consider that he is speaking][120] to [someone incurable, and] he will [communicate] {his errors} ....
not to all, but to some.[121] And what has been said concerning vulgarity too [must be attuned] > [122]...

---

[118] Supply, e.g., "although they say..."

[119] Prior to this topic heading (apparently as the concluding words of the discussion of the previous topic) the disegni read τοῖς εἰρημένοις ἀναλόγως, "analogously to the things that have been said" (Ware).

[120] Or "he {i.e., the student} will [consider] that the wise man [does not speak]" (Ware).

[121] G. suggests "to one."

[122] Gigante, *Ricerche filodemee*, 102 n. 240, judges Ph.'s restoration [ἁ]ρμοσ[τ]έον to be "uncertain."

ἀ]ρμος[τ]έον
·

1-7 suppl. Ph.   4 ἐν[ίοιc: ἐν[ί G. 102

Fr. 82 (=85 N)   πρὸc τὰc ἐπιτιμή[cειc
παρρηcιαζόμενο[c ὁ co]φὸc
οὐκ ἐπὶ πάντων κ[ᾆι]τ᾽ εὐ[ερ-
γ]ετήcειν πέποιθεν. ὃν
5   δ᾽ οὖν [τ]ῆc πείραc [ο]ὐ[κ ἠξί-
ωc]εν,   [τοῦ
φαινομ]ένου λυποῦ[ντοc

4-7 ὃν κτλ. suppl. Ph.

Fr. 83 (=86 N)   κ]αὶ τὸ κα-
τα]λέ[γειν] "κα[ὶ τ]ότε μὲν οὐ-
χ᾽ ἥ]μαρτον, τ[ὸ] νῦν δὲ παρρηcίαc ἀξιώcει καταλαβών; εἰ
5   μ]ὴ νὴ Δία φοβήcεται <αὐ> τάc· οὐ
γ]ὰρ καὶ [π]ρώην ἡμαρτηκέ-
ναι] με λέγω, [ἀλλ᾽] ἔπεcον [ἐθε-
λο]ντὴc εἰc τ[ὴν] τῶν νέω[ν
ἀμαθίαν καὶ διὰ το]ῦτο μαcτι-
10   γοῦν με δεῖ]ν νομ[ίζει"

10 δεῖ]ν νομ[ίζει Ph. δεῖ] O.

Fr. 87 N   [χρὴ
δὲ] λέγειν, αἷc [χρ]ω[μένουc ὁρῶ-
μεν [π]ωλοδάμ[ν]αc θ[ωπείαιc
ὑπὸ τῶν πώ[λων καταφρονου-
5   μένουc, τόν [γε co]φ[ὸν ἀν-
θρωποδάμ[νην] ὄντ[α δια-
κι]νεῖν ἀπειθίαν <ν> έου <ὑ> περη[φά-
νου] ὄντο[c] * καὶ δὴ γὰρ α[ὐ]τοῖc

....
....
....

Fr. 82 (=85 N): ...[the wise] man, when speaking frankly {in reply} to reproaches, {but} not in the presence of all,[123] [and then] he is confident that he will do a service. <Therefore the one whom he [did not think worthy] of the attempt... [one who is shown to] hurt>...

Fr. 83 (=86 N): ...[and repeating,] "and then I did not err, but now will he grasp {me} and think me worthy of frank criticism? Unless, by Zeus, he will fear them {i.e., my reproaches};[124] for I deny that I have erred just now, [but rather] I slipped [voluntarily] into the [ignorance] of young people [and because of this] <[he] thinks> that [it is necessary] to whip [me]..."[125]

Fr. 87 N: ... <[it is necessary] to say that with [the wheedlings] which, when colt-tamers [employ] them, [we see] them [being despised] by the colts, the [wise man], being a person-tamer,[126] [probes] the disobedience of a young man who is [arrogant].[127] For in fact to them...

....
....
.... [128]

but surely not [through irony]>...

---

[123] Or "not in all cases."

[124] Cf. fr. 82.1. O. understands "errors."

[125] For a somewhat different understanding of this fragment, see Nussbaum, "Therapeutic Arguments," 42.

[126] For the metaphor, cf. fr. 71.6-8; Philo De agric. 34; Plutarch De liber. educ. 13DE. On Philodemus' treatment of this topos, see Gigante, "Motivi paideutici."

[127] G.'s quite different restoration may be translated: "to say that ... the [young are] tamed like colts ... [reared] by the [colt-tamers], [but] that the wise man [truly] tames human beings, [endures] disobedience..."

[128] In the missing lines (unrestored by Ph.) G. is able to read only the following complete words: ἀπεγνῶσθαι, "given up", and παυσαμένου, "ceasing."

13   οὐ μὴν̣ [δι᾿ εἰ]ρωνε[ίας

1-8, 13 suppl. Ph.   2-7 λέγειν αιc. [τ]ο[ὺc]
ν[έουc] | μὲν πωλοδαμ[ν]ᾶcθ[αι......] | ὑπὸ τῶν
πω[λοδαμνῶν τρεφο]|μένουc, τὸν [δὲ c]οφ[ὸν
ἀν]|θρωποδαμ[νᾶν] ὄντ[ωc, ὑπο|μέ]νειν ἀπειθίαν
emend. G. 103

Fr. 84 (=88 N)   κἀνταῦθα
ἐπὶ φίλων πλειόνων ὑ[πε-
ρο]κνουμ[ένη]ν ἕξει τὴν
π[αρ]ρη[cί]αν καὶ πάλιν ἀν-
5 ε[λευθέ]ρωc· * καὶ ἐφ᾿ ὧν οὐκ ἐ-
χρῆ ν[ου]θετ[ήcει], ἐφ᾿ ὧν [δ᾿ ἔ-
τυ[χεν τ]ῆc [ἐ]πιτιμήcεω[c
μετ[αc]τήcεται· * καὶ τῶν
ἄλλω[ν δ]ὲ γινομένου τι-
10 νὸc ἀ[ν]εφοδεύτου πρότερον ἢ παρεθέντοc ἀθερα-
πεύτου, μετὰ ταῦτ᾿ ἐπε[ι-
δὰ]ν γνωcθῆ <ι> προνοίαc γε-
νομέν]ηc ε[ὐ]λόγωc

Fr. 85 (=89 N)   δι[αν-
ο]ρθούμενοι· καὶ ταῦτα μὲν
εἰc τὸν [αἰ]cχ[υ]νό[μενον
καὶ πάλιν παρρηcιάcεcθαι
5 καὶ πάλ[ι]ν εἴρηται. δ[ια]τ[ι-
θέcθω δ᾿ ὅτι καὶ τ[ῆι δια-   5
θέcει π[λ]ε[ῖ]cτον ἑαυτοῦ τ[ού-
των ὁ [κ]αθηγούμενοc ε[ὐη-
μέρωι καὶ φιλοφίλωι [καὶ
10 ἠ]πίωι

1-2 δι[αν|ο]ρθούμενοι suppl. Ph.

Fr. 86 (=90 N)   διαθέc[εων] αἰcχρο[τέρων ἀ-
μελῶν τ[ιc], τιθαcε[ύειν
προcκαρτερητικῶc ἀν-
θρώπουc εἰc φιλ[ότ]ητας

Fr. 84 (=88 N): ...and here, in the presence of many friends, he will practice a [very tentative] frankness and, again, [abjectly];[129] [he will] also [admonish] in the presence of those {where} he ought not to have, [and] in the presence of those {where} [he has met] with reproach, he will desist. And when some one of the others appears who was unexamined earlier or was disregarded[130] as untreatable, after this, when he is recognized, since [there was] foresight, {he} reasonably[131]...

Fr. 85 (=89 N): ... <they are being restored fully>. And it has been said that he will speak frankly again and again about these things to the one [who is ashamed]. Let it be [stated] that the teacher of these men, by means also of his extremely cheerful and friendly [and] gentle [dis]position...

Fr. 86 (=90 N): ...[someone] neglecting their very shameful conditions, {the teachers try} persistently [to] tame people into love for themselves, [subt]ly[132] helping [through] doctors even those who are indifferent to being treated. If [for the sake] of shame or [fear]...

---

129 Or "in a niggardly way."
130 Or "discharged."
131 Or "since foresight was taken reasonably."
132 Or "in diverse ways."

5 ἐ[αυ]τῶν καὶ τοῖc ἀ[πα]θοῦ-
ci θερ]απεύε[c]θαι πο[ικί]λωc
βο]ηθοῦντεc [δι'] ἰατ[ρῷ]ν. * εἰ
μὲν αἰδοῦc ἢ [φόβου ἕνεκεν

Fr. 91 N   ὄντοc δὲ φαν[εροῦ
τοῦτο δι]ὰ μεταθεcίαc [δύνα-
cθαι] οὐ μικρὸν κουφίcα[ι
πᾶν δὲ] οὔπω λῦc[αι π]ροβή[cε-
5 cθαι δὲ τὸ] κακὸν οὔ, κἂν ἀπρόc-
ληπτοc] ἦι νουθετηc[ία

1-6 suppl. Ph.   2 ἀμεταθεcίαc G. 108   4 οὔπω
λῦc[αι: οὐ κωλυc. G.

Fr. 87 (=92 N)   Ἡρα-
<κ>λῆc δ' ὡc μουcιάζων
καὶ ἐπ]ιρρείπτων ἀγέλη<ι>c
πτηνῶν μαθητῶν· * ἐ-
5 ἂν δ' ἀνεκ[τὴ]ν καὶ λήξειν
προcδοκω[μ]ένην, οὐκ ἀν-
<ε>πορυιεῖτα[ι τ]ὴν μιcοῦcαν
ὀργήν, ἀλλὰ τὴν μεμφο-
μ]έ[νη]ν τὰ[c] ἀβελτερίαc

Fr. 93 N   ἐ]φέξεcθαι μέχρ[ιc ἂ]ν
ἢ παύcωνται τῆc κολ[ακείαc
ἢ τρέπεcθαι καθα[πτόμενοι
ἐαθῶcιν * ἐὰν δ[ὲ τὴν ἀcθέ-
5 νειαν
ἀναλήψετα[ι
μάλα τ[οιοῦτ]ον ἐπ[ελθ]ὼν
μετρίαιc ὑπ[ο]μνήcεcιν

1-8 suppl. Ph.   1 ἐ]φέξεcθαι: ἀφέξεcθαι G. 109
2 κολ[ακείαc sive κομ[ψείαc Ph. κοι[νωνίαc G.
3 καθα[πτόμενοι: καθ' ἃ G.   7 τ[ὸν νέ]ον ἐπ[ιτιμ]ῶν
G.   9 καὶ ταῖc suppl. G.

Fr. 91 N: ... < it being clear [that it is possible through] a change[133] to relieve [this] no small amount, [but] not yet to undo[134] [all of it], [and that the] evil [will] not [advance], even if admonition is unac[cepted] > [135]...

Fr. 87 (=92 N): ...like Heracles making music [and] casting at flocks of winged disciples.[136] But if {the teacher is responding to an error or reproach that is} bearable and expected to cease, he will not be angry with an anger that hates, but rather with one that blames foolishness...

Fr. 93 N: ... < that they will be restrained[137] until they either cease from [flattery][138] or are allowed to change their minds [as they upbraid {others}].[139] But if {he perceives} [weakness].. ... ...he will resume ... [approaching such a person][140] with moderate reminders > [141]...

---

[133] G. proposes "changelessness."

[134] G. restores "[but] not prevent" (aorist or future).

[135] Gigante, *Ricerche filodemee*, 108 n. 275, is skeptical of Ph.'s restoration of lines 4–6.

[136] An allusion to the labor of Heracles in which he drove away man-eating birds from the Stymphalian Lake in Arcadia, scaring them with the noise of a bronze rattle and shooting them as they flew off; the vocabulary suggests that Philodemus is drawing on a poetic account.

[137] Or "that they will restrain themselves." G. reads "that they will refrain."

[138] Ph. suggests also the alternative, "daintiness." G. restores "community," which would give the sense "cease from {participating in} community."

[139] G. suggests "in accordance with the things which."

[140] G. restores "reproaching the young man."

[141] G. adds "and with the..."

Fr. 88 (=94 N)			τὴν τ]οῦ ὁμή[λικος παρ-
				αίνεс]ιν περιέχουс[ιν
				καὶ προ[сη]μείωсιν ἢ χε[ιρι-
				смὸν споυδ]αῖον. * πῶс ἐ[πι-
			5	γνωсόμεθα τὸν ἐνηνοχ[ό-
				τα δεξιῶс παρρη[cία]ν καὶ
				τὸν проспоιούμ[ε]νον; ἐ-
				πιγνωсόμεθα τοίν[υ]ν						5
				τὸν ἐνη < νο > χότα δεξιῶ[с
			10	παρρηсίαν καὶ τὸ[ν π]ρο[с-
				поιούμενον, ἵνα καὶ φρα-
				ζώμεθα προсέχοντεс εἰ
				παρ' ἡμῖν ἦν ἀλα[ζ]ών. *					10

1-4a suppl. Ph.

Col. Ia			[διαλαβεῖν] τὸν
				ἀπὸ διαθέсεωс ἀсτείαс [παρ-
				ρηсιαζόμενον καὶ τὸν ἀ-
				π]ὸ φαύληс. * ἔсτιν δὲ καὶ
			5	τοῦ παρρηсίαν ἄγοντος
				ἀπὸ διαθέсεωс ἀсτείαс καὶ
				τοῦ πάλιν ἀπὸ μοχθηρᾶс
				φύсιν διαλ]αβεῖν. [κ]αί τινες

Col. Ib			[ἀπὸ μὲν ἀсτείαс
				πᾶс [τίс] ποτε εὐνοῶν καὶ
				сυνετ[ῶс] κα[ὶ сυν]εχῶс φι-
				λοсοφῶν καὶ μέγας ἐν ἕ-
			5	ξει καὶ ἀφιλόδοξοс καὶ [δη-
				μαγωγὸс ἥκιστα καὶ φθό-
				νου καθαρὸс καὶ τὰ прос-
				όντα μόνον λέγων καὶ
				μὴ сυνεκφερόμενος,
			10	ὥсτε λοιδορεῖν ἢ πομπε[ύ-
				ε[ιν] ἢ [κ]αταβάλλε[ιν ἢ] βλά-
				πτ[ειν], μηδ' ἀс[ε]λγε[ί]αιс
				κα[ὶ κολ]ακευτ[ι]καῖс χρώ-
				μενοс τέχναιс].

Fr. 88 (=94 N): ... <they contain the [advice of one's age-mate] and a prognostication or [serious handling]>. *How will we recognize the one who has endured frank criticism graciously and the one who is pretending {to do so}?* We shall, then, recognize the one who has endured frank criticism graciously and the one who is pretending, so that, by paying attention, we may consider too whether among us he was a boaster...

Col. Ia: ...[to distinguish] *one who is frank from a polite disposition and one who is so from a vulgar one.* It is indeed possible to [dist]inguish [the nature] of one who practices frankness from a polite disposition and that of one who in turn {does so} from a base one. And some...

Col. Ib: ...[from a polite one], everyone who bears goodwill and practices philosophy intelligently and [con]tinually and is great in character and indifferent to fame and least of all a politician and clean of envy and says only what is relevant and is not carried away so as to insult or strut or show contempt [or] do harm, and does not [make] use of insolence and [flattering arts].[142]

---

[142] Insolence and flattery represent the two extremes of which frankness is the mean.

Col. IIa   [μηδὲ

γ[λ]ώ[ccη]c [ἀκ]ρ[ατ]ὴ[c μηδὲ
μενψ[ίμοι]ρος (οὐδὲ [γὰρ ἀνόη-
τος ὥcτ[ε κ]ᾶν [μι]κρά τ[ιc
5   βλάψηι [θυμ]ωθῆναι) μη[δ'
ἐρεθιcτὸc μηδὲ τραχὺc
μηδὲ πικρόc. * ἀπὸ δὲ μο-
χθηρίαc ὁ τοῖc ἐναντίοιc
κεχρημένοc. * εἰ δέ τιc ἐ-
10 πιζητώιη, πότερον ὁ co-
φὸc εὐεπιφορώτερόc ἐc-
τι πρὸc ψόγ]ου[c ἢ ἐπαί]νουc τῶν

12 suppl. Ph.

Col. IIb   ἐρ[ρω-

μένωc. εἰ μὲν πυνθάνο[ι-ι
το, τί μᾶλλον ἡ[δ]έωc πο-
εῖ, φανερόν τι ζητεῖ· φανε-
5   ρὸν γὰρ ὅτι τὸ μὲν ὑπερ-
ηδέωc πράτ[τει], τὸ δ' ὡc   5
ἀηδῶc ὑπομένει καὶ κα-
θάπερ ἀψίνθιον· * εἰ δὲ πότερον ποεῖ πλεοναζόν-
10 τωc μᾶλλον, οὐ[δ]έτερον
φήcο[μεν]· οὐδὲ γὰρ ἀ[νάγκη   10
προcάγειν πάντωc τ[ὴν
παρρηcίαν· * εἰ δέ, πότ[ε-
ρον οἴεται δεῖν

1–2 ἐρ[ρω]|μένωc Ph.   6 ὡc <μάλιcτα> O., omit.
G. 70

Col. IIIa   π[ερὶ] μὲν οὖν το[ύ-

των ἀπόχρη τὰ λελεγμέ-
να. [ζη]τουμένου δ᾽, εἰ πα[ρ]αλ-
λάξουcιν ἀλλήλων καὶ
5   cοφοὶ κατὰ παρρηcίαν,
ῥητέον, ὅτι τοιαῦται μὲν
οὐκ ἔcονται διαφορ[α]ὶ περὶ

Col. IIa: ...[nor without control] over his [tongue nor] carping (for he is not [foolish] so as to be [enraged] if someone harms him slightly) nor irritable nor harsh nor bitter. But one who has employed the opposite {means is frank} from baseness. If one should inquire further whether the wise man is more prone < to [censure than praise] of the > ...

Col. IIb: ... < vigorously > . If one should inquire which he {the wise man} does more pleasurably, one is seeking something obvious: for it is obvious that he performs the one {i.e., praising} most pleasurably, but he endures the other {i.e., blaming} pleasurelessly[143] and as though {he were drinking} wormwood. If {one should ask} which {i.e., praise or blame} he does more predominantly, we shall say neither: for there is no [necessity] to apply frankness in every case. But if {one should ask} which he thinks it is necessary...

Col. IIIa: Concerning these things, then, what has been said suffices. If one is exploring whether wise men too will diverge from one another in respect to frankness,[144] it must be said that there will not be such differences concerning...

---

[143] Omitting O.'s supplement ("as pleasurelessly *as possible*"), with G.

[144] Despite the fact that the first part of this sentence is underlined in the Greek, it does not appear to be a section heading; see Introduction, pp. 8–9, esp. n. 25.

Col. IIIb

καὶ κ]αθάπερ ἐντ[έχνως
χοροδ[ι]δασκαλούντ[ω]ν,
ἐν φιλοσοφίαι· καὶ τὸ[ν] μὲν
ἀκράχολον εἶναι κα[ὶ] κυνώ-
5   δη πρὸς ἄπαντας, ὡς πάλιν
ἄλλοι [τ]ινές εἰcιν· τ[ὸ]ν δ' ἀ-
εἰ βληχρόν· καὶ τὸν μὲν εὖ
κατὰ πᾶν, τὸν δ' ἐλλε[ι]πόν-
τως κατά τι παρρηcιάζε-
10 cθαι. πάντες γὰρ ὁμοίως
καὶ φιλοῦcι κατ' ἀξίαν ἑκά-
cτου καὶ τὰc ἁμαρτίαc
βλέπουcι καὶ τὰc διὰ παρ-
ρηcίαc]

---

1 ἐντ[έχνως O. ἐν τ[έχνηι sive ἐν τ[ῆι τέχνηι fortasse
Konstan

Col. IVa

πρὸ[c cυγ-
κεχυμέ[νον ἢ πρὸc με]μειωμέ-
νον [ἢ] πρ[ὸc ἀνα]τεταμέ-
νον ἢ πρὸ[c ἄλ]λον αἰδη-
5   μονέcτερον [ἢ] δ' ἄλ[λον
ἀτενέcτερο[ν ἐκ] πολλῶν
διοίcουcιν ἀλλήλων τε
καὶ ἑαυτῶν νῦν ἢ νῦν. ἔc-
τα[ι] δὲ τοῦτ[ο κενεὰν] ἀπομάc-
10 cειν]

8b–10 suppl. Ph.

Col. IVb

ἐκ τῶν ὑπ' αὐτῶν ῥηθέντων] τε
καὶ [π]ρα[χθ]έν[των] οἶδεν βα-
θυτέρως [οἵα]c πρὸc ἑκάτε-
ρον κοινότηταc προcοί-
5   co]νται[ι] καὶ τελειωθέν-
τεc· καὶ πάλιν οἶδ[ε]ν <τίνεc> ἐξ   5
αὐλικωτέρων γονέ[ων
εἰcὶν ἢ cυνετράφηcάν τ[ι-
cιν οἳ παρρηcίαν ἦγον ἐ-

Col. IIIb: [And] {not}[145], as in the case of those who train choruses [skillfully],[146] in philosophy: both that one {teacher} is irascible and snappish toward everyone, as certain others are in turn, while another is always mild; and that one speaks frankly about everything in a good way, but another does so deficiently on some matter. For all {wise men} both love {their students} alike in accord with the worth of each and see their faults alike and, through [frankness], the...

Col. IVa: ...toward a confused[147] [or] a weakened or a puffed up person or one too shy or another too intense they {wise men} will differ for many {reasons} from one another as well as from themselves at one time and another. < But this will be to skim [an empty] {measuring cup} > .[148]

Col. IVb: ... < [from the things said and done by them] {the students} > he {the wise man} knows more deeply in regard to each [what kinds of] common traits they will exhibit even when they are perfected. And in turn he knows which ones are from excessively courtly parents or were brought up with people who practiced frankness mildly in regard to the more humble;[149] equal[ly], he knows the birth and the up[bringing] that the many had.[150]

---

[145] A contrast seems to be required between the chorus-trainer and the wise man; cf. col. IIb.9–10, IIIa *fine*.

[146] Or perhaps, reading ἐν τέχνῃ (or ἐν τῇ τέχνῃ) for O.'s ἐντέχνως, "in the art of those who train choruses."

[147] Preceding the "confused" student there may have been mention of a corresponding type at the other extreme (e.g., "self-assured"); the next four examples appear to be grouped in two such pairs.

[148] A proverbial phrase meaning to do useless labor.

[149] The constrast is between those who flatter people better off than themselves and those who act graciously toward those who are worse off.

[150] Οἱ πολλοί are those who are in a position neither to fawn upon the rich nor to act graciously toward the poor, i.e., the majority.

10   πιεικῶc πρὸc τοὺc ταπει-
        νο]τέρουc· οἶδεν <ἐξ> ἴcου ἦ[ν   10
        οἱ] πολ[λοὶ] καὶ τὴν γένε-
        cιν ἔcχον καὶ τὴν ἐκ[τροφήν.

1-2 ἐκ - [π]ρα[χθ]έν[των] suppl. Ph.

Col. Va   ὥcτε θαρcέω[c παρρηcίαι
                 χρήcο]νται πρὸc [ἀργίαc
                 κα]ὶ ἀ[να]βολάc. [δι]ὸ ἀ[κρι-
                 βέcτεροι πωc ὑπά[ρξουcιν
        5   ἐν cπάνει τῶν πρὸc [εὔνοι-
                 αν καὶ φιλίαν εὐθέτων
                 γενηθέντεc καὶ παρ[ὰ τὴν
                 ἀπομίμ[ν]ηcιν δὲ τὴν πο-
                 λυχρόνιον τῶν καθηγηcα-
        10   μένων. cφόδρ[α

1 ΘΑΡCΕΩ. pap. θαρcέω[c Neap. edd., Ph. θραcέω[c
O.   4 πωc Konstan πῶc O.

Col. Vb   κατὰ] τὸ καθηγεῖ[cθα]ι δ' ἢ [τὸ
                 κ[αθη]γήcαcθαι ο[ὐ]δ[ὲν Κλε-
                 άν[θου]c οὐδὲ Μητρ[οδώ-
                 ρο[υ] διοίcουcιν (ὁ γὰρ ἐφεc-
        5   τηκὼc δαψιλεcτ[έ]ραι χ[ρ]ή-
                 cεται δηλονότι) * καὶ πα-
                 ρὰ πλείω] χρόνον δὲ προcει-
                 ληφότεc πλειόνων ἱcτο-
                 ρίαν τῶν οὐ προcε[ιλη-
        10   φ[ότων π]εριτοττέρα[ι
                 τ[ούτων] παρὰ ταῦτ[α παρρη-
                 cία<ι> χρήcοντα[ι

11-12 suppl. Ph.

Col. Va: ...so that they [will employ frankness] aggressively in regard to [laziness and] procrastination. Therefore, they [will be] rather[151] too strict {in the application of frankness} if they were born in want of things conducive to [goodwill] and friendship and toward the long-term imitation of those who taught {them}.[152] Vehemently...

Col. Vb: ...[in] the process of teaching or moments of teaching they[153] will in no way differ from Cleanthes or Metrodorus (for it is obvious that an attentive {teacher} will employ a more abundant {frankness}); and after [more] time, when they have gained knowledge of more matters than those who have not gained it, they will employ more lavish < frankness than [these latter] in these matters >...

---

[151] Philodemus is illustrating the type of character given too readily to employing frankness (cf. οἱ πολλοί in IVb.11). O.'s text translates: "How, then, will they be more strict...?"

[152] Contra O. in the *apparatus criticus*, this passage is not evidence that Philodemus thinks common people cannot be taught; Philodemus says rather that such people will tend to be harsh teachers and will need to exercise restraint.

[153] I.e., the type, described above, who are given to employing frankness rather freely.

Col. VIa

[δῆλον δὲ γέγονε ἐκ τῶν
εἰ]ρημέ[νων, ὅτι καθ᾽ ἕκασ-
το]ν ὁ μὲ[ν] μακρά, [ὁ δὲ μικρὰ
διοίϲ]ουϲ[ι]ν, ὥϲπερ γ[υναι-
5 κὸϲ μειράκιον δια[φέρει
γυναικῶν] τε καὶ νε[ανίϲ-
κων γέροντεϲ ἅμ[α διοί-
ϲουϲιν. * κἂν ἦι δ᾽ ὁ μ[ὲν ἀ-
ποφθεγματίαϲ μᾶλ[λον,
10 ὡϲ Πολύ[α]ινόν φη[ϲι] Μ[η-
τ]ρόδωροϲ, "πολλάκι δὲ καὶ
παρυποδύνων ὁμιλίαι
μᾶλλον καὶ ποτιμώτεροϲ,"
ἔτι δ᾽ ἀξιοπιϲτότερο[ϲ
15 ἔ[ϲτ]αι.

6 γυναικῶν] τε Ph. ἑκάϲτο]τε Ο.

Col. VIb

[τοῖϲ
προϲ]οίϲουϲ[ι τὰϲ ἁμαρ-
τί]αϲ ἐξερε[ῖ διὰ] π̱α̱ρ̱ρ̱[ηϲί-
αϲ] καὶ καθ᾽ [ἕκα]ϲτα πρ[ὸϲ
5 ἐ[ν]ίουϲ [ἐρεῖ κ]αὶ πρὸϲ τὸ χα-
ρ[ι]εντίζεϲ[θαι τῶ]ν αὐ[τῶν
τῶν πραγμάτων ὄν-
των· κἂν ὁ μὲν ἥκι[ϲ]τα
παρρηϲία[ϲ] ἦι δεδεημέ-
10 νοϲ, ὁ δὲ διὰ ταύτηϲ ϲεϲω<ι>ϲ-
μένοϲ, ὁ μὲν ἧττον, ὁ [δ]ὲ
μᾶλλον προϲάγει τ[ι] δι᾽   5
ὃ] τέλειοϲ ἐγ[έ]νετο. δι[ὸ
κ[α]ὶ Πολ[ύαι]νοϲ οὐ πάν[υ
15 δε]δεη[μ]ένοϲ οὐδὲ προϲ·

1–8a suppl. Ph.

Col. VIa: [It has become obvious from what has been said] that they {teachers} will differ for each {student}, one much, [one little,] just as a lad differs from a woman and old men will differ from < [women] > [154] and youngsters alike. Even if one is rather sententious, as Metrodorus says Polyaenus was, "often rather insinuating himself into conversation and quite sociable,"[155] he will be still more worthy.[156]

Col. VIb: ... < [to those] who will bring forward [their errors], he will speak out [with] frankness, and to some he [will speak] on individual matters and with a view to being ingratiating, though the actions are the same. > [157] And if one has needed frankness minimally, while another has been saved by means of this, then the one {i.e., the former} applies less, the other more of that through which he became perfect. Thus Polyaenus too, who had not needed it much, did not {apply much frankness} toward...

---

[154] "Women" translates Ph.'s conjecture; O.'s "each time," is according to Ph. too short for the space and introduces hiatus (it also does not make sense).

[155] Fr. 45 Koerte.

[156] For this sense of ἀξιόπιστος, cf. Aspasius *in Aristotelis Ethica Nicomachea* 159.13; LSJ gives "trustworthy," "plausible," which do not seem pertinent here. An alternative translation is "he will still be quite worthy."

[157] I.e., he will ingratiate those who respond to such treatment, while to those who manifest their faults he will employ frankness, though the actions in need of correction are the same for both.

Col. VIIa

δι[ὸ] παρρησιάζεσθαι τὸν
σοφὸν δ]ε[ῖ, δ]ιότι πρεσβύ-
τερος ἢ καθηγητὴς ἢ πα-
τὴ]ρ οὐ δεῖ παρεμβάλλειν
5 κατα]φορὰς ὑπαρχούς[α]ς
μὲ]ν σοφοῖ[ς], καθάπερ τινὲς   5
κ]αὶ ταύτας συνκαταριθμοῦ-
σιν]. γέγονε δὲ ἐκ τῶν εἰρη-
μέ]νων [δῆ]λον, ὅτι καὶ κα-
10 θ' ἕκ]αστο[ν] ὑπερέχοντας
ἄνδρας τε] καὶ δήμους   10
νουθετέον.]

1–2a suppl. Ph.

Col. VIIb

καταφορὰς σοφι]στικὰς ἐ-
νίων [πάντω]ς παραλλά-
ξουσι[ν]· ἐφα[ρ]μόσαι γὰρ
μόνον δεῖ τὰ πλεῖστ[α] τῶν
5 εἰρημένων ταῖς τοιαύ-
τ]αις παρρησίαις. ἔργον
δὲ τοὺς ἐπιτομικῶς ἐξ-
εργαζομένο[υ]ς πᾶν εἶ-
δος ἀκρειβοῦν ὡς τοὺς ἀν-
10 ελλι[πῶς] ἕκαστον ἐξοικο-
νο[μ]οῦντας, [οἷο]ν [ὃν τ]ρό-
πον διατεθήσεται σοφὸς
ἀγόντων τ[ι]νῶ[ν] παρρησί[αν

9–10 ἀν|ελλι[πῶς] Ph. ἂν | ἐλλι[πῶς] O.   11 [οἷο]ν
[ὃν Ph. [πά]ν[τα O.

Col. VIIIa

ποτὲ καὶ σοφὸς
πρὸ[ς σ]οφόν· εἰ δ' ὁ [μὲ]ν σοφὸ[ς
καὶ γινωσκόμενο[ς, τέ-
λειος πρὸς τέλειον ἀπ[αντᾶι
5 (ὅ τι τέ[λ]ειο[ς] καὶ ἀγνοούμ[ε-
νος, καὶ τάχα γινωσκόμε-
νος ὡ[ς] σοφὸς πρὸς ἀ[γ]νοού-
μεν[ο]ν καὶ φιλόσοφος δὲ

Col. VIIa: < Therefore, the [wise man]¹⁵⁸ [ought] to be frank, > because an older man or a teacher or a father ought not to inflict [jabs] appropriate for wise men, in the way that some enroll these too.¹⁵⁹ It has become obvious from what has been said that [one must admonish] prominent [men] and peoples according to each...

Col. VIIb: ...they will [wholly] diverge from some {who inflict} [sophi]stical [jabs]. For one need only adapt the majority of what has been said to such {kinds of} frankness.¹⁶⁰ It is hard work for those who are handling {a topic} by way of an epitome to be precise about every kind, in the manner of those who dispose of each {kind} exhaustively,¹⁶¹ < [for example in what] > way¹⁶² a wise man will be disposed when some are practicing frankness...

Col. VIIIa: ...a wise man also {will be frank} to a wise man sometimes. If the wise man is also recognized, a perfect man con[fronts] a perfect man (because he is perfect, {he will be frank} even if unrecognized, and surely if recognized as a wise man and a philosopher and a scholar {but is speaking} to one who is not recognized); because a wise man receiving praise or jabs about himself...

---

¹⁵⁸ Sc. "only."

¹⁵⁹ Sc., perhaps, in their epitomes or tractates.

¹⁶⁰ I.e., the kind applied by the authority figures mentioned in col. VIIa and the sophistical kind mentioned here.

¹⁶¹ Instead of O.'s "in the manner of those who would dispose of each one selectively"; Ph.'s reading (see also next note) eliminates the lacuna indicated by O. in line 12.

¹⁶² O.'s reading translates "in every way."

καὶ φιλόλογος)· διότ[ι c]οφὸς
10   αἴνεcιν ἢ καταφορ[ὰ]c ὑπὲρ
αὐτοῦ λαμβάνων·

Col. VIIIb   ἴcωc
δὲ κα[ὶ φιλ]οcτοργίαν ἔ-
χοντεc ἰδιωτικὴν ἢ θέ-
λοντεc ἔ[χ]ειν ἔνιοι παρρη-
5   cιάcαιντ᾽ [ἃ]ν πρὸc αὐτόν.
ἂν μὲν οὖν οἱ cοφοὶ γινώc-
κωcιν ἀλλήλουc, ἡδέωc
ὑπομνηcθήcονται πρὸc
ἀλλήλων ἐν οἷc διεcαφή-
10   cαμεν, ὡc καὶ ὑφ᾽ ἑαυτῶν,
καὶ δή[ξον]ται δηγμὸ[ν
ἑαυτοὺc τὸν ἠπιώτα-
τον καὶ χάριν ε<ἰ>δήcου[cι
τῆc ὠφελίαc.]

Col. IXa   ἢ [μεγάλη]ν ἀcθένειαν
ἢ πόν[ων ἀηδίαν] αὐτῶ[ι] παρα-
πεπτω[κυῖα]ν καὶ τὰc αἰτίαc αἷ[c παρε]λογίcθη cυνό-
5   ψεται κἀκείνωι δείξει καὶ
πεί[c]ει, καὶ πολὺ δώcει τοῦ-
τ᾽ αὐτὸ πρὸc ἐπ[ί]γνωcιν τῆc
ἀλλήλων τελ[ει]ότητοc. οὐ

Col. IXb   ἀλλὰ τῶι πολλὰ γίνεcθαι καὶ
παρὰ μεμπ[τ]ὰc αἰτίαc καὶ
παρ᾽ οὐ μεμπτὰc ὑπολήψε-
5   ται παρὰ μεμπτ[ὰc τοῦτο] γε-
γονέναι. διότι μὲν cοφὸc
ο]ὔπω κατειληφώc, ὑπὸ δὲ
κοινοτήτων παραλογιc-
θείc†, ἂν δ᾽ ὁ ἐπιτιμηθεὶc
10   παρυπονοῆ<ι> cοφὸν εἶναι
τὸν ὑπειληφότα τὸ μὲν

Col. VIIIb: Some, perhaps, having a private affection {for the wise man} or wishing to have it, may be frank toward him. If, then, the wise men recognize each other, they will be reminded pleasurably by one another in the ways we have made clear, as also by themselves, and they will sting each other with the gentlest of stings and will acknowledge gratitude [for the benefit].

Col. IXa: ...he will perceive that a [great] weakness or [dislike] for toil has befallen him and the causes on account of which he has reasoned [falsely] and he will point {these} out to him and persuade him, and this itself will contribute much toward the recognition of one another's perfection. Not...

Col. IXb: ...but because many things happen for both blameworthy and non-blameworthy reasons he will assume that [this] happened for blameworthy ones. Because the wise man has not yet grasped {the matter} but was reasoning falsely on account of common traits,[163] if the one who has been reproached suspects that the one who assumed that he had erred is wise, he will chide the [blameworthy] reason, {but} himself[164]...

---

[163] O. posits a lacuna here.

[164] Sc. "he will excuse" (O. in app. crit.); but for O.'s αὐτόν, "himself," perhaps read αὐτὸν [δέ], "[but] him."

ἡμαρτηκέ[να]ι, μ[εμπτὴν
κακολο[γεῖ αἰ]τίαν, α[ὐ]τὸν

Col. Xa   τὸν ὑπ[ο]νοή[c]-
cόντα κατ᾽ [α]ὐτοῦ τα[c αἰτίαc. * ἐὰ[ν] δὲ φιλόcοφοc
ἢ φιλόλ[ο]γοc, οὐ τῶν ὑπ᾽ αὐ-
5   τοῦ δέ, κατ[ὰ τοιοῦ]το μέ-
τ[ρ]ον παρρηcιάζηται πρὸc
αὐτόν, οὐκ ὀργ[ιεῖτα]ι μέν,   5
ὡc ὁ Ζεὐc τῶ[ι] Καπανεῖ, τοὐναντίον δὲ γινώcκων ταύ-
10   την [ο]ὖca[ν] δίκ[η]ν τῶν ἀ-
φρ[όνω]ν καὶ μ[ὴ] τελείων
ἀνέξεται, καθά]περ ὁ Cω[κράτηc   10

―――――――――
1-3 τὸν - αἰτίαc suppl. Ph.   12 Cω[κράτηc suppl. Ph.

Col. Xb   "ὥcπερ ἄνθρ]ωπο[c] οἴ-
cων δὴ νῦν καὶ τὴν παρρη-
c[ί]αν;" οὐκ ἐξερεῖ καὶ ἀπο-
τ]ρέψει προcεπειπών· "οὐ
5   μὴ ἐπὶ ταύτη < ι > c, ὥcπερ
ὦν ἐν ἀνδράcιν, καὶ μει-
cοῦcαί με γινώcκουcιν,"
ἀλλὰ καὶ ἀνέξεται καὶ
ἀποδέξεται τὴν εὔνοιαν,
10   ἀφ᾽ ἧc ὅ ποτ᾽ ἐφαίνετο cυν-
φ[έ]ρον ὑπέδειξε, καὶ χάριν
ἕ[ξ]ει κατὰ τ[οῦ]το καὶ ἀπο-
λ[ο]γιεῖται δὲ πεῖcαι φιλό-
cοφον]

Col. XIa   πολλάκιc δὲ καὶ παρ᾽ ὑπόμνη-
c[ι]ν ἤ, [ὡc] φάν᾽, ὑπεροχήν,
ἐ[κ]φήναc διαβλέπειν τὰ
μεγάλα, καὶ μὴ προχείρωc
5   ἁμαρτήματα νομίζειν
τὰ μέcηc προcβάλλοντα.

Col. Xa: ...< the one who will suspect the reasons {alleged} against him >.... But if a philosopher or a scholar, but not one of those {instructed}[165] by him, is frank toward him in such measure, he [will] not be angry, like Zeus toward Capaneus, but on the contrary he will tolerate it, knowing that this is the way of those who are foolish[166] and not perfect, just as So< [crates] >[167]...

Col. Xb: "...is he indeed going to endure frankness now too [like a human being]?"[168] He will not speak out and turn away {the other}, telling him, "not in the presence of these {women} as though you were among men![169] They {the women} know me and hate me." But he will both tolerate it and accept the goodwill, from which he exhibited whatever seemed advantageous, and he will have gratitude for this and will say in his defense that a philo[sopher] has persuaded {him}...

Col. XIa: ...many times even by a reminder, or, [so] to speak, by his superiority, having shown that he looks to serious things and does not promptly believe to be errors things that smack of the mean.[170] {One} would not be amazed that {he is} [wise][171]...

---

[165] Κατασκευασαμένων or the like is understood; cf. col. XIIb.6–7.

[166] The diction is elevated, and perhaps reflects a poetic source in which the story of Zeus and Capaneus was related.

[167] Socrates' patience with Xanthippe (cf. Xenophon *Mem.* 2.2) anticipates col. Xb.

[168] Ἄνθρωπος, i.e. "a human being," as opposed to a slave; cf. Headlam-Knox on Herodas 15.5. The topic here is apparently whether a wise man will endure criticism in public; the phrase does not seem to be a quotation from tragedy (contra O. in app. crit.).

[169] Ἄνδρες, i.e., "males."

[170] Retaining the papyrus reading with Ph., and removing the comma after νομίζειν and inserting a full stop after προσβάλλοντα. O. emends to "puts forward" (modifying σοφόν?).

[171] It is possible that σοφός should be read in place of O.'s σοφόν.

co[φὸν μὲν] οὐκ ἂν θαυμά-
c[ειε

---

6 προ[c]βάλλοντα O.

Col. XIb

        τῶν δ' ἰ[δ]ιω-
τῶν, ἐὰν γονεῖc ὦcιν ἤ τινα τοιαύτην ἔχοντεc
ἀναλογίαν, cύνπαc ὅc-
5   τιc προcέξει. καὶ διὰ τὸ πα-
ραδεδομένον ἔθοc καὶ
διὰ τὴν ἄρρητον εὐχα-
ριcτίαν καὶ τιμὴν καὶ
μᾶλλον φιλήcει τὴ[ν] εὔ-
10   νοιαν καὶ π[αν]τὶ τρόπω[ι]
μεταθήcει [τ]ὴν ὑπόλη-
ψ[ι]ν ἀπο[λογ]ούμενοc.

Col. XIIa

καὶ π[οιήcεται ἐάν τιc ἁ-
μάρτηι ....
δ]ὴ παρὰ μέγα καὶ ὑπερβαί-
νων [τὴν] cυνπεριφοράν.
5   ἐὰν δὲ μηδὲν μὲν ἐπι-
φέρωνται τῶν τοιούτων
(cυνοίδαcιν ἄλλο[ι] τε καὶ [οἱ   5
οἰκέται), νὴ τὸν Δία λέγειν
μὲ]ν ἐάcε[ι] ποτ' αὐτοὺc

1-2 suppl. Ph.   3 δ]ή suppl. G. 90 μ]ή Ph.   4 [τὴν]
cυνπεριφοράν G. [ἄν]ουν περιφοράν O.   7 cυνοίδαcιν
ἄλλο[ι] τε καὶ [οἱ Konstan cυνοίδαcιν ἄλλο[ι τε] καὶ O.
cυνοίδαcιν ἄλλω[c] κἂν [οἱ Ph. cυνοιδῶcιν ἄλλω[ι] κἂν
G.

Col. XIIb

     ποή[c]ει δ' αὐτοῖc φα-
νερόν, ὅτι [c]υνπεριφερό-
μενοc αὐτ[οὺ]c φέρει. "ἄ-
λ[υ]ποc γὰρ ὁ Μαίcων φρε-
5   ν]ούμενοc καὶ ἀπάγει τοῦ
χωρίου." τῶν δ' ὑπ' αὐτοῦ

Col. XIb: ...but of laymen, if they are parents or have some such relationship, everyone who will pay attention.[172] And through the habits that have been transmitted {to him} and through his unspoken thankfulness and honor he will love the more the {other's} goodwill and in every way will, in defending himself, change the assumption {of the other}...

Col. XIIa: ... < and [he will make, if someone] errs ... indeed[173] > even going greatly beyond < [accommodation] > .[174] But if they bring up no such things (< the others > and even < [the] > slaves know), by Zeus he will allow them to speak at times...

Col. XIIb: ...he will make it clear to them that he is bearing with them in an accommodating way.[175] "For a cook who is informed is harmless and he withdraws from the spot."[176] But he will not much tolerate the frankness of those who are to be instructed by him, nor will he be pleasurably bemused and < [choose] > [177] to change his mind toward them...

---

[172] The verb is lost in the preceding lacuna.

[173] Instead of Ph.'s μή, "not."

[174] Reading τὴν συνπεριφοράν with G. (a common term in Philodemus) instead of O.'s ἄνουν περιφοράν, "silly sociability."

[175] Instead of O.'s "now sociably"; cf. col. XIIa.2 and note.

[176] Perhaps a paraphrase of a line in New Comedy (see Athenaeus 14.659A); the term μαίσων (perhaps Maison, a proper name) may have designated the mask or persona of the cook, who was traditionally an irascible stage character. See Marcello Gigante, "Testimonianze di Filodemo su Maison," CErc 1 (1971) 65-68.

[177] Instead of O.'s "agree".

κατασκευασομένων οὐ
πάνυ μὲν ἀνέξεται παρ-
ρηςίας, οὔτ᾽ αὐτὸς ἡδέως
10   κ]αταναρκ[ώ]μεν[ος] π[ρὸς] ἐ-
κείνους τ[ετ]ράφθαι [πρ]ο-
αιρήσεται]

2-3 [c]υνπεριφερό|μενος G. 90 Konstan [ν]ῦν περιφερό-
μενος O.   11-12 [πρ]ο|[αιρήσεται Ph. [ὁμ]ο|[νοήσει O.

Col. XIIIa   κα]ὶ κατα[φ]ρόνησιν
ὑ]ποπτεύων κ[ατ᾽] ὀλίγον
διδάξει] καὶ δι᾽ ἀ[γ]άπης ἐ-
πηθρ]οιςμέν[ους] αὐτοὺς
5   καθ᾽ ὑπερβολήν, ὅταν πρ[ο-
βάντες [πά]θη κ[αὶ] φωνὰ[ς
ἀνανεῶνται. * [τά]χα δὲ
καὶ ὑπ᾽ αἰςχύνης περιςτή-
ςεται τὸν ςοφὸν καὶ τὴ[ν
10   παρὰ τοῖς ἄλλοις φίλοις ο[ἵ-
η]ς[ιν] προνοούμενος καὶ
τὴ]ν ἀπομίμηςιν φυλάτ-
των

---

3 διδάξει] Ph. φιλήςει] O.   3-4 ἐ|πηθρ]οιςμέν[ουc
suppl. Ph.   6 [πά]θη κ[αὶ] φωνὰ[ς suppl. Ph.

Col. XIIIb   καὶ μεγάλα
παρεςχημένος καὶ τῶι
γένει, καθαπερεὶ ςυνβου-
λε]υτικὸν ποῆται τὸ τά-
5   γμα τῆς παρρηςίας, καὶ πε-
ρ[ὶ] ποιῶν πραγμάτων, οἷ-
ον μ[ὴ] καταχαρίζεςθαι
ῥαιδίως παντάπαςι μηδὲ
πιςτεύειν προχείρως, ἤ
10   τινος τῶν τοιούτων·
ἀνέξεται [μ]ὲν καὶ τὸ κη-
δεμονικ[ὸ]ν ἐπαινέςει.
διδάξει δ᾽ [ὡ]ς ὀρθόν ἐςτιν

Col. XIIIa: ...[and] he will <[teach]> [178] little by little if he suspects contempt, and abundantly if they {the students} are <[gathered together]> through love, when they proceed and renew their <[feelings and]> words. But perhaps out of shame {a student} will avoid the wise man, if he foresees the [opinion] {of him that obtains} among the other friends and if he keeps up the imitation {of the teacher}...

Col. XIIIb: ...and if he has made claims for great things both in the genre {of frankness}, as if he were making the status of frankness deliberative,[179] and concerning the kinds of acts, for example absolutely not to show favoritism lightly nor to believe {what is said} promptly or one of these sorts of things; he {the wise man} will tolerate {him} and will praise his concern. But he will teach that it is right...

---

[178] Instead of O.'s "will love."

[179] I.e., that branch of rhetoric concerned with giving counsel.

Col. XIVa

κεν[ὸ]ν θρυλλ[όν·] ἐπὶ δὲ τὸν
βίον μὴ μεταφέρειν ἄλ-
λ᾿ [ἢ ἀγα]θὸν ἀεὶ καὶ τῶν τοσού-
τ[ωι κ]αταδεεστέρων καὶ
5   μνημονεύειν τίς ἐςτι καὶ
τίνι λαλεῖ παραινέςει. * τὰ
δ᾿ ἀνάλογα χρὴ καὶ περὶ τοῦ
μεγάλου καὶ βαδίζοντος
ἐπὶ φιλοσοφίαν ὑπολαμ-
10   βάνει<ν>. καὶ γὰρ οὗτος τῶν
μὲ]ν ἔξωθεν καταφρον[η-
τέον]

---

1 κεν[ὸ]ν θρυλλ[όν·] suppl. Ph.

Col. XIVb

κα[ὶ
μετὰ πά[ς]ης δέξεται χά-
ριτος τὴν ὑπόμνηςιν,
προβαλὼν ἃ προεί<ρη>ται πε-
5   ρὶ τῆς παρρηςίας καὶ τῶν,
ὡς προςήκει, χ[ρ]ωμένων
αὐτῆι. * ζητουμ[έ]νων
τοίνυν ἐνίων κατὰ τὸν
τόπον, ἀφ᾿ ἧς αἰτίας γίνε-
10   ται, μεταβάντες ἀπὸ τῶν
ἁδροτέρ[ω]ν ἐπ᾿ ἐκεῖνα, προς-
μένου[ςι] τὸν ἀπ[αι]τοῦν-
τα]

Col. XVa

λυποῦντα[ι,
ὅτι] τῶν ὑπονοουμένω[ν
ὑπ᾿ ἄλλου γί[ν]εςθαι καὶ ςυν-
βήςεςθαι οὐθὲν νομίζου-
5   ςιν ἐξ α[ὐ]τῶν εἶναι [κα]ὶ γε-
νήςεςθαι. καλῶς δ᾿ ἂν ἔχοι
καὶ καθ᾿ ἕκαςτον ἐπελθεῖν.
καὶ τὸ τ[ῆ]ς ἁμαρτία[ς] οὐ λυ-
πεῖ τος[οῦ]τον αὐτοὺς [ὥ]ς-
10   περ

Col. XIVa: ... < empty chatter >.... But he {the wise man} will advise {him} never to transfer to his life anything [but what is good], and, {as one} of those who are so much more in need, both to remember who he is and to whom he is speaking. It is necessary to assume analogous things also concerning a great man, even if he is coming to philosophy. For in fact he {may say} that external things [must be] despised...

Col. XIVb: ...and he will receive the reminder with total gratitude, putting forward what has been said previously concerning frankness and those who employ it as is suitable. Thus, if some things are explored in regard to the topic—from what cause they occur—when they {the students} have moved on from the larger {issues} to those things and they are waiting for the one {the wise man} who asks in return...

Col. XVa: ...they are hurt [because] they believe that none of the things of which it is suspected that they are occurring and are going to happen by {the agency of} another are and will occur by their own {agency}. But it would be well also to go over each point individually. The fact of their error does not hurt them as much as...

Col. XVb

[τὴν ἀλήθει-
α]ν ὡ[ς ἀ]κούειν, οὐ [μόνον
ἐδεή[θ]ηςαν ἄλλων, [ἀ]λ-
λὰ δέο[ν] μηδὲν ἐξαμαρ-
5   τάνε[ιν], τὸν δεύτερον
πλοῦ[ν] ἐπορεύθηςαν αὐ-
τοὺς διορθώςαντες· ἐκεῖ
δὲ κα[ὶ] τὸ δυςκίνητον ἐν-
οχλεῖ, καὶ μηδὲ τῶν οἰ[κ]ε[ί-
10   ων ἁμαρτημάτων ἐπαι-
ςθάνεςθαι, καὶ πρὸς ἄλ-
λων μὲν ἐπιτιμώμε-
νοι, τ[ὸ] νομίζειν ὡς ἐπὶ
τὸν π[λ]εῖςτον οὐχ ἡμα[ρτή-
15   καςι.]

_____

4 δέο[ν] Ph. δ᾿, ἔφ[η] O.

Col. XVIa

ἀςτόχως
ἐντ[υχ]ὼν κατὰ τὴν παρ-
ρηςίαν, αὐτοὺς δὲ βέλτις-
τα γι[ν]ώςκοντας τὰ κα[θ᾿
5   ἑα[υ]τοὺς ἐν μηδενὶ τ[ίθηςιν. ἄλλοι δὲ καὶ ςυνετωτάτους
ἑαυτοὺς διαλαμβάνον-
τες καὶ πραέως μὲν α[ὐ]τοῖς
ἐπιτιμῶςι καὶ πρὸς ἡδο-
10   ν]ήν· ὑπὸ δὲ τῶν ν[έ]ων
τὰ πολλὰ πικρό[τ]ερ[ον] ἐ[πι-
πλ]ήττοντα[ι.

Col. XVIb

ἄχθονται [π]αρρη-
ςιαζομένων, * ὅτι οὐ λέ-
γ[ο]υςιν ἐξ ὅλης ψυχῆς, ἀ[λ-
λ[ὰ] φαντασίαν ἐκκόπτον-
5   τ[ε]ς, ὥς εἰςι δὴ φιλοπαρρη-
ςιάςται. [γε]νομένης δὲ
τ[ῆ]ς ἐπιπλήξεως, ἐλεγχό-
με]νον ἔχουςι τὸ πλάς-

Col. XVb: ...as to hear [the truth], not [only] did they need others, but since < [it is necessary] > [180] that one not err, they made the second sailing, [181] having corrected themselves. But there {i.e., the other case}, their obduracy too gives them trouble and the fact that they are not aware of their own errors, and, though they reproach others, that they believe that for the most part they have not erred.

Col. XVIa:...missing the mark, [182] when he encountered {them}, in respect to frank criticism, and though they themselves best know what concerns them [he sets] them at naught. Others, who distinguish themselves as most intelligent, reproach them {their pupils} gently and to their liking. But for the most part they are rebuked more sharply by the young.

Col. XVIb: ...they are vexed at those who speak frankly, because they do not speak from their entire heart but rather by stamping [183] the image that they are indeed lovers of frankness. But when the rebuke comes, they have their pretense exposed, just like those who are compelled to dine together for the sake of politeness, when they < [correct somewhat] > {their fellow diners}. But sometimes they call upon [184] [not?]...

---

[180] O. supplies ἔφη, "he {sc. Zeno} said."

[181] For the proverbial expression, cf. Plato *Phd.* 99D, *Plt.* 300C, *Phlb.* 19C; *Paroemiographi Graeci* 1.359 Leutsch-Schneidewin (Gregory of Cyprus 2.21) explains it as referring to the breaking out the oars when the wind fails. O. sees a reference to Plato's visits to the court of Dionysus in Syracuse (Plato *Ep.* 7.323D–352A; cf. Plutarch *Quomodo adulator* 7.52F, 26.67C–E), denied by Ph.

[182] The reference may be to the teacher or, perhaps, the students. There is a possible reference here to Plato and Dionysius II of Syracuse (Clay).

[183] The term is employed in the stamping of coins.

[184] Or perhaps, if the image of the dinner is maintained, "invite."

μ[α], καθάπερ τῶν ἀπευφη-
10   μ[ι]cμοῦ χάριν cυναριc-
τᾶ]ν βιαζομένων, ὅταν
τ[ι διο]ρθῶcιν. ἐν[ί]οτε δὲ
π[α]ρακαλοῦcιν μὲν ου

---

12 τ[ι διο]ρθῶcιν suppl. Ph.

Col. XVIIa   ἀλλ᾽ ὅ-
τ]αν τὴν διάθε[cιν] αὐτ[ῶ]ν
ἀμ]αρτωλὸν ἐπιβ[λέπ]ωcι,
δ]άκνονται· * καὶ [κ]αθάπερ
5   c[οφ]οὺc ἰατροὺc ἐπὶ διαίρε-
cιν παρακαλοῦντες ὅταν
δῶcι τὸ ζμίλιον νο[c]οῦ-
cιν, οὕτωc ὅταν <τ>ο[ύ]τοι<c> τὸ
δηκτικὸν ἐν ὄμματι γέ-
10   νηται τῆc παρρηcίαc καὶ
νομίζουcιν οὐθὲν ἀμάρτη-
μα ποιήcειν, ἢ λήcεcθαι κᾂν
πολλάκιc ἡμαρτηκότας,
παρακαλοῦcι νο[υ]θετεῖν

Col. XVIIb   [οὐ δια-
λαμβάνουc[ι], καὶ μόνοιc
καὶ κατὰ καιρὸν καὶ ἀπ᾽ εὐ-
νοίαc καὶ πάντα προcφε-
5   ρομένουc ὅcα παρη<ι>ν[ο]ῦ-
μεν. τότε δὲ διαλαμβά-
νοντεc ἔν τε τιμῆι προcεῖ-
ναι, δυcχεραίνουcι. καὶ
πρότερον μὲν βλέπουcιν
10   τὴν ἐκ τῆc παρρηcίαc ὠφε-
λίαν, τότε δὲ cυνχεόμενοι
διὰ πολλὰc αἰτίαc οὐχ [ὁ]ρῶ-
cι[ν], ὡc ἔνιοι διαπαίζ[ο]ν-
τεc, ἄ[λλ]ουc [ο]ὐ φέροντε[c

Col. XVIIa: ...but when they observe that their character is prone to error, they are stung. And just like those who call skilled doctors to an operation when they apply the scalpel to those who are ill, so too when what is stinging in frank criticism meets the eye of these people and they believe that they will commit no error, or that they will escape notice even if they have erred many times, they call upon {their teachers} to admonish...

Col. XVIIb: ...{earlier they see that} they {the teachers} apply to them {the students}, when they are [not dis]tinguishing {themselves from others} and to them only, both at the right moment and out of goodwill, all the things that we were advising. But then, when they do distinguish {themselves and feel} that they are there in {a position of} honor, they are annoyed. And earlier they see the benefit of frank criticism, but then, because they are confused for many reasons, they do not see it, like some people who make jokes but do not endure others {making jokes at their expense}...

Col. XVIIIa

μό-
νον κα........ γ᾿ εἰc cκῶμ-
μά τι κινε[ι .....]ν . ιc ἐκτε-
λῶν (?) μαίνε[ται cκω]φθεὶc
5   καὶ τὸν c[οφὸν κ]α[τασκ]ευά-
ζων ἐνίοτε δ[ι]αίτηc αὐτῆc
ἐρᾶι. * τούτ[ου δ᾿] αἴτιον ὅ-
τι τῶι μὲν λαλεῖν ἐπιθυ-
μίαc ἀντιτεινούcαc οὐκ ἔ-
10   χουcιν, ὅθεν ἀκεραίωc λέ-
γουc[ι] τὸ φαινόμεν[ον,   5
τῶι δὲ πράττε[ι]ν πικρῶc
ἀμυττούcαc, ὥcτ᾿ ἐνμέ-
νε[ι]ν [ο]ἷc ἐπή<ι>νουν᾿ ἀδύνα-
15   τον

1–7a suppl. G. 96   4 cκω]φθεὶc Clay   7 τούτ[ου G.
τοῦτ[ο O.

Col. XVIIIb

οὐ λόγουc cυν]φέρον-
ταc ἀποδέχοντ[α]ι, διὰ δὲ
δοξοκοπίαν λέγουcι μό-
νον, ὡc ἂν "οὐκ ὠνούμε-
5   νοι τοὺc λόγουc, ἀλλ᾿ ἐκ βα-
θείαc α[ἰθ]έροc ἀμοχθεὶ λαμ-
βάνοντεc"· ὅταν δὲ τὸ πον-
οῦν κνιcθῇ<ι>, πηδῶc[ι]ν, ἀ-
δυνατοῦντεc ἐφ᾿ ἑαυτῶν
10   τὸ πλάcμα τηρεῖν. ἐνίοτε δὲ κἀκείνουc μὲν δεόν-
τωc νο[υ]θετεῖcθ[αι] νομίζουcιν, ἑαυτοὺc δὲ πα[ρὰ
λόγον οὐχ ἡμαρτηκόταc.

1–2 οὐ λόγουc cυν]φέρον | ταc G. 96 οὐ cυν]φέρον | ταc
O. 7–8 πον | οῦν G. πολι | οῦν O.

Col. XVIIIa: ... < only ... moves {them} to a kind of mockery ... he {a student} ends up (?) being furious {[when he has been mocked]}, and, [as he instructs the wise man], he is sometimes passionate for this very way of life>. The reason for this is that, in {merely} talking, they have no desires that resist {such a life}, and hence they say sincerely what seems the case {to them}, but in acting {they have desires} that chafe bitterly, so that it is impossible {for them} to continue in what they were {previously} praising {in words}...

Col. XVIIIb: ...they do not accept advantageous < [words]>, but solely through a desire for reputation they talk as if they were "not purchasing their words but taking them effortlessly from the deep heavens."[185] But when < [what hurts]>[186] is piqued, they flinch, unable on their own to keep up the pretense. Sometimes they believe that those people {who are all words} indeed are fittingly admonished, but that they themselves, contrary to reason, have not erred.

---

[185] Quoted as Euripidean in Plutarch *Mor.* 539B; also quoted in Philodemus *Rh.* II 101.8-13; cf. Gigante, *Ricerche filodemee*, 92-93.

[186] O. reads "turning grey," presumably a reference to old men.

Col. XIXa
πρὸς ὧι φασι μ[έμ-
φεcθ[αι], καὶ οὐχὶ τῆι παρρηcία[ι] κοινῶc· καὶ τὸ cυνφέρον
ὁρῶcι]ν αὐτοὶ διατρανῶc, [μᾶλ-
5   λον δ᾽ ἔ]τι βλέπουcιν. * διὰ τί
μᾶλλον ἔτ᾽ ἐπι[τηδει]ότεροι
πρὸς τὸ παρρη[cιά]ζειν
εἰcίν; ἢ δ < ιὰ τὸ > οἴεcθαι [ἄλλω]ν cυν-
ετώτεροι, νομίζου[c]ιν αὐ-
10   τοῖc εἶναι παρρηcία[c] μέ-
ρος] πρὸς ἄλλους ἐπιτιμῶ-
cι [καὶ] νωθροτέρ[ους ἐπ]εί-
γουcι.]

Col. XIXb
φιλικὸν μὲν γὰρ οἴονται τὸ παρρηcί-]
α]ν ἐπι[φέρειν καὶ τὸ νου-
θετεῖν ἄλλους, τὸ δ᾽ αὐτὸν ἄ-
ξια ποιε[ῖ]ν ἐπιπλήξεωc, ἀ-
5   δοξίαν καὶ κατάγνω[c]ιν.
κ]αὶ φιλικὸν ἔργον ἐπι[τ]η-   5
δεύειν οἰόμενοι χαίρου-
c]ι, νουθετούμενοι δ᾽ οὐ[θ]έν,
καὶ τῶν ἁμαρτημάτων
10   ἐκτὸς εἶναι· μὴ γὰρ ἂν βλέ-
πειν καὶ μετ[α]τιθέναι τῶν   10
ἄ]λλων τότ᾽ ἐ[φ᾽ ἑ]αυτ[οὺς

1-2 φιλικὸν - καὶ τὸ suppl. Ph.

Col. XXa
πῶ[c ἐπιγιγνώcκοντεc
ἐξ] αὐτῶν cυν[ε]τωτέρουc
τινὰc εἶναι καὶ [δὴ] καὶ κ[α]θη-
γητὰc ἐξ αὐτῶ[ν παρρηcί-
5   αν οὐ φορ[οῦ]cιν; [δι]ό[τι] νομίζουcιν ἐν τοῖc κατὰ πρόβλη-
μα λόγοιc ὑπερέχεcθαι μό-
νον, ἐν δὲ τῆι διαθέcει κ[α]ὶ
τῶι cυνορᾶν τὰ κρείττω
10   καὶ μάλιcτα τἀν τῶ[ι] βίωι,

Col. XIXa: ...in which they say they blame {them}, and not by frank criticism {practiced} jointly. And they themselves [see] what is advantageous clearly, {or} [rather] they [still] look to it. Why is it that they are now more suited to speaking frankly?[187] Because they think that they are more intelligent than [others], they believe that they have a [share] in frankness when they reproach others [and urge on] the more sluggish.[188]

Col. XIXb: ... < [for they think that it is the part of a friend to apply frank criticism and to] > admonish others, but that to do oneself what is deserving of rebuke is a disgrace and crime. And those who think that they are performing the office of a friend rejoice, being in no way admonished, and {they think} that they are free of errors. For {they think} that they would not then see and transfer {errors} of others [to themselves].

Col. XXa: ...*how, [when they recognize] that some of their number are more intelligent, and in particular that some of them are teachers, do they not abide frank criticism?* It is because they believe that they are surpassed only in {regard to} theoretical arguments, but that in point of character and in perceiving what is preferable, and most especially affairs in {real} life, they themselves are far better. Sometimes in...

---

[187] Despite the fact that this question is underlined in the Greek, it does not appear to indicate a section heading; see Introduction, pp. 8–9, esp. n. 25.

[188] Cf. Plato *Ap.* 30E.

πολὺ βελτείους ἐαυτοὺς ὑ-
πάρχειν· * ἐ[ν]ίοτε δὲ κατ[ὰ

Col. XXb   καὶ πανπόλλωι δια-
φέρειν αὐτοὺς νομίζου-
cιν· ὡς Τιμοκράτης καὶ φιλεῖν ἔφη τὸ[ν ἀδ]ελφὸν ὡς
5   οὐδεὶς καὶ μιcεῖν ὡς οὐ-
δείc. πολλὰ γὰρ ἐκ τῶν
ἐναντίων πάcχουcι καὶ
πράττουcι αἱ τοῦ cυνφέ-
ροντοc ἀδιαλόγιcτοι ψυ-
10   χαί, * καὶ διειλημμένωc
μὲν ἔcτιν ὅτε δοξά[ζ]ου-
cι]ν εἶναι φρονιμώτε[ρ]οι,
ἀδιαλήπτω[c] δὲ

Col. XXIa   πολλά-
κιc δὲ καὶ cυνχυθέντεc ὑπὸ
τῆc ἐπιτιμήcεωc οὐ βλέπουcι τὴν φρόν[ηcι]ν· ποτὲ δὲ
5   παραλελογ[ί]cθαι νομίζουcιν αὐτοὺc ο[ὐ]χ ἡμαρτηκό-
cιν ἐπιτιμῶντας ἢ παρεωρα-
κέναι τι τῶν καὶ cοφ[ῶ]ι παρο-
ο[ρ]ωμένων, ἢ cυνετωτέ-
10   ρουc μὲν εἶνα[ι], μὴ φιλεῖν
δέ, ἢ μιcεῖν ἢ φθονεῖν ἢ cυν

Col. XXIb   ὧ[ιπ]ερ κολούειν καὶ
θερ]απεύε[ιν] καὶ τῶν ἄλλων
ἐπ[ι]φέρειν [τ]ι τῶν ἐκ τῆc παρρηcίαc καλῶν. οὐδέν τε πε-
5   ρᾶ[ναι] τὸ cυνετωτέρ[ουc καλ]εῖ-
cθα[ι] καὶ cοφοὺc τοὺc νου[θ]ε-
το[ῦ]ντας πρὸc τὸ μὴ δάκνε-
c[θαι], τῶν δ[έ] τινων ἀποcπω-
μένουc, [ο]ἷ[ον] καὶ ἐ[πι]θυμίαι
10   πονηραὶ κ[αὶ] γλυκύτητε[c

Col. XXb: ...and they believe that they are vastly different. Just so, Timocrates[189] said that he both loved his brother as no one else did and hated him as no one else. For souls that are unable to calculate what is advantageous suffer and do many things by opposites. And there are times when they have the opinion that they are distinctly wiser, but {they suffer and do things}[190] without distinction...

Col. XXIa: ...and often, since they are confused by the reproach, they do not look to prudence. Sometimes they {the students} believe that they {the teachers} have reasoned falsely in reproaching them when they have not erred, or that they have overlooked some of the things that are overlooked even by a wise man, or that they are indeed more intelligent, but they {the teachers} do not like them or they hate them or envy them or...

Col. XXIb: ...by which[191] they deflate {them} and treat {them} and apply some of the other fine things that derive from frank criticism, and that it accomplishes nothing for those who admonish {others} to be called more intelligent or wise with a view to their not being stung, but that, of others, those who are drawn away from certain things, [for example] base desires and delights...

....

.... [*Why does womankind not accept frank criticism with pleasure?*]

---

[189] The renegade brother of Epicurus' closest associate, Metrodorus of Lampsacus. The comment seems to derive from a letter of Metrodorus to his older brother Metrodorides; cf. Philodemus *Ir.* col. XII.26–29 Indelli.

[190] Understanding πάσχουσι καὶ πράττουσι or the like.

[191] Instead of O.'s "so as to." The infinitives are presumably in indirect discourse.

....
.........................διὰ τί]
τὸ τῶν γυ[ναικῶν γένος οὐχ ἡδέ-
[ως τὴν παρρησίαν προσδέχεται;

1 ὤ[ιπ]ερ Clay ὤ[cπ]ερ O.

Col. XXIIa   καὶ] μᾶλλον
ὑ[π]ολαμ[βά]ν[ο]υcιν ὀνειδίζεc-
θαι καὶ [μᾶλ]λον ὑπὸ τῆc ἀδο-
ξίαc θλίβον[τ]αι καὶ μᾶλλον ὑ-
5   πονοοῦcιν πονηρὰ περὶ τῶν
νουθετούντων καὶ καθό-
λου πάντα, δι' ἅ τινεc δάκνον-
ται, μᾶλλ[ο]ν ἔχουcιν χειμά-
ζοντα, * καὶ θραcύτεραι δ' εἰ-
10   cὶ κα[ὶ] χαυν[ό]τεραι καὶ φιλοδο-
ξότεραι]

Col. XXIIb   καὶ ἀξιοῦcι]
τὴν τῆc φύ[cεωc] ἀcθένειαν
ἐλεεῖcθαι καὶ cυνγνώμηc
τυγχάνειν καὶ μὴ προπηλα-
5   κίζεcθαι πρ[ὸ]c τῶν ἰcχυροτέ-
ρων ἐξεπί[τη]δεc. ὅ[θε]ν καὶ
ταχέωc ἐπὶ τ[ὰ] δάκρυα καταν-
τῶcιν, ἀπὸ καταφρονήcεωc
ἐπικ[ό]πτεcθαι νομίζουcαι.
10   διὰ τί, τῶν ἄλλων ἐπ' ἴcηc ἐχόν-
των, ἧττον φορ�οῦc[ι]ν < οἱ κ > αὶ ταῖc
περιουcίαιc κα[ὶ] ταῖc δόξαιc
λαμπ[ρ]οί; δ[ι]ότι νομίζου-
c[ι] τοὺc εὐτυχ[ε]cτέρου[c] καὶ
15   φρονιμωτέρ[ουc κα]ὶ δυc-
χεραίνεcθαι καὶ μιcεῖcθαι]

15–16 δυc|[φημεῖcθαι καὶ φθονεῖcθαι fortasse Clay

Col. XXIIa: ...[and] they {i.e., women} assume rather that they are being reviled and they are all the more crushed by the disgrace and they rather suspect evil things concerning those who admonish and in general they rather deem upsetting everything by which some {of their sex} are stung, and they are too impulsive and too vain and too fond of their [reputation]...

Col. XXIIb: ...[and they {i.e. women} think it right] that the weakness of their [nature] be pitied and that they meet with pardon and not be intentionally ridiculed by those who are stronger {than they are}. Hence they quickly reach {the point of} tears, believing that they are being reproved out of contempt. *Why is it that, when other things are equal, those who are illustrious both in resources and reputations abide {frank criticism} less well {than others}?* Because they believe that those who are more fortunate and more wise are [offensive and hated][192]...

---

[192] O.'s supplements are doubtful; Clay's suggestion translates "are spoken badly of and envied."

Col. XXIIIa   ἐ]ξελέγχοντας [ο]ὺχ ἡδέω[ς
                προσδέχονται, [ὅτι] διὰ φθό-
                νον πολλοὺς ἐπιτ[ι]μᾶν ἑαυ-
                τοῖς νομίζουσι, [κ]αὶ συνειθισ-
           5   μένοι ε[ἰ]σί πως [ὐ]πὸ πάντων
                πρὸς χάριν ὁμιλεῖσθαι· δ[ι]όπερ
                αὐτοὺς κινεῖ καὶ τὸ παράλογον

Col. XXIIIb   ἀπορήσειν, ὃ φ[ο]βούμενοί
                τινες ὑποφέρουσι παρρησί-
                αν. * καὶ διὰ τὴν ἐπιφάνειαν
                δὲ τού[τ]ου καὶ τὰς ἁμαρτίας
           5   ἀοράτο]υς αὐτῶν γενομ[έ-
                νας βλ[έπ]ειν ὑπολαμβάνου-
                σι μᾶλλον καὶ φιλοδοξεῖν
                τοὺς ἀν[υ]ποστόλως ὁμιλοῦν-
                τας ὑπονοοῦσιν, ἵνα καλῶν-
          10   ται παρρησιάσται, καὶ πα[ρ'] ὕ-
                β]ριν ἡγο[ῦ]νται[ι] τὸ τοιοῦτο
                καὶ ἀτιμ[ί]αν ἑαυτῶν. οἱ δὲ
                βασιλε[ῖς διὰ τὸ] καθόλου δύν[α-
                σθ]αι π[ρὸ]ς το[ὺ]ς [ε]ἰρημένο[υς
          15   οὐχ ἡδέως τρέψονται]

Col. XXIVa   κ]αὶ τὴν ἐπι-
                τ[ί]μησιν ἀ[ν]υποταξίαν ἡ-
                γ]οῦνται. θέ[λ]ους[ι δ]ὲ καὶ νό-
                μίζουσι συνφέρειν ἄρχειν
           5   πάντων κ[α]ὶ πά[ν]τα [δ'] αὐ-
                τοῖς ἐναπ[ερείδε]σθ[αι] καὶ
                ὑποτετάχθαι. * διὰ τί μᾶλ-
                λον οἱ πρεσβύτεροι δυσχε-
                ραίνουσιν; * ὅτι συνετωτέ-
          10   ρους οἴοντ[α]ι διὰ τὸν χρόνο[ν
                ἑαυτοὺς καὶ νομίζουσιν ἀπ[ὸ
                καταφρονήσεως τῆς ἀσθε-
                νείας ἐπὶ τὴν παρρησίαν τι-
                ν[ὰ]ς ἔρχεσθαι καὶ μεγάλην
          15   ὕβριν.]

Col. XXIIIa: ...they {the illustrious} do not gladly accept others confuting them, [because] they believe that many people reproach them out of envy, and they have become accustomed in a way to being conversed with graciously by everyone. Therefore the unexpected too disturbs them...

Col. XXIIIb: ...will be at a loss, and some people, fearing this, submit to frank criticism. And because of the revelation of this {error?}, they both assume that they see better their own errors, which have become [invisible?], and they suspect that those who converse with them forthrightly are eager for reputation, so that they may be called frank speakers, and they consider such {conduct} as tending to insolence and their own dishonor. Kings, [because] they are totally powerful, [will not gladly change their minds?] in regard to the abovementioned people...

Col. XXIVa: ...and they {kings} consider reproach to be insubordination. They wish, and believe that it is advantageous, to rule over everything and that everything [depend on] and be subordinated to themselves. *Why is it that old men are more annoyed {by frankness}?* Because they think that they are more intelligent because of the time {they have lived} and they believe that some people proceed to frankness and great [insolence?] out of contempt for their weakness.

Col. XXIVb

ἀ[μαρ]τάν[ο]υσι, καὶ θ[αυ]μαζ[ό-
μενοι καὶ τιμώμενοι πα-
ρὰ τοῖς πλ[ε]ίοσι παράδοξον
ἡγοῦνται τὸ πρός τινων ἐ-
5   πι[τιμ]η[θῆναι], καὶ καταξ[ιού-
μενόν τ[ι]νων τὸ γῆρας θ[ε-
ωροῦντε[ς] εὐλαβοῦνται
μὴ τούτων ἀποστερῶνται
φανέντες ἀνάξιοι. καὶ τὸ
10 "δὶς παῖδες οἱ γέροντες" ὑ-
ποδύνον αὐτοὺς νύ[τ]τει,
φοβουμένους μὴ [τοῖς] ἤθεσ[ι

APPENDIX

Tab. I fr. 2

                  [ὀρ-
γίζεσθ[αι] καὶ μ[ὴ πείθειν
καὶ μηδὲ φιλ[εῖν] ἢ σ[τέργειν
ἀλλὰ κολακ[εύειν

Tab. II fr. 6

περὶ [τοῦ ἐκ τῶν καθηγη-
τῶν βυβλίων μὴ κ[αταμα-
θεῖν, πρὸς οὕς τε γὰρ εὐ[λα-
β]ῶς εἰ κ[αὶ] μ[ά]λιστα ταύτ[ηι
5   κέχρηνται, Λεοντέα καὶ
Ἰδομενέα καὶ Πυθοκλέα
καὶ Ἕρμαρχον καὶ Δωσί[θεον, ἐ-
χόμενοι παντοδαπ[ῶς πρὸς
αὐτού[ς ......]θοαν[
10 μενου[

1-2 [τοῦ ἐκ τῶν καθηγη | τῶν, 2-3 κ[αταμα | θεῖν, 3-
4 εὐ[λα | β]ῶς suppl. Ph.   3 οὕς Ph. οἷς O.
7-8 Δωσί[θεον, ἐ | χόμενοι suppl. Ph.

Col. XXIVb: ...they err, and since they are revered and honored among most people they consider it untoward to have been reproached by some people, and because they observe that old age is deemed worthy of certain things, they are careful not to be deprived of these by having been shown to be unworthy of them. And the {proverb} "Old age is a second childhood"[193] gets under their skin and irks them, since they fear that, because of [their] character...

APPENDIX[194]

Tab. I fr. 2: ...to be angry and not [persuade] and not even like or [love] but to flatter...

Tab. II fr. 6: ...about not <[learning]> from the books of <[the teachers]>, for they have employed this {frankness} <[cautiously]>, albeit especially, toward <them>—Leonteus and Idomeneus and Pythocles and Hermarchus and <Dosi[theus]>,[195] <[behaving>] in all sorts of ways [toward] them...

---

[193] Literally, "Old men are a second time children"; cf. the comic poet Philemon, fr. 147 Koerte; *Paroemiographi Graeci* 2.66 Leutsch-Schneidewin (Gregory of Cyprus 1.89).

[194] The Appendix includes those dissociated scraps of papyrus that O. did not integrate into his edition. He associated these scraps with some of the 21 Tabulae into which the papyrus was divided when opened in 1808. They are often so unyielding that we have not translated every possible word.

[195] Cf. Anna Angeli, "I frammenti di Idomeneo di Lampsaco," *CErc* 11 (1981) 64; Hermarchus fr. 46 Krohn and fr. 14 Longo-Auricchio.

Tab. II fr. 8   [
       φοβ[ηθήϲ]εται [
       ἐπιλόγιον [ἀ]νά[γ]εϲθαι τὰ
       ἀλλ[ότ]ρ[ι]α [ποι]εῖ κα[ὶ] ο[
    5   con[.....δι]όπερ[
       ἀλλ[.......]διο[
       αὐτὰϲ [...... μέγ]εθ[οϲ λέ-
       ληθεν[.... πρ]ὸϲ αὐτῶ[ν ὀφλιc-
       κάνει[......] ἥμαρτ[εν ὥϲ τι-
   10 ναϲ ὑ[βρίζειν

Tab. II D   καὶ τὴν [τοῦ βίου
       cωτη]ρίαν προβ[εβληκό-
       τεϲ
       ....
    5 .... κα]ὶ τὴν ὅλην φευξό-
       μεθα cυμ]βίωcιν ἀπὸ τῶν
       ὅλων βυ]βλίων τεκμαιρό-
       μενοι], παραπληϲίωϲ δ' οὐ

Tab. III F   δι]ά τε τὴν [ἀρετ]ὴν
       προϲφέρε[τ]αι καὶ [διὰ] τὴν
       δ[ύναμι]ν
       ....
    5   καὶ παρὰ τῶν ἔξωθεν
       περι]cτάcειϲ

Tab. III G   ἐπὶ πολ-
       λῶν ἢ πάντων ἐξελ[έ]γ[ξ]ει
       καὶ τοὺϲ ἁ[παλοὺϲ] καὶ

Tab. III H   οὐ μέντοι τῶν τυ[χόντων] <μόνον>
       ἀλλὰ καὶ cτεργόν[των αὐ-
       τοὺϲ καὶ cυνετῶν

Tab. IV I   ὅτε δὲ πρ[ῶ]τον
       δακὼν διὰ τῆϲ ἐπιτ[ι]μή-
       cεωϲ ἐ[π]ὶ τὸν ἔπαιν[ον] ἤ-

Tab. II fr. 8: ...he will fear ... to draw the conclusion, he does what is foreign {to him} and ... therefore ... escaped notice ... he is [liable] in their eyes ... has erred so that some...

Tab. II D: ...having [propounded[196] the salvation of their life]...

....

...[and] we shall avoid their company entirely, inferring from [entire?] books, and in a like manner not...

Tab. III F: ...he exhibits {it}[197] through [virtue] and power...

....

...and according to [conditions] of external things...

Tab. III G: ...in many or all cases he will test even the [tender?] ones and...

Tab. III H: ...not, however, [only] of those who [happen by] but also those who love them and are intelligent...

Tab. IV I: ...when he first has stung {the student} by his reproach he will come to praise, and just as he will resume...

---

[196] Or, perhaps, "having given up."
[197] Or, perhaps, "it {i.e., frankness} is applied."

ξει καὶ καθά[περ ἀ]ναλ[ή]ψε-
5 τ]α[ι
. .

post fr. 15:   λω[
                  μόνον[
                  προϲδεχ[/4 ὀρθῶϲ /5 .]ων επ /6 ʒουϲιν /7 κ[αὶ]
                  διότ[ι /8 τοϲωϲυ /9 ...οαιτ[
                  .

Tab. IV J   ἐξανιϲτάμενον, οὐ
                  δὲ c[οβ]αρῶϲ ἐπενγελῶντα
                  τὰϲ ἀϲθενείαϲ [.]κ[...]ον οἰό-
                  με[ν]ον, ὅτι πολ[λοῖ]ϲ ὑ[πά]ρχ[ει
                  .   .

                  3 [ἄ]κ[αιρ]ον suppl. Ph.

Tab. V extrem. fr.   βού[λεται μὲν δ]ιὰ φ[ιλίαϲ
                     νουθετεῖν]

Tab. VIII L   τῶ]ν
                  προϲηκ[όντων τὰϲ ἔχθραϲ] καὶ
                  τὰϲ δια[φορὰ]ϲ ἵνα διορ-
                  θῶϲι
5   ἀ-
                  νι[έ]ντεϲ αὐ[τῶ]ν [ἐ]πιθυ-
                  μίαϲ καὶ μ[ανίαϲ

Tab. XII M   οἱ ϲοφοὶ ἀμαρτάνουϲιν, ἐὰν μὴ]
                  πρὸϲ ἐρεθιϲ[μὸν] πολλάκιϲ
                  κ]αὶ πρὸϲ [ὀργὴν με]τ[ρίωϲ
                  μένωϲι κ[α]θ᾽ ἑκάτερον
5   τῶ]ν εἰρημ[ένω]ν κ[α]ὶ περὶ
                  .
                  τοὺϲ ἄκρουϲ [ἰα]τροὺϲ [δ]ιά-
                  .
                  π]τωϲιϲ γίνεται

                  1 suppl. Ph.   3 [ὀργὴν Ph. [ἡδονὴν O.   με]τ[ρίωϲ O.
                  ἀ]τ[ενῶϲ Ph.

after fr. 15: ...only ... accept rightly ... and because...

Tab. IV J: ...rising, nor haughtily laughing at his weaknesses ... thinking that it [belongs] to many...

Tab. V, end of fr.: ...[he] wishes [to admonish on] account of [friendship]...

Tab. VIII L: ...in order to correct [the enmities] and differences among kinsmen ... relaxing their desires and [follies]...

Tab. XII M: ... < [wise men err unless] > they [moderately][198] abide irritation and often < [anger] >[199], in accord with each of the above-mentioned {methods?}, and failure occurs with the foremost doctors...

---

[198] Ph. supplies "resolutely."
[199] O. supplies "pleasure."

Tab. XII extrem. fr.

> ..]υc παρ[εμπ]ίπτειν κα[ὶ
> πίνο]ντας ἐλλέβορ[ον μὴ εἶναι
> ἰατ]ροῖc καταγε[λάcτουc·
> κα]τατυχὼν μὲν ὑπὲρ [
> 5   ....]c ἔcται πεπο[ιθ]ὼc
> .....]ν, ἀποτυχὼ[ν δὲ] διὰ
> τὴ]ν παρρηcίαν

---

3 ἰατ]ροῖc Clay ἐτέ]ροιc O.

Tab. XIV extrem. fr.

>   [μη-
> δ[ὲ πεί]cαc ἱcτορίαι διά τ'
> ἄλλ[α]c αἰτίαc καὶ παρὰ τὸ[ν
> χ[ρ]όνον· διὸ καὶ πρὸc Π[ολύ-
> 5   αινον Ἐπίκουροc κανό[νοc
> ἀπ[ό]ντοc [μύ]θ[ουc ἔ]φ[η
> διὰ τὸν χρόνο[ν μὴ φ]έρ[οντα
> περὶ αὐτῶν ὥc τι[.]αc
> διαφέρουcι παρρη[cι]άζεc-
> 10   θαι πρὸc τοὺc μὴ ποιοῦν-
> ταc *

1–2 [μη]|δ[ὲ πεί]cαc suppl. Ph.   6 ἀπ[ό]ντοc Ph.
ἄπ[α]ντοc O.   [μύ]θ[ουc ἔ]φ[η suppl. Ph.   7 μὴ
φ]έρ[οντα suppl. Ph.   8 τι[ν]αc suppl. Ph.

Tab. XII, end of fr.: ...that it happens that even those who [have drunk] hellebore are not ridiculous to {[doctors]}.[200] Hitting the mark above ... he will be, being confident, ... [but] missing the mark because of frankness...

Tab. XIV, end of fr.: ...<[nor having persuaded]>[201] by means of knowledge, both for other reasons and during the {available?} time. Therefore even to Polyaenus, when a rule <[was absent]>, Epicurus <[uttered words {?}]> concerning these things which he <[did not endure?]> on account of the time; thus ... they differ {as to whether} to speak frankly in respect to those who do not do...

---

[200] Instead of O.'s "to others."
[201] Ph.'s supplement; another possibility is $\delta\eta\lambda\omega\sigma\alpha\varsigma$, "having revealed."

BIBLIOGRAPHY

Amoroso, F. "Filodemo Sulla conversazione." *CErc* 5 (1975) 63–76.

Angeli, Anna. "I frammenti di Idomeneo di Lampsaco." *CErc* 11 (1981) 41–101.

Arrighetti, Graziano, ed. *Epicuro: Opere.* 2d ed. Biblioteca di cultura filosofica 4. Turin: Einaudi, 1973.

Asmis, Elizabeth. "Philodemus' Epicureanism." *ANRW* 2.36.4 (1990) 2369–2406.

Capasso, M. *Trattato etico epicureo (PHerc 346).* Naples: Giannini, 1982.

Crönert, W. *Memoria Graeca Herculanensi.* Leipzig: Teubner, 1903.

——. *Kolotes und Menedemos.* Leipzig, 1906. Reprint, Amsterdam: Hakkert, 1965.

De Lacy, E. A. and P. H. De Lacy. *Philodemus: On Methods of Inference.* 2d ed. La scuola di Epicuro 1. Naples: Bibliopolis, 1978.

De Witt, Norman W. "Organization and Procedure in Epicurean Groups." *CP* 31 (1936) 205–11.

Erler, Michael. "Epikur." In *Die Philosophie der Antike 4: Die Hellenistische Philosophie,* edited by Hellmut Flashar, 29–202. Basel: Schwabe, 1994.

Fitzgerald, John T., ed. *Friendship, Flattery, and Frankness of Speech: Studies on Friendship in the New Testament World.* NovTSup 82. Leiden: Brill, 1996.

Gargiulo, T. "PHerc. 222: Filodemo Sull' adulazione." *CErc* 11 (1981) 103–127.

Gigante, Marcello. "Philodème: Sur la liberté de parole." In *Actes du VIIIe Congrès, Association Guillaume Budé,* 196–217. Paris: Les Belles Lettres, 1969.

——. "Testimonianze di Filodemo su Maison." *CErc* 1 (1971) 65–68.

——. "Per l'interpretazione dell'opera filodemea 'Sulla libertà di parola.'" *CErc* 2 (1972) 59–65.

——. "Motivi paideutici nell'opera filodemea *Sulla libertà di parola.*" *CErc* 4 (1973) 37–42.

——. "'Philosophia medicans' in Filodemo." *CErc* 5 (1975) 53–61.

——. *Ricerche filodemee.* 2d ed. Biblioteca della Parola del Passato 6. Naples: Macchiaroli, 1983.

Glad, Clarence E. *Paul and Philodemus: Adaptability in Epicurean and Early Christian Psychagogy.* NovTSup 81. Leiden: Brill, 1995.

——. "Frank Speech, Flattery, and Friendship in Philodemus." In *Friendship, Flattery, and Frankness of Speech: Studies on Friendship in the New Testament World,* edited by John T. Fitzgerald, 21–59. NovTSup 82. Leiden: Brill, 1996.

Indelli, G., ed. *Filodemo: L'Ira.* La scuola di Epicuro 5. Naples: Bibliopolis, 1988.

Kondo, E. "Per l'interpretazione del pensiero filodemeo sulla adulazione nel P. Herc. 1457." *CErc* 4 (1974) 43–56.

Konstan, David. "Patrons and Friends." *CP* 90 (1995) 328–42.

——. "Friendship, Frankness and Flattery." In *Friendship, Flattery, and Frankness of Speech: Studies on Friendship in the New Testament World,* edited by John T. Fitzgerald, 7–19. NovTSup 82. Leiden: Brill, 1996.

——. "Greek Friendship." *AJP* 117 (1996) 71–94.

——. "Problems in the History of Christian Friendship." *JECS* 4 (1996) 87–113.

———. *Friendship in the Classical World*. Cambridge: Cambridge University Press, 1997.

Momigliano, Arnaldo. "Freedom of Speech in Antiquity." In *Dictionary of the History of Ideas: Studies of Selected Pivotal Ideas*, edited by P. P. Wiener, 2:252-63. New York: Charles Scribner's Sons, 1973-74.

Nussbaum, Martha. "Therapeutic Arguments: Epicurus and Aristotle." In *The Norms of Nature: Studies in Hellenistic Ethics*, edited by Malcolm Schofield and Gisela Striker, 31-74. Cambridge: Cambridge University Press, 1986.

Obbink, Dirk, ed. *Philodemus: On Piety*. Part 1. Oxford: Clarendon, 1996.

Olivieri, Alexander, ed. *Philodemi Περὶ παρρησίας libellus*. BT. Leipzig: Teubner, 1914.

Philippson, R. Review of *Philodemi Περὶ παρρησίας libellus*, edited by Alexander Olivieri. *Berliner Philologische Wochenschrift* 22 (1916) 677-88.

———. "Philodemos." PW 19.2 (1938) 2444-82.

Riley, Mark T. "The Epicurean Criticism of Socrates." *Phoenix* 34 (1980) 55-68.

Scarpat, Giuseppe. *Parrhesia: Storia del termine e delle sue traduzioni in latino*. Brescia: Paideia, 1964.

Sedley, David. "Epicurus and the Mathematicians of Cyzicus." *CErc* 6 (1976) 23-54.

Vooijs, C. J. and D. A. van Krevelen. *Lexicon Philodemeum*. 2 vols. Murmerend: Muuses; Amsterdam: Swets & Zeitlinger, 1934-41.

Wilke, C., ed. *Philodemi de ira liber*. BT. Leipzig: Teubner, 1914.

INDEX VERBORUM

GREEK-ENGLISH

N.B.   unmarked words are legible in papyrus or restored with a high degree of probability

*   indicates word conjectured in Olivieri's text, or a supplement proposed on the basis of the disegni

\#   indicates word conjectured in apparatus or footnote

or   indicates alternate translation offered in notes

V   initial Arabic numeral = fragment

5   initial Roman numeral = column

T5   T + Arabic numeral = tabula; second numeral or letter = fragment

5.5   line numbers are our own, based on editors' supplements

ἀβελτερία	fatuity	87.9
ἀγαθός	good	36.8–9, 39.7, *43.2, *43.5, 68.6–7, 75.6, *XIVa.3
ἀγαπάω	be content	18.3–4
ἀγάπη	love	XIIIa.3
ἀγάπηϲιϲ	love	80.9–10
ἀγέλη	flock	87.3
ἀγένητοϲ	groundless	71.5–6
ἀγνεύω	purify	55.11
ἀγνοέομαι	be unrecognized	VIIIa.5–6, VIIIa.7–8
ἄγνοια	ignorance	53.9
ἀγνόω	be ignorant	8.5
ἀγνώμων	senseless	19.5
ἀγνώϲτωϲ	unbeknownst	61.2–3
ἄγω	practice	22.7, Ia.5, IVb.9, VIIb.13
ἀδεήϲ*	fearless	71.12
ἀδελφόϲ	brother	XXb.4
ἀδιαλήπτωϲ	without distinction	XXb.13
ἀδιαλόγιϲτοϲ	unable to calculate	XXb.9
ἀδικέω*	wrong	12.10
ἀδοξία	ill repute, disgrace	3.8, XIXb.4–5, XXIIa.3–4
ἀδρόϲ	large	XIVb.11
ἀδυνατέω	be unable	XVIIIb.8–9
ἀδύνατοϲ	impossible	56.14, XVIIIa.14–15
ἀηδία*	dislike	IXa.2
ἀηδῶϲ	pleasurelessly	IIb.7

ἀθεράπευτος	untreatable	84.11-12
ἀθυμόω	dishearten	12.5-6
αἰδήμων	shy	IVa.4-5
αἰδώς	shame	86.8
αἰθήρ	heavens	XVIIIb.6
αἴνεσις	praise	VIIIa.10
αἱρέομαι	choose	17.6, 45.9, *48.1-2
αἵρεσις*	choice	42.12
αἱρέω	induce	57.12
αἴσθησις*	awareness	29.3-4
αἰσχρός	shameful	39.8, 86.1
αἰσχύνη	shame	XIIIa.8
αἰσχύνομαι	be ashamed	85.3
αἰτία	reason, cause	59.9, 62.12, IXa.3-4, IXb.3, IXb.13, *Xa.2-3, XIVb.9, XVIIb.12, T14.end.3
αἰτιάομαι	accuse	58.3, 73.6-7
αἴτιον	reason	XVIIIa.7
αἰφνίδιος	sudden	32.5
ἀκεῖον	medicine	30.6
ἀκέομαι*	heal	78.8
ἀκεραίως	sincerely	XVIIIa.10
ἀκεστικός*	healable	77.7-8
ἀκίνητος	unmovable	19.3
ἀκμάζω	be at its height	65.9
ἀκόλουθος	consequent	68.6
ἀκούω	listen, hear	27.9-10, 28.9-10, *31.11, 51.1, XVb.2
ἀκρατής*	without control	IIa.2
ἀκράχολος	irascible	IIIb.4
ἀκρειβόω	be precise	VIIb.9
ἀκριβής	strict	Va.3-4
ἀκριβῶς	exactly	50.9
ἄκρος	foremost	T12.M.6
ἄκρως	strictly	57.8
ἀλαζών	boaster	88.13
ἀλγέω*	suffer	30.11
ἀλγίων	more painful	62.5
ἀλήθεια	truth	XVb.1-2
ἀληθινός*	truthful	73.7
ἀλλότριος	foreign	*66.2-3, T2.8.4
ἀλλοτριόω	repel	18.2
ἄλυπος	harmless	XIIb.3-4
ἀμαθία*	ignorance	83.9
ἁμαρτάνω	err	6.2, 46.6, *46.10, 62.9-10, 63.2, 64.2-3, 83.3, 83.6-7, IXb.12, *XIIa.1-2, XVb.14-15, XVIIa.13, XVIIIb.14, XXIa.6-7, XXIVb.1, T2.8.9,

		*T12.M.1
ἁμάρτημα	error	*9.1, 9.7-8, 55.9, 76.9-10, 77.5, 79.6-7, XIa.5, XVb.10, XVIIa.11-12, XIXb.8
ἁμαρτία	error	1.3, 49.7, 79N.8-9, 79.10, IIIb.12, *VIb.2-3, XVa.8, XXIIIb.4
ἁμαρτωλόc	prone to error	XVIIa.3
ἀμελέω*	neglect	86.1-2
ἀμεταθεcία#	changelessness	91N.2
ἀμοχθεί	effortlessly	XVIIIb.6
ἀμύνομαι*	ward off	19.11
ἀμύττω	chafe	XVIIIa.13
ἀναβολή	procrastination	Va.3
ἀναγκαίωc	necessarily	41.2
ἀνάγκη*	necessity	IIb.11
ἀνάγομαι	draw	T2.8.3
ἀναιρέομαι*	take up	5.5
ἀνακάκχεcιc*	ridicule	15.5
ἀνακρίνω	interrogate	42.9
ἀναλαμβάνω*	resume	93N.6, T4.I.4-5
ἀναλθήc	incurable	59.10-11, *84N.2
ἀναλογία	resemblance, relationship	80.3, XIb.4
ἀνάλογοc	analogous	XIVa.7
ἀναλόγωc#	analogously	81.1
ἀνανεόομαι	renew	XIIIa.7
ἀναξιοπαθέω*	suffer undeservedly	73.11-12
ἀνάξιοc	unworthy	XXIVb.9
ἀναπλάττω	restore or feign	61.6-7
ἀνάπτω	ascribe	76.6
ἀνάταcιc	stress	60.9-10
ἀνατεταμένοc	puffed up	IVa.3-4
ἀνατίθεμαι	communicate	81.2-3, 81.7, *84N.3
ἀνεκτέον	one must bear	80.5-6
ἀνεκτόc	bearable	87.5
ἀνελευθέρωc*	abjectly	84.5
ἀνελλιπῶc*	exhaustively	VIIb.9-10
ἀνεποργίζομαι	be angry	87.6-7
ἄνετοc	intemperate	9.8
ἀνεφόδευτοc	unexamined	84.10
ἀνέχομαι	tolerate	#2.6, *74.1, Xa.12, Xb.8, XIIb.8, XIIIb.11
ἀνήκεcτοc*	incurable	70.2-3
ἀνήρ	man	43.13, *VIIa.11, Xb.6
ἀνθρωποδαμνάω#	tame human beings	87N.6-7
ἀνθρωποδάμνηc*	person-tamer	87N.6-7
ἄνθρωποc	human being, person	56.12, 86.3-4, *Xb.1
ἀνίημι	relax	65.10, T8.L.5-6
ἀνόητοc*	foolish	IIa.3-4

ἀνοικείωc*	inappropriately	81.9
ἄνουc#	silly	XIIa.4
ἀντέχω	resist	5.7-8, *71.12
ἀντιδοκεύω	be on the look-out	66.13
ἀντικρούω	hinder	66.8-9
ἀντιλέγω*	talk back	13.10
ἀντιστρόφωc	conversely	65.4
ἀντιτάττομαι	oppose	30.7
ἀντιτείνω	resist	XVIIIa.9
ἀνυποcτόλωc	forthrightly	40.2-3, XXIIIb.8
ἀνυποταξία	insubordination	XXIVa.2
ἀνύω	accomplish	12.5, 64.10
ἀξία	worth	IIIb.11
ἀξιόλογοc	worthy of discussion	48.9
ἀξιόπιcτοc	worthy	VIa.14
ἄξιοc	worth, deserving of	*78.6, XIXb.3-4
ἀξιόω	think worthy, think right	*82.5-6, 83.4, *XXIIb.1
ἀόρατοc*	invisible	XXIIIb.5
ἀοργήτωc	without anger	12.7
ἀπαγγέλλω	report	52.10-11
ἀπαγορεύω*	give up	66.4-5
ἀπάγω	withdraw	XIIb.5
ἀπαθέω	be indifferent	86.5-6
ἀπαθῶc*	dispassionately	48.2
ἀπαιcχύνομαι	be ashamed	71.3
ἀπαιτέω	ask in return	XIVb.12-13
ἀπαλλάττω	recover	69.6-7
ἀπαλόc	tender	7.2, *T3.G.3
ἀπαντάω*	confront	VIIIa.4
ἀπάντηcιc*	rejoinder	73.12
ἀπαντλέω	jettison	74.9
ἀπαυχενίζω	rear the neck	71.7
ἀπειθέω	disobey	#1.5, 65.9, 65.11-12, *66.2
ἀπειθία*	disobedience	87N.7
ἄπειμι*	be absent	T14.end.6
ἀπειροκαλία*	vulgarity	84N.5-6
ἀπεργάζομαι	accomplish	21.3-4
ἀπευφημιcμόc	politeness	XVIb.9-10
ἀπέχομαι#	refrain	93N.1
ἀπιcτέω*	distrust	1.5
ἁπλῶc	simply	*10.4, 35.8-9
ἀποβαίνω	turn out	57.6-7
ἀπογινώcκω	give up	3.4, #87N.10
ἀπογνώcιμοc	desperate	46.7
ἀποδέχομαι	accept	Xb.9, XVIIIb.2
ἀποδιαcτρέφω	divert	60.10-11
ἀποδίδωμι	respond (with)	6.4
ἀπόθεcιc*	setting right	77.7
ἀποθνῄcκω	die	29.7-8

ἀποκνητέον*	one must shrink from	80.12
ἀπόλλυμαι	come to ruin	72.6
ἀπολογέομαι	defend oneself	XIb.12
ἀπολογίζομαι	say in one's defense	Xb.12–13
ἀπομάσσω*	skim	IVa.9–10
ἀπομίμησις	imitation	Va.8, XIIIa.12
ἀπόνοια	madness	21.12
ἀπορέω	be at a loss	XXIIIb.1
ἀποσπασμός	separation	3.10–11
ἀποσπάω	draw away	XXIb.8–9
ἀποστερέω	deprive	XXIVb.8
ἀποστρέφεται	be alienated	13.8–9, 27.3
ἀποστροφή	recourse	21.9
ἀπότομος	offshoot	45.6
ἀποτρέπομαι	turn away	67.7
ἀποτρέπω	turn away (active)	Xb.3–4
ἀποτυγχάνω	miss the mark	T12.end.6
ἀπόφασις#	denial	1.5
ἀποφέρω	turn away	24.2–3
ἀποφθεγματίας	sententious	VIa.8–9
ἀποχράω	suffice	IIIa.2
ἀπρεπής*	improper	39.1–2
ἀπρόςληπτος*	unaccepted	91N.5–6
ἀπρόςωπος	impersonal	61.11
ἀπροφασίςτως	unhesitatingly	80.8–9
ἀργία*	laziness	Va.2
ἀρέσκω	please	26.7–8
ἀρετή*	virtue	T3.F.1
ἁρμοστέον*	must be attuned	84N.7
ἄρρητος	unspoken	XIb.7
ἀρχή	point of departure, beginning	6.11, *32.2, *47.4
ἄρχω	rule	XXIVa.4
ἀσέλγεια	insolence	Ib.12
ἀσθένεια*	weakness	93N.4–5, IXa.1, XXIIb.2, XXIVa.12–13, T4.J.3
ἀσθενής	weak or sick	59.9
ἀστεῖος	polite	Ia.2, Ia.6, *Ib.1
ἀστείως*	politely	80.6
ἀστόχως	missing the mark	XVIa.1
ἀσύμβλητος*	incomparable	77N.3
ἀσφάλεια	security	78.2–3
ἀταράχως	calmly	18.3
ἀτενής	intense	IVa.6
ἀτενῶς#	resolutely	T12.M.3
ἀτιμία	dishonor	XXIIIb.12
ἀτόπως*	wrongly	62.12
αὐλικός	courtly	IVb.7
ἀφανής*	concealed	14.4–5
ἀφιλόδοξος	indifferent to fame	Ib.5

ἄφιλος	unfriendly	41.3, 78.2
ἀφίσταμαι	shun	4.8, 59.2
ἀφόρητος*	unendurable	34.4–5
ἀφορμή*	capacity	68.12
ἀφρονέω*	be foolish	21.6
ἀφροσύνη	foolishness	55.8–9
ἄφρων	foolish	Xa.10–11
ἀχαιός	Greek	31.4
ἄχθομαι	be vexed	30.9, XVIb.1
ἀψίνθιον	wormwood	IIb.8
βαδίζω	come	XIVa.8
βάθος	depth	53.11
βαθύς	deep	IVb.2–3, XVIIIb.5–6
βαρβαρικῶς	in a barbarian language	24.11
βασιλεύς	king	*47.3, XXIIIb.13
βέλτιστα	best	XVIa.3–4
βελτίων	better	58.10–11, XXa.11
βιάζω	treat roughly, compel	12.8–9, XVIb.11
βίος	life	XIVa.2, XXa.10, *T2.D.1
βλάβη	injury	30.3, 37.2–3
βλάπτω	harm	*47.5, *78.10, Ib.11–12, IIa.5
βλασφημέω	malign	*13.2, 18.7
βλέπω	see, look to	IIIb.13, XVIIb.9, XIXa.5, XIXb.10–11, XXIa.3–4, XXIIIb.6
βληχρός	mild	IIIb.7
βοήθεια	assistance, assisting	18.5, 67.8–9
βοηθέω	help	43.9–10, 86.7
βοηθός	helper	71.10
βούλομαι	want	T5.end.1
βυβλίον	book	T2.6.2, T2.D.7
γέλως	laughter	23.2
γένεσις	birth	IVb.12–13
γένος	genre, kind	XIIIb.3, *XXIb.13
γέρων	old man	XXIVb.10
γῆρας	old age	XXIVb.6
γηράσκω	grow old	29.9
γινώσκω	know, recognize	23.10, 44.8, 46.7–8, 84.13, VIIIa.3, VIIIa.6–7, VIIIb.6–7, Xa.9, Xb.7, XVIa.4
γλυκύτατος	sweetest	14.9–10
γλυκύτης	delight	XXIb.10
γλῶσσα*	tongue	IIa.2
γνώριμος*	acquaintance	77.10
γόης	charlatan	60.8
γονεύς	parent	IVb.7, XIb.2

γράφω	write	6.9, 72.3
γυμνόω*	strip	78.11
γυνή	woman	VIa.4–5, *VIa.6, *XXIb.13
δάκνω	sting	16.2, 26.9, VIIIb.11, XVIIa.4, XXIb.7–8, XXIIa.7–8, T4.I.2
δάκρυον	tear	XXIIb.7
δαψιλής	plentiful, abundant	68.4, Vb.5
δείκνυμι*	show, point out	1.9, 19.7–8, 40.2, 40.14, IXa.5
δεινός*	terrible	77N.4
δεινῶς*	terribly	77N.7
δελεάζω	entice	26.11
δεξιά	welcoming (n.)	44.9–10
δεξιῶς	graciously	36.8, 88.6, 88.9
δέομαι	need	7.4–5, 34.7, 40.13, 46.5, VIb.9–10, VIb.15, XVb.3
δέον	be wanting, necessary	54.9, *XVb.4
δεόντως	fittingly	XVIIIb.11–12
δέος*	fear	47.5
δεσποτικῶς*	tyrannically	34.3
δεύτερος	second	XVb.5
δέχομαι	receive	XIVb.2
δηγμός	sting	VIIIb.11
δηκτικός	stinging	XVIIa.9
δηλονότι	it is obvious that	Vb.6
δῆλος*	obvious	VIa.1, VIIa.9
δηλόω*	reveal	71.10, #T14.end.2
δημαγωγός	politician	Ib.5–6
δῆμος	people	VIIa.11
διαβάλλομαι	be discredited	35.9
διαβάλλω	slander	51.7–8
διαβλέπω	look to	XIa.3
διαβολή	slander	17.7
διάβολος	slanderer	50.3
διαγελάω#	laugh at	31.9–10
διαγίνομαι	go through	31.9–10
διαγινώσκω	discern	1.4–5
διάθεσις	condition, disposition, character	30.5–6, 36.6, 48.9–10, 72.8, 85.6–7, 86.1, Ia.2, Ia.6, XVIIa.2, XXa.8
διαίρεσις	operation	XVIIa.5–6
δίαιτα*	way of life	XVIIIa.6
διάκειμαι	be disposed	80.5
διακελεύομαι	encourage	8.10–11
διακινέω*	probe	87N.6–7
διαλαμβάνω	treat or memorize, suppose, distinguish	3.5, 59.6, *Ia.1, Ia.8, XVIa.7–8, XVIIb.1–2

διαλανθάνομαι	forget	61.11–12, *65.12–13
διαλέγω	examine	27.6
διαμαρτάνω	err	51.4–5
διαμαρτία	error	40.3–4
διάνοια	intellect	13.8
διανορθόω	restore fully	85.1–2
διαπαίζω	make jokes	XVIIb.13–14
διαπίπτω	slip up, make a mistake	20.7, 56.1–2, 56.4–5, 56.13, 63.7–8, 67.8
διαπράττω*	accomplish	47.2
διαπρέπω	be eminent	45.4–5
διάπτωcιc*	failure	4.1–2, 58.8, T12.M.6–7
διαρρήγνυμαι	burst	54.7–8
διαcαφέω	make clear	*25.9–10, VIIIb.9–10
διαcτρέφω	distort	66.11
διαcυρτικόc	disparaging	37.8–9
διατεταμένωc	contentiously	37.5–6
διατίθεμαι	be disposed	*2.2, 27.11, 70.12, 73.2–3, VIIb.12
διατίθημι	set forth, state	47.10, 85.5–6
διατρανῶc	clearly	XIXa.4
διαφέρω	differ, be different	80.1, IVa.7, Vb.4, VIa.4, VIa.5, VIa.7–8, XXb.1–2, T14.end.8
διαφιλοτεχνέω	practice an art	10.2
διαφορά	difference	26.5–6, 50.8–9, IIIa.7, T8.L.3
διάχυcιc	merriment	79.9
διδάcκω	teach	*XIIIa.3, XIIIb.13
δίδωμι	give, present, contribute, apply	22.6, 55.1–2, 68.10–11, IXa.6, XVIIa.7
διειλημμένωc	distinctly	XXb.10
διερεθίζομαι	be very irritated	31.2
δίκαιοc*	just	33.6
δίκη	way	Xa.10
διορθόω	correct	44.4, 62.6–7, 75.8, XVb.7, *XVIb.12, T8.L.3–4
διόρθωcιc	correction	50.6, 55.6, 55.10
διcτάζω	doubt	47.7–8
δοκέω	seem	32.3, 32.7, 32.8, 52.8, *56.1, 56.4, 62.4–5, *78.11
δόξα	reputation	XXIIb.12
δοξάζω	have the opinion	XXb.11–12
δοξοκοπία	desire for reputation	XVIIIb.3
δραcτικόc*	effective	32.12
δριμύ	harsh	78.3
δύναμαι	be able, can, be powerful	20.3–4, 56.10–11, 58.10, 79.1, *91N.2–3, XXIIIb.13–14

ἐναπερείδομαι	depend on	XXIVa.6
ἐνέχομαι	be involved	44.2
ἐνοχλέω	give trouble	XVb.8–9
ἐντέχνως*	skillfully	IIIb.1
ἐντυγχάνω	encounter	XVIa.2
ἐξαμαρτάνω	err	XVb.4–5
ἐξανίσταμαι	rise	T4.J.1
ἐξελέγχω*	test, confute	42.4–5, XXIIIa.1, T3.G.2
ἐξεπίτηδες	intentionally	XXIIb.6
ἐξεργάζομαι	handle	VIIb.7–8
ἐξερέω*	will speak out	VIb.3, Xb.3
ἐξετάζω	examine	48.10
ἕξις	character	Ib.4–5
ἐξοικονομέω	dispose	VIIb.10–11
ἔξοχος	outstanding	41.7–8
ἔξωθεν	external	30.4–5, XIVa.11, T3.F.5
ἐπαγρύπνησις	watchfulness	11.4
ἐπαθροίζω*	gather together	XIIIa.3–4
ἐπαινέω	praise	49.1–2, XIIIb.12, XVIIIa.14
ἔπαινος	praise	68.4–5, *IIa.12, T4.I.3
ἐπαίρω	lift up	74.4
ἐπαισθάνομαι	be aware of	XVb.10–11
ἐπανέρχομαι*	return	76.11
ἐπείγω*	urge on	XIXa.12–13
ἐπεγγελάω	laugh at	T4.J.2
ἐπέρχομαι	go, approach, go over	70.3–4, *93N.7, XVa.7
ἐπέχω	present, restrain	39.5, *93N.1
ἐπιβλέπω	observe	XVIIa.3
ἐπιγινώσκω	recognize	88.4–5, 88.7–8, XXa.1
ἐπίγνωσις	recognition	IXa.7
ἐπιδείκνυμι	exhibit, show	15.6, 16.4, 77.2
ἐπιεικῶς	pretty much, mildly	26.8, IVb.9–10
ἐπιζητέομαι	inquire further	11.3, IIa.9–10
ἐπιζητέω	seek	25.2
ἐπιθυμέω	desire	50.4–5
ἐπιθυμία	desire	XVIIIa.8–9, XXIb.9, T8.L.6–7
ἐπικόπτω	reprove	XXIIb.9
ἐπικραυγάζω	shout at	7.7
ἐπιλανθάνομαι	forget	14.8
ἐπιλόγιον	conclusion	T2.8.3
ἐπιλογιστικῶς	logically	28.4
ἐπιμέμφομαι	cast blame	35.7
ἐπιπαρρησιάζομαι	speak frankly	1.6
ἐπίπληξις	rebuke	XVIb.7, XIXb.4
ἐπιπλήττω	rebuke	XVIa.11–12
ἐπιρρ(ε)ίπτω	cast	39.4, 87.3
ἐπισημαίνω	indicate	68.2–3
ἐπίσταμαι	understand	50.9, 58.9

ἐπίcτακιc	treatment	7.4
ἐπιcτολή	letter	6.11
ἐπιcτρέφομαι	pay attention	30.1–2, 31.5–6
ἐπιτείνω	intensify, heighten	7.5, 25.4–5, 67.2, 79N.2
ἐπιτεταμένοc	strained, intense	38.3, 74.7
ἐπιτήδειοc	be suited	XIXa.6
ἐπιτηδέω	perform	XIXb.6–7
ἐπιτιμάω	reproach	6.8, 31.3, 38.7–8, *62.1, #93N.7, IXb.9, XVb.12–13, XVIa.9, XIXa.11–12, XXIa.7, XXIIIa.3, XXIVb.4–5
ἐπιτίμηcιc*	reproach	30.11, 75.2, 82.1, 84.7, XXIa.3, XXIVa.1–2, T4.I.2–3
ἐπιτομικῶc	by way of an epitome	VIIb.7
ἐπιτυχία*	success	4.4
ἐπιφάνεια	revelation	XXIIIb.3
ἐπιφέρομαι	bring up	XIIa.5–6
ἐπιφέρω*	apply	XIXb.2, XXIb.3
ἐπιφορά*	reproach	66.3–4, 73.4
ἐπιφωνέω	cite	40.9, 73.13–14
ἐπιφώνηcιc	charge	27.7
ἐπίχειρον	wage	44.10–11
ἔπομαι	accompany	40.10
ἐράω	be in love, be passionate for	*42.3, 48.5, 57.2, *XVIIIa.1
ἔργον	deed, action, hard work, office	*16.6, *40.8, VIIb.6, XIXb.6
ἐρεθίζω*	irritate	13.4
ἐρεθιcμόc	irritation	T12.M.2
ἐρεθιcτόc	irritable	IIa.6
ἐρέω	will say	28.8–9
ἐρρωμένωc	vigorously	IIb.1–2
ἔρχομαι	proceed	*32.3, XXIVa.14
εὐγένεια	nobility	4.6–7
εὐεπίφοροc	inclined, prone	19.8, IIa.11
εὐεργετέω	do a service	4.4–5, 82.3–4
εὐήμεροc	cheerful	85.8–9
εὔθετοc	conducive	Va.6
εὐθήνηcιc	richness	22.3
εὐκαταφρόνητοc	contemptible	62.6
εὐλαβέομαι	be careful	XXIVb.7
εὐλαβῶc	cautiously	53.9, *T2.6.3–4
εὐλογία	reasonable argument	1.9, 57.10
εὐλόγιcτον	reasonable	57.5
εὔλογοc	reasonable	63.5, 69.2
εὐλόγωc	reasonably	69.5, 69.10, 84.14
εὐνοέω	bear goodwill	52.8–9, Ib.2
εὔνοια	goodwill	25.6, 31.12, 36.3, 74.6–7,

		*79N.2, *80.11, *Va.5-6, Xb.9, XIb.9-10, XVIIb.3-4
εὐνόως	favorably	80.4
εὑρίσκω*	discover	63.2
εὐτυχέω	fare well	19.7
εὐτύχημα	well-being	61.7
εὐτυχής	fortunate	XXIIb.14
εὐφορία	contentment	36.2
εὐφραίνω	rejoice	11.2
εὐφρονέω*	be cheerful	66.16
εὐφροσύνη	good cheer	43.7
εὐχαριστέω*	be thankful	74.12-13
εὐχαριστία	thankfulness	XIb.7-8
εὔχομαι	pray	72.4
ἐφαρμόζω	adapt	VIIb.3
ἐφεστηκώς	attentive	Vb.4-5
ἐφίημι*	remit	77.10
ἐφικνέομαι	succeed	65.3
ἐφόδιον	supplies	36.3-4
ἔχθρα	enmity	T8.L.2
ζάω	live	45.9, 72.4, #77.3-4
ζητέω*	seek, explore	35.1, 81.6, IIb.3, IIIa.3, XIVb.7
ζμίλιον	scalpel	XVIIa.7
ζωή	life	21.5
ἡγέομαι	consider	36.4, 40.5-6, 50.4, *84N.2, XXIIIb.11, XXIVa.2-3, XXIVb.4
ἡδέως	pleasurably, with pleasure, gladly	IIb.3, VIIIb.7, XIIb.9, *XXIb.13-14, XXIIIa.1, *XXIIIb.15
ἥδιον	more pleasantly	8.4-5
ἡδονή	liking, pleasure	XVIa.9-10, #T12.M.3
ἦθος	character	XXIVb.12
ἥκω	come	27.10, T4.I.3-4
ἡλικιώτης*	peer	77.9
ἤπιος	gentle	85.10, VIIIb.12-13
ἡσυχία*	silence	77N.5-6
θαυμάζω	be amazed, revere	XIa.7-8, XXIVb.1-2
θέλω	wish	*78.10, VIIIb.3-4, XXIVa.3
θεός	god	6.6-7
θεραπεία	treatment	39.10
θεράπευσις	treatment	40.13-14
θεραπεύω	treat	8.6, *20.2, 23.5-6, *32.10, 40.11, 44.8-9, 69.8, 79.3-4, 86.6, XXIb.2

Greek	English	References
θέсιс	hypothesis	57.10
θεωρέω	observe	26.2, 51.2, 71.1–2, XXIVb.6–7
θηρευτής	hunter	28.2
θηριόομαι	be bestial	52.2–3
θλίβω	crush	XXIIa.4
θρασέωс	aggressively	Va.1
θρασύс	impulsive	XXIIa.9
θρυλλόс*	chatter	XIVa.1
θυμόομαι*	be maddened, enraged	74.2, *IIa.5
θυμόс	passion, spirit	10.10–11, *27.1
θωπεία*	wheedling	87N.3
ἰάομαι	heal	32.6–7
ἰατρόс	doctor	39.12, 63.4, 64.5, 69.8, 86.7, XVIIa.5, T12.M.6, *T12.end.3
ἴδιος	(one's) own, suitable	14.7, 18.5, 37.2
ἰδίωμα	individual trait	22.2
ἰδιώτης	individual character, layman	14.3, #31.11, XI.b.1–2
ἰδιωτικόс	private	VIIIb.3
ἰλαρῶс	cheerfully	61.4
ἴσοс	equal	52.1, 77.4, XXIIb.10
ἴσου, ἐξ*	equally	IVb.10
ἵσταμαι	maintain, halt	20.8–9, 69.3–4
ἱστορία	knowledge	Vb.8–9, T14.end.2
ἰσχυρόс	strong	7.2–3, 7.6, 10.9, XXIIb.5–6
καθάπτομαι	upbraid	51.8–9, *93N.3
καθαρεύω	be pure	16.3–4, 44.6–7
καθαρόс	clean	Ib.7
κάθαρcιс	purification	46.4–5
καθηγέομαι	teach	Va.9–10, Vb.1, Vb.2
καθηγητής	teacher	*31.11, 45.5, 52.6–7, 80.2–3, VIIa.3, XXa.3–4, *T2.6.1–2
καθηγούμενος	teacher	8.6–7, 39.2–3, 42.10, 46.3–4, 61.10, 70.6, 75.3–4, 76.5–6, 85.8
καθίстημι	establish	32.10–11
καθόλου	in general, totally	1.5–6, *9.1, *13.1, 17.3, 38.3–4, 42.11–12, XXIIa.6–7, XXIIIb.13
καθορθόω*	succeed	77N.8
καθυβρίζω	scorn	79.11–12
καινόс#	new	8.1
καιρόс	opportunity, critical or right moment	22.5, 25.1, XVIIb.3
κακία	vice	57.3

κακίζω	blame	77N.4-5
κακισμόc*	blame	10.11
κακολογέω	chide	IXb.13
κακόν	evil	23.4, 91N.5
κακόc	bad	43.4
κακόφιλος	bad friend	50.11
κακῶc	evilly, badly	23.2-3, 51.10, 72.5
καλέω	call	XXIb.5-6, XXIIIb.9-10
καλόc	fine	28.5, 33.8, 44.11, XXIb.4
καλῶc	nicely, nobly, well	*28.1, 29.7, XVa.6
κανών	rule	T14.end.5
καταβάλλω	show contempt	Ib.11
καταβλητικόc	contemptuous	37.7-8, 38.2
καταβλητόc#	comtemptible	77N.3
καταγέλαστος	ridiculous	T12.end.3
καταγνοέω	ignore	33.4
κατάγνωcιc	crime	XIXb.5
καταγωγή#	return	33.4
καταδεήc	in need	XIVa.4
καταλαμβάνω	catch, grasp	57.2, 83.4, IXb.7
καταλέγω*	repeat	83.1-2
καταμανθάνω*	learn	T2.6.2-3
καταναρκάομαι	be bemused	XIIb.10
καταντάω	reach	XXIIb.7-8
καταξιόω	judge right, deem worthy	60.1, XXIVb.5-6
καταποδίζω	obstruct	30.8
κατάρα	malediction	21.10
κατάρχομαι	begin	29.1, 37.2
κατασκευαζόμενοc	student	55.3-4
κατασκευάζω	instruct	2.3, 25.6-7, 71.2-3, 76.7-8, XIIb.7, *XVIIIa.5-6
κατάσχετος	possessed	57.3
κατατυγχάνω	hit the mark	T12.M.end.4
κατάφημι*	assent	72.11
καταφορά*	jab	VIIa.5, *VIIb.1, VIIIa.10
καταφρονέω*	despise	87N.4-5
καταφρόνησιc	contempt	XIIIa.1, XXIIb.8, XXIVa.12
καταφρονητέον*	must be despised	XIVa.11-12
καταχαρίζομαι	show favoritism	XIIIb.7
κατελπίζω	expect	57.7-8
κατεγχειρέω	treat fully	57.12
κατεπᾴδω	enchant	60.12
κατήγοροc	accuser	51.3-4
κελεύω*	order	47.4
κενεόc*	empty	IVa.9
κενόc*	empty	XIVa.1
κενόω	purge	63.9, 64.8
κέντρον*	goad	17.10
κένωμα	purge	63.7

κεράννυμι	combine	68.3–4
κεφαλή	head	24.3
κηδεμονία	concern	42.11
κηδεμονικόν, τό	concern	XIIIb.11–12
κηδεμονικόc	caring	26.6–7
κινέω*	move, disturb	XVIIIa.3, XXIIIa.7
κλυcτήρ	clyster	64.6–7
κνίζω	pique	XVIIIb.8
κνίcμα	irritation	32.9
κοινόc	sociable	8.1
κοινότηc	common trait	IVb.4, IXb.8
κοινωνία#	community	93N.2
κοινῶc	publicly, generally, jointly	40.4, 66.8, XIXa.3
κολακεία*	flattery	93N.2
κολακευτικόc*	flattering	Ib.13
κολακεύω	flatter	T1.2.4
κολούω	deflate	XXIb.1
κομίζομαι	obtain	44.11
κομψεία#	daintiness	93N.2
κόcμοc	world, orderliness	26.3, 33.6–7
κουφίζω	relieve	66.9, *91N.3
κρείττων	better, preferable	44.5–6, 44.7–8, XXa.9
κρύπτω	hide	41.9, 79N
κυνίδιον	little dog	19.4
κυνικόc*	Cynic-like	73.12–13
κυνώδηc	snappish	IIIb.4–5
κύριοc	important	45.7–8
κωλύω	prevent	*34.10, 35.6, #91N.4
κωμῳδέω	ridicule	18.9–10
κωμῳδογράφοc*	comic poet	29.4
λαθραιοπραγέω	act in secret	41.2–3
λαλέω	utter, speak, talk	*47.6, *48.3, XIVa.6, XVIIIa.8
λαμβάνω	take, receive	6.11, 32.1, VIIIa.11, XVIIIb.6–7
λαμπρόc	famous, illustrious	6.10, XXIIb.13
λανθάνω	escape notice	41.10, 61.9–10, XVIIa.12, T2.8.7–8
λήγω	cease	87.5
λιτή#	entreaty	29.2
λογίζομαι	reason	78.4
λογιcμόc	reason	56.3, 56.6
λόγοc	reason, speech, argument, word	27.8, 40.7, 42.4, 54.6, 57.11, *XVIIIb.1, XVIIIb.5, XVIIIb.14, XXa.7
λοιδορέομαι	insult	60.6–7
λοιδορέω	insult	79.12, Ib.10
λοιδορία	insult	21.11, 60.5–6

λυμαίνομαι	abuse	18.7-8
λύμη	offense	13.5
λυπέω	hurt	61.1, 82.7, XVa.1, XVa.8-9
λύω*	undo	91N.4
μαθητής	disciple	87.4
μαίνομαι*	be furious	XVIIIa.4
μαίcων	cook	XIIb.4
μακρότης	long stretch	58.11-12
μανία*	folly	T8.L.7
μαcτιγόω	whip	83.9-10
μεγάλως	very	14.6
μέγας	serious, great	58.13, *73.10, Ib.4, *IXa.1, XIa.4, XIIIb.1, XIVa.8, XXIVa.14
μέγεθος*	magnitude	77N.7-8, 77.8
μεθίcταμαι	desist	84.8
μεικτός	mixed	58.7
μειόομαι	deteriorate, weaken	58.11, IVa.2-3
μειράκιον	lad	VIa.5
μέμνημαι*	remember	39.1
μεμπτός	blameworthy	IXb.3, IXb.4, IXb.5, IXb.12
μέμφομαι	blame	13.2-3, 87.8-9, XIXa.1-2
μεμψίμοιρος	carping	IIa.3
μένω	stay, abide	43.11-12, T12.M.4
μερίζω	mete out	20.5-6
μέρος*	share	XIXa.10-11
μέcος	mean	XIa.6
μεταβαίνω	move on	15.3, XIVb.10
μετάγω	transfer	9.6, 72.11
μεταγωγή	transfer	21.2
μεταδίδωμι	share, give away	47.8, 50.11
μεταθεcία*	change	91N.2
μετακαλέω	call back	65.10-11, *65.14
μεταποιέω*	reform	43.2-3
μετατίθεμαι	change	7.7-8
μετατίθημι*	change, transfer	22.1, XIb.11, XIXb.11
μεταφέρω	transfer	XIVa.2
μετρέω	measure out	52.2
μέτριος*	moderate	20.1, 93N.8
μετρίως	in moderation, moderately	6.8, 71.4, *T12.M.3
μέτρον	measure	Xa.5-6
μηνύω	disclose	42.7-8, 49.6
μιμέομαι	portray, imitate	29.5, 69.4
μιμνήcκω*	remind	46.9
μιcέω	hate	46.5, 59.3, 87.7, Xb.6-7, XXb.5, XXIa.11, *XXIIb.16
μνημονεύω	remember	XIVa.5
μόνιμος*	fixed	19.2

μόνος	only	21.3, 39.4–5, 40.8–9, XVIIb.2
μουςιάζω	make music	87.2
μοχθηρία	baseness	IIa.7–8
μοχθηρός	base	Ia.7
μῦθος*	word	*T14.end.6
μύριοι	ten thousand	24.12
μωρός	foolish	78.3
νεανίςκος	youngster	VIa.6–7
νέος	young	31.2, 36.5, 52.4–5, 71.8, 83.8, *87N.7, #87N.3, #93N.7, XVIa.10
νεότης	youth	9.8–9
νοέω	think, judge	17.5–6, 28.12, 63.11
νομίζω	believe	10.6, 69.6, *83.10, XIa.5, XVa.4–5, XVb.13, XVIIa.11, XVIIIb.12–13, XIXa.9, XXa.5–6, XXb.2–3, XXIa.5–6, XXIIb.9, XXIIb.13–14, XXIIIa.4, XXIVa.3–4, XXIVa.11
νοςέω	be ill	XVIIa.7–8
νόςημα	disease	69.7–8
νόςος	disease	63.10, 64.6
νουθετεία*	admonition	66.5–6
νουθετέον*	one must admonish	VIIa.12
νουθετεύω#	admonish	20.2
νουθετέω	admonish	13.4–5, 23.5, 35.2, *38.9–10, 45.3, 61.2, 73.1–2, 84.6, XVIIa.14, XVIIIb.12, XIXb.2–3, XIXb.8, XXIb.6–7, XXIIa.6, T5
νουθετηςία*	admonishment	91N.6
νουθέτηςις	admonishment	26.7, 32.4, 36.7–8, *39.15, *40.14, *73.1–2, 77.6–7
νύττω	irk	XXIVb.11
νωθρός	sluggish	XIXa.12
ὁδηγία*	approach	21.7
ὁδηγός	guide	40.6–7
ὀδυνάομαι	be pained	61.5–6
ὀδυνηρός	painful	30.9
οἶδα	know, acknowledge	44.4, 75.5, 78.6, IVb.2, IVb.6, IVb.11, VIIIb.13
οἴηςις*	opinion	XIIIa.10–11
οἰκεῖοι	family	3.10
οἰκεῖον	appropriately	2.9
οἰκεῖος	one's own	XVb.9–10

οἰκειόω*	acknowledge as one's own	73.8-9
οἰκέτης	slave	XIIa.8
οἰκονομέω	administer, manage	2.7-8, 22.3-4
οἶμαι	think	27.7-8, IIb.14, XIXa.8, XIXb.1, XIXb.7, XXIVa.10, T4.J.3-4
ὀλίγον, κατά	little by little	XIIIa.2
ὁμῆλιξ*	age-mate	88.1
ὁμιλέω	converse	24.2, 72.9, XXIIIa.6, XXIIIb.8-9
ὁμιλία	conversation	*43.3, VIa.12
ὄμμα	eye	26.4-5, *42.1, 77.3, XVIIa.9
ὁμοιότης	similarity	60.4-5
ὁμοίωσις	simile	54.10
ὁμολογέω	agree	57.11
ὁμονοέω#	agree	XIIb.11-12
ὀνειδίζω	revile	XXIIa.2-3
ὀνίναμαι	profit	80.8
ὄντως*	truly	41.10, #87N.8
ὁράω	see	*70.1, *87N.2-3, XVIIb.12-13, *XIXa.4
ὀργή	anger	87.8, *T12.M.3
ὀργίζομαι	be angry	38.4-5, 58.2, 58.4, *71.9-10, Xa.7, T1.2.1-2
ὀργίλος*	irascible	67.12
ὀργίλως*	angrily	2.1, 70.8, 70.13
ὀρέγομαι	desire	28.10-11
ὀρθός	right	40.7, XIIIb.13
ὀρθῶς	rightly	35.10, App. after fr. 15
ὀφλισκάνω*	be liable	T2.8.8-9
παγίως	rigidly	1.9
πάθος	passion, feeling	48.4, 65.8, 66.7-8, *XIIIa.6
παιδεύω	teach	26.2
παῖς	child	18.1, XXIVb.10
παραδείκνυμι	point out	72.5
παραδίδωμι	give over, transmit	40.10-11, XIb.5-6
παράδοξος	untoward	XXIVb.3
παραίνεσις*	advice	88.1-2
παραινέω	advise	XIVa.6, XVIIb.5-6
παρακαθαρεύω*	be cleansed	42.3-4
παρακαλέω	exhort *or* invite, call, call upon	38.11, XVIb.13, XVIIa.6, XVIIa.14
παρακινδυνευτέον	it must be risked	10.5-6
παρακολουθέω	accompany, follow	11.5-6, *42.5-6
παραλάττω	diverge	IIIa.3-4, VIIb.2-3
παραλλήλου, ἐκ*	analogously	71.1
παραλογίζομαι	reason falsely	62.10-11, *IXa.4, IXb.8-9, XXIa.5

παράλογος	unexpected	XXIIIa.7
παραμελέω	slight	35.4-5
παραπίπτω	befall	IXa.2-3
παραπλήςιον (adv.)	like	35.4
παραπλήςιος*	like	22.6, 63.3
παράπτωςις	slip	35.8
παραςειτική*	agitating	17.2-3
παραςκευή	provision	39.6-7
πάρειμι	be present	79.8
παρελπίζω	be disappointed	14.5
παρεμβάλλω	inflict	VIIa.4
παρεμπίπτω	happen	T12.end.1
παρέρχομαι	pass	56.10
παρεφάπτομαι	touch upon	8.3
παρέχομαι	make claims for	XIIIb.2
παρέχω	present, exhibit	19.9, *74.3, 75.7
παρίημι	admit, disregard	6.7, 84.11
παροράω	overlook	XXIa.7-8, XXIa.8-9
παρρηςία	frank criticism, frankness	2.7, 7.10, 10.5, 12.3-4, 15.7-8, 16.8, 17.5, *17.10, 22.9, 25.4, *27.2, 31.7, *47.3, *47.9, 55.2, *56.13-14, 59.11, *60.4, 62.11, 64.4, 65.2, 67.10, 68.11, 70.8, 70.14-15, 72.8-9, 75.10, 76.8-9, 79N.1, 81.3-4, 81.8-9, 83.3-4, 84.4, 88.6, 88.10, Ia.5, IIb.13, IIIa.5, *IIIb.13-14, IVb.9, *Va.1, *Vb.11-12, *VIb.3-4, VIb.2, VIIb.6, VIIb.13, Xb.2-3, XIIb.8- 9, XIIIb.5, XIVb.5, XVIa.2-3, XVIIa.10, XVIIb.10, XIXa.2-3, XIXa.10, *XIXb.1-2, XXa.4-5, XXIb.3-4, *XXIb.14, XXIIIb.2-3, XXIVa.13, T12.end.7
παρρηςιάζομαι	speak frankly, be frank	*5.1-2, *6.2-3, 25.7-8, 37.6, 48.1, 58.4-5, 58.5-6, 60.2, 62.7-8, 63.12-13, 64.4-5, 64.9, 67.10-11, 70.11, 82.2, 85.4, Ia.2-3, IIIb.9-10, *VIIa.1, VIIIb.4-5, Xa.6, XVIb.1-2, T14.end.9-10
παρρηςιάζω*	speak frankly	43.11, XIXa.7
παρρηςιάςτης	frank speaker	XXIIIb.10

παρυποδύνω	insinuate oneself	VIa.12
παρυπονοέω	suspect	IXb.10
πάσχω	experience, suffer	62.3, XXb.7
πατήρ	father	VIIa.3–4
παύομαι	stop, cease	15.2, #87N.11, *93N.2
πειθαρχέω	obey	36.6, 66.5
πείθω	persuade	16.5, 44.5, *73.8, IXa.6, Xb.13, *T1.2.2, *T14.end.2
πεῖρα*	attempt	82.5
πειράομαι	try	18.9, 39.14
πέλας	nearby	61.3
πέποιθα	be confident	82.4, T12.end.5
πεποίθησις	confidence	45.2
περαίνω*	accomplish	64.1, 64.7, XXIb.4–5
περιαθρέω	scrutinize	80.7
περιαυτίζομαι*	show off	81.10
περιβάλλομαι	be clothed	31.4–5
περιγίνομαι	result	28.6
περιγράφω	determine *or* limit	21.9–10
περιδείκνυω	demonstrate	28.3
περιέχω	circumscribe, contain	78.2, *88.2
περιίσταμαι	avoid	50.2–3, XIIIa.8–9
περιλύπως*	painfully	71.9
περιουσία	resource	XXIIb.12
περιπατέω	stride	23.3
περίστασις*	condition	T3.F.6
περιστέλλω	cover up	41.6
περιττός*	lavish	Vb.10
περιφερόμενος#	sociably	XIIb.2–3
περιφορά#	sociability	XIIa.4
πηδάω	flinch	XVIIIb.8
πικρός	sharp, bitter	60.4, IIa.7, XVIa.11
πικρότης*	bitterness	6.3–4
πικρῶς	bitterly	XVIIIa.12
πίνω*	drink	T12.end.2
πίπτω	slip	83.7
πιστεύω	believe	XIIIb.9
πίστις*	belief	6.6
πλανωδῶς	wandering about	66.14
πλάσμα	pretense	XVIb.8–9, XVIIIb.10
πλεοναζόντως	predominantly	IIb.9–10
πλῆθος	multitude	75.5–6
πλοῦς	sailing	XVb.6
ποικίλος	subtle	60.11, 68.1
ποικίλως	subtly	86.6
ποιότης	quality	14.2
πολεμέω	make war	19.10–11
πολιός*	grey	24.3
πολιόω#	turn grey	XVIIIb.7–8

πολυχαρής	graceful	54.9–10
πολυχρόνιος	long-term	Va.8–9
πομπεύω	strut	Ib.10–11
πονέω	labor, hurt	12.4, 21.6, *XVIIIb.7–8
πονηρός	base, evil	19.6, *23.11–12, XXIb.10, XXIIa.5
πόνος	toil	IXa.2
πορεύομαι	make (a trip)	XVb.6
πόρρωθεν	from afar	32.2
πότιμος	sociable	VIa.13
πρᾶγμα	action, act	*VIb.7, XIIIb.6
πραέως	gently	XVIa.8
πρᾶος*	mild	74.2–3
πράττω	perform, act, do	IIb.6, XVIIIa.12, XXb.8
πρεσβύτης	old	29.6, VIIa.2–3, XXIVa.8
προαιρέομαι*	choose	XIIb.11–12
προβαίνω*	proceed, advance	70.3, 91N.4–5, XIIIa.5–6
προβάλλω	put forward, propound *or* give up	#XIa.6, XIVb.4, *T2.D.2–3
πρόβλημα, κατά	theoretical	XXa.6–7
προθυμία*	eagerness	20.2–3
προκατασκευή*	preparation	32.11–12
προκοπή	progress	10.10, *33.3
προλαμβάνω	preconceive	*56.3, 56.5–6
προνοέομαι	foresee	XIIIa.11
πρόνοια	foresight	84.13
πρόοιδα	know beforehand	71.6
προπηλακίζω	ridicule	XXIIb.4–5
προσαγορευτέον	one should address	24.11–12
προσάγω	apply	IIb.12, VIb.12
προσαναθετέον	to be ascribed	77.4–5
προσαναπαύομαι*	rely	71.11–12
προσαναφέρω*	report	41.4–5
προσβάλλω	attack, smack of	65.12, XIa.6
προσδέομαι	be in need	30.3–4, 63.6
προσδέχομαι*	accept	2.6, 31.8, *40.14, *XXIb.15, XXIIIa.2, App. after fr. 15
προσδοκάω	expect	69.2–3, 87.6
προσδοκία*	expectation	32.6
πρόσειμι	be there	XVIIb.7–8
προσεκκάω	inflame further	44.1
προσεπεῖπον	tell	Xb.4
προσεπέρχομαι*	come on	73.10–11
προσέχω	pay attention	88.12, XIb.5
προσηκόντως	suitably	38.10–11, *73.2, *76.3
προσήκω	be suitable	43.8, XIVb.6
προσήκων	kinsman	T8.L.2
προσημείωσις*	prognostication	88.3
προσκαρτέρησις	persistence	67.4–5

προσκαρτερητικῶς	persistently	86.3
προςλαμβάνω	accept, gain	#17.8–9, Vb.7–8, Vb.9–10
προςμένω	wait for	XIVb.11–12
προςπάςχω	be devoted	8.2
προςποιέομαι	pretend	88.7, 88.10–11
προςτίθημι	add	54.8
προςτροχάζω	run up	52.7
προςυφίςταμαι	ascribe	9.4–5
προςφέρομαι	present, exhibit	3.2–3, 55.12, IVb.4–5, T3.F.2
προςφέρω	apply, bring forward	3.6, 54.3–4, *62.13, *72.10, *VIb.2, XVIIb.4–5, #T3.F.2
πρόςφορος*	fitting	36.9
προςχαρακτηρικῶς	in accord with one's character	8.3–4
προςών	relevant	Ib.7–8
πρόςωπον	person	8.1
πρότερον	first, earlier	65.6, *66.2, 66.12, 84.10–11, XVIIb.9
προτρέπομαι	exhort	68.5–6, 69.9–10
προφέρω	declare	*23.1, 53.6
προχείρως	promptly	XIa.4, XIIIb.9
πρώην	just now	83.6
πτηνός	winged	87.4
πυνθάνομαι	learn, inquire	9.4, 24.9, IIb.2–3
πωλοδαμνάω#	tame like a colt	87N.3
πωλοδάμνης	colt-tamer	87N.3, #87N.4
πῶλος*	colt	87N.4
ῥᾳδίως	lightly	XIIIb.8
ῥαθυμέω	be remiss	49.9–10
ῥᾷον	more easily	8.5
ῥητέον	must be said	IIIa.6
ῥυθμικός	expert in rhythms	54.6–7
ςεβαςμός	reverence	4.5–6
ςεμνότατα*	most solemnly	74.1
ςημεῖον	sign	63.5
ςημειόομαι	infer from signs	57.4–5
ςημείωςις	interpretation of signs	63.8
ςήμερον	today	29.1
ςκληρός	harsh	7.9
ςκῶμμα*	mockery	XVIIIa.2–3
ςκώπτω	mock	18.10, *XVIIIa.4
ςοβαρότης*	swagger	23.3–4
ςοβαρῶς	haughtily	37.5, T4.J.2
ςοφιςτικός*	sophistical	VIIb.1
ςοφός	wise, skilled	1.7, 9.7, 15.8, 18.8, 22.8, 35.3, *39.15, 46.2–3, 59.4, 62.8–9, 70.12, 81.1, 81.6,

		*84N.1, 82.2, *87N.5, IIa.10–11, IIIa.5, *VIIa.2, VIIa.6, VIIb.12, VIIIa.1, VIIIa.2 bis, VIIIa.7, VIIIa.9, VIIIb.6, IXb.6, IXb.10, *XIa.7, XIIIa.9, XVIIa.5, *XVIIIa.5, XXIa.8, XXIb.6, *T12.M.1
cπάνιοc	occasional	22.8–9
cπάνιc	want	Va.5
cπανίωc*	seldom, sparingly	16.8, 21.7
cπουδαῖοc*	serious	88.4
cτέργω	love	44.7, T1.2.3, T3.H.2
cτερέω	bereave	53.11–12, 72.6–7
cτέρηcιc#	loss	29.3–4
cτοργή	love	54.1–2
cτοχάζομαι	conjecture	1.8, 23.12
cτοχαcτόν	conjecture	57.5–6
cτυγέω	hate	26.3–4
cυγγνώμη	pardon	20.6, XXIIb.3
cυγκαταριθμέω	enroll	VIIa.7–8
cυγκαταcκευαζόμενοc	fellow-student	53.4, 53.7–8
cυγχέω	confuse	IVa.1–2, XVIIb.11, XXIa.2
cυλλογίζομαι	infer	53.2–3
cυμβαίνω	happen	13.7, 58.13, 70.10, 78.5, XVa.3–4
cυμβίωcιc	company	T2.D.6
cυμβουλευτικόc	deliberative	XIIIb.3–4
cυμπαθία	sympathy	43.9
cυμπαθῶc	sympathetically	79.9–10
cυμπαραλαμβάνω	bring in	61.12
cυμπεριφερόμενοc*	accommodating	XIIb.2–3
cυμπεριφορά*	accommodation	XIIa.4
cυμπίπτω	occur	59.7–8
cυμφέρω	be advantageous	1.4, 47.7, Xb.10–11, XVIIIb.1–2, XIXa.3, XXb.8–9, XXIVa.4
cυμφορά#	mishap	66.3–4
cυναιcθάνομαι	perceive (in oneself) *or* perceive in common	1.2–3
cυνανάπτομαι	be attached	11.6–7
cυναντάω	confront	71.4–5
cυναντιλαμβάνομαι	help (oneself to)	39.10–11
cυναριcτάω	dine together	XVIb.10–11
cυνδείπνω	dine together	48.8
cυνεθίζομαι	grow accustomed	XXIIIa.4–5
cυνεκφέρομαι	be carried away	Ib.9
cυνελόντι (εἰπεῖν)	in short	15.6–7
cυνεμπίπτω	come together	8.7–8

σύνεσις	understanding	53.12
συνετός	intelligent	XVIa.6, XIXa.8– 9, XXa.2, XXIa.9–10, XXIb.5, XXIVa.9-10, T3.H.3
συνετῶς	intelligently	Ib.3
συνέχω	encompass, afflict	45.7, 63.10–11, 66.6-7
συνεχῶς	continually	79.4, Ib.3
συνήθης	companion	42.7, 52.12
σύνοιδα	recognize, know	67.5, XIIa.7
συνοίδησις	swelling	67.1
σύνολος	whole	35.10
συνοράω	perceive	XXa.9
συντίθεμαι	conclude	57.9
συντρέφω	bring up	IVb.8
συσχολάζων	fellow-student	75.4–5, 79.3
σφάλλω#	trip up	37.4
σφάλμα*	failing	23.1
σφόδρα	vehemently, strongly	14.6, 28.10, *78.9, Va.10
σφοδρός*	vehement	14.1
σφοδρῶς*	vehemently	5.7, *34.4
σῴζω	save	34.5, 36.1–2, *43.13, *77.3-4, 78.6-7, VIb.10-11
σῶμα	body	39.9
σωτήρ	savior	40.8
σωτηρία	security, salvation	4.9, *T2.D.2
τάγμα	status	XIIIb.4-5
ταπεινός	humble	IVb.10-11
ταπεινῶς*	humbly	75.9
ταχέως	quickly	67.6-7, XXIIb.7
τεθαρρηκότως	boldly	27.6-7
τεκμαίρομαι	infer	T2.D.7-8
τέλειος*	complete, perfect	42.12, 46.9, VIb.13, VIIIa.3-4, VIIIa.4, VIIIa.5, Xa.11
τελειότης	perfection	*56.2, 56.6-7, IXa.8
τελειόω	perfect	74.10-11, IVb.5-6
τελεσφορέω	succeed	#64.13, 65.7-8
τελέως	completely	39.8
τέλος	perfection	56.9
τέλους, διά	consistently	20.9
τέχνη	art	*Ib.14, #IIIb.1
τηρέω	keep up	XVIIIb.10
τιθασεύω	tame	86.2
τίθεμαι	deem, put	49.4-5, 55.4-5
τίθημι	set, place, put	26.4, *29.2, *42.1, XVIa.5
τιμάω*	honor	27.4-5, XXIVb.2
τιμή*	honor	22.6-7, *34.9, XIb.8, XVIIb.7
τολμάω	dare, endure	2.5, 31.12

τόνος	tone	38.4
τόποc	place, topic	77.2, 81.5, XIVb.9
τραχύc	harsh	IIa.6
τρέπομαι	change one's mind	*93N.3, XIIb.11, *XXIIIb.15
τρέφω#	rear	87N.4–5
τρόπον, κατά	properly	53.2
τρόποc	way, character	10.3, 25.3, *43.4, 58.8, VIIb.11–12, XIb.10
τροφή	food	18.1, 18.5
τυγχάνω	encounter, obtain, chance (to, upon), happen by, attain, meet with	12.2–3, 18.4, 23.10, 50.5–6, 56.9, 66.10, 66.12, 76.4, 84.6–7, XXIIb.4, T3.H.1
ὕβρις	insolence	XXIIIb.10–11, *XXIVa.15
ὑβριστικόc*	insolent	37.7
ὑγιήc*	sound	13.9–10
υἱόc	son	29.8–9
ὕμνος	accolade	*15.3, 74.3
ὑπακούω	(pay) heed	10.7, 64.3, 66.9–10
ὑπάρχω*	be, be appropriate, belong	Va.4, VIIa.5, XXa.11–12, *T4.J.4
ὑπερβαίνω	go greatly beyond	XIIa.3–4
ὑπερβαλλόντωc	exceedingly	10.8–9
ὑπερβάλλω#	surmount	66.3
ὑπερβολήν, κατά	abundantly	XIIIa.5
ὑπερέχω	surpass	XXa.7
ὑπερέχων	prominent	VIIa.10
ὑπερηδέωc	most pleasurably	IIb.5–6
ὑπερήφανοc*	arrogant	87N.7–8
ὑπεροκνέομαι*	be very tentative	84.2–3
ὑπεροράω*	disdain	66.3
ὑπεροχή	superiority	XIa.2
ὑποδείκνυμι	exhibit	Xb.11
ὑποδύνω	get under one's skin	XXIVb.10–11
ὑπολαμβάνω	assume, take up	63.4, 79.10–11, IXb.4–5, IXb.11, XIVa.9–10, XXIIa.2, XXIIIb.6–7
ὑπολέγω#	take into account	13.10–11
ὑπόληψιc	assumption	XIb.11–12
ὑπομένω	endure	IIb.7, #87N.7–8
ὑπομιμνῄcκω	remind	38.5–6, VIIIb.8
ὑπόμνηcιc	mention, reminder	68.9–10, *93N.8, XIa.1–2, XIVb.3
ὑπονοέω*	suspect	Xa.1–2, XVa.2, XXIIa.4–5, XXIIIb.9
ὑποπίπτω	happen	1.1
ὑποπτεύω	suspect	46.1–2, XIIIa.2
ὑποcπάω	shy away	48.7–8

ὑποτάττω*	subject, subordinate	34.2, XXIVa.7
ὑποτίθεμαι*	propose for consideration	76.10–11
ὑποφείδομαι	be sparing	51.6
ὑποφέρω	submit	59.4, XXIIIb.2
ὕcτερον	later	66.4, 66.15, 74.4
φαίνομαι	be seen, be shown,	65.3, *82.7, Xb.10,
	seem (the case)	XVIIIa.11, XXIVb.9
φανερόc	clear, obvious	*12.1–2, 13.6, 41.5, 61.8,
		*91N.1, IIb.4, IIb.4–5,
		XIIb.1–2
φαντacία	image	19.6–7, XVIb.4
φάcιc	statement	61.5
φαῦλοc	vulgar	Ia.4
φέρω	endure, bear with	15.5–6, 16.8–9, 36.8, *38.8,
		38.9, 67.10, 88.5–6, 88.9,
		Xb.1–2, XVIIb.14
φεύγω	avoid	T2.D.5–6
φευκτόc*	to be avoided	77.9
φθονέω	envy	62.2, XXIa.11, #XXIIb.16
φθόνοc	envy	Ib.6–7, XXIIIa.2–3
φιλάργυροc*	avaricious	42.2
φιλέω	like, love	44.3, IIIb.11, XIb.9,
		#XIIIa.3, XXb.3–4, XXIa.10,
		T1.2.3
φίληcιc	fondness	48.2–3
φιλία	friendship	28.5, Va.6, *T5.1
φιλικόc	of a friend	*XIXb.1, XIXb.6
φίλιοc	friendly	52.4
φιλοδοξέω	be eager for reputation	XXIIIb.7
φιλόδοξοc*	fond of reputation	XXIIa.10–11
φιλόκακοc	friend of the bad	50.12
φιλόλογοc	scholar	37.4, VIIIa.9, Xa.4
φιλοπαρρηcιάcτηc	lover of frankness	XVIb.5–6
φίλοc	friend	8.10, 15.8–9, *43.4, *43.14,
		50.5, 70.5, 81.3, 81.8, 84.2,
		XIIIa.10
φίλοc (adj.)	pleasing	55.7
φιλοcοφέω	practice philosophy	Ib.3–4
φιλοcοφία	philosophy	59.1–2, IIIb.3, XIVa.9
φιλόcοφοc	philosopher	1.7, 35.3, VIIIa.8, Xa.3,
		*Xb.13–14
φιλοcτοργία	affection	VIIIb.2
φιλοτεχνία	artistry	68.1–2
φιλότηc	love	86.4
φιλότροποc#	attached to character	43.4
φιλόφιλοc	friend to one's friend,	50.8, 85.9
	friendly	
φιλοφροcύνη	kindness	60.11–12

φιλόφρων	well disposed	14.4. 74.5
φίλτατος	dearest	14.9
φοβέομαι	fear	58.12–13, 83.5, XXIIIb.1, XXIVb.12, T2.8.2
φόβος*	fear	86.8
φοιτάω	go	49.10
φορέω	abide	XXa.5, XXIIb.11
φράζομαι	consider	88.11–12
φρενόω	inform	XIIb.4–5
φρονέω	think	51.9
φρόνησις	prudence	56.7–8, XXIa.4
φρόνιμος	wise	XXb.12, XXIIb.15
φυλάττω	guard, defend, keep up	*8.11, 56.12, *78.9, XIIIa.12–13
φύσις	nature	10.9, 19.4, 28.10, *Ia.8, *XXIIb.2
φύω*	be naturally inclined	2.9
φωνή	saying, word	5.3, 20.1, XIIIa.6
φωράω	detect	66.15
χαίρω	rejoice	XIXb.7–8
χαλεπός	difficult	25.8, 34.6
χαριεντίζομαι	be ingratiating	34.8, VIb.5–6
χάριν, πρός	graciously	XXIIIa.6
χάρις	gratitude	VIIIb.13, Xb.11, XVIb.10
χαῦνος	vain	XXIIa.10
χειμάζω	upset	XXIIa.8–9
χειρισμός*	handling	88.4–5
χλευάζω	scorn	62.2
χοροδιδασκαλέω	train a chorus	IIIb.2
χράομαι	employ, handle, make use of	7.9, 14.2, *15.8, 17.2, 21.8, 64.1– 2, 65.2, 70.7, *71.11, *87N.2, Ib.13, IIa.9, *Va.2, Vb.5–6, *Vb.12, XIVb.6, T2.6.5
χρεία	need	39.13
χρή	it is necessary, must, ought	40.1, 51.8, 79.8, *87N.1, 84.5–6, XIVa.7
χρόνος	time	58.12, Vb.7, XXIVa.10, T14.end.4, T14.end.7
χωρέω	give way	2.4
χωρίον	spot	XIIb.6
ψέγω*	censure	33.5–6
ψόγος*	censure	IIa.12
ψεύδομαι	pretend	65.13
ψυχή	soul, heart	39.14, XVIb.3, XXb.9–10
ὠνέομαι	purchase	XVIIIb.4–5

| ὠφελέω | benefit | 32.8–9, 53.10–11, 54.5, 59.5–6, 59.6–7 |
| ὠφελία | benefit | 20.4, 49.5, *VIIIb.14, XVIIb.10–11 |

INDEX VERBORUM

ENGLISH-GREEK

abide	μένω, φορέω
abjectly	ἀνελευθέρως
able, be	δύναμαι
absent, be	ἄπειμι
abundant	δαψιλής
abundantly	καθ᾽ ὑπερβολήν
abuse	λυμαίνομαι
accept	ἀποδέχομαι, προσδέχομαι, προσλαμβάνω
accolade	ὕμνος
accommodating	συμπεριφερόμενος
accommodation	συμπεριφορά
accompany	ἕπομαι, παρακολουθέω
accomplish	ἀνύω, ἀπεργάζομαι, διαπράττω, περαίνω
accuse	αἰτιάομαι
accuser	κατήγορος
accustomed, be	εἴωθα
acknowledge	οἶδα
acknowledge as one's own	οἰκειόω
acquaintance	γνώριμος
act	πρᾶγμα
act (v.)	πράττω
act in secret	λαθραιοπραγέω
action	ἔργον, πρᾶγμα
adapt	ἐφαρμόζω
add	προστίθημι
address, one should	προσαγορευτέον
administer	οἰκονομέω
admit	παρίημι
admonish	νουθετεύω, νουθετέω
admonish, one must	νουθετέον
admonishment	νουθετησία, νουθέτησις
admonition	νουθετεία
advance	προβαίνω
advantageous, be	συμφέρω
advice	παραίνεσις
advise	παραινέω
afar, from	πόρρωθεν
affection	φιλοστοργία

afflict	cυνέχω
age-mate	ὁμῆλιξ
aggressively	θρασέωc
agitating	παραcειτική
agree	ὁμολογέω, ὁμονοέω
alienated, be	ἀποcτρέφεται
allow	ἐάω
amazed, be	θαυμάζω
analogous	ἀνάλογοc
analogously	ἀναλόγωc, ἐκ παραλλήλου
anger	ὀργή
anger, without	ἀοργήτωc
angrily	ὀργίλωc
angry, be	ἀνεποργίζομαι, ὀργίζομαι
annoyance	δυcχεραcμόc
annoyance, with	δυcχερῶc
annoyed, be	δυcχεραίνω
apply	δίδωμι, ἐπιφέρω, προcάγω, προcφέρω
approach	ὁδηγία
approach (v.)	ἐπέρχομαι
appropriate, be	ὑπάρχω
appropriately	οἰκεῖον
argument	λόγοc
arrogant	ὑπερήφανοc
art	τέχνη
artistry	φιλοτεχνία
ascribe	ἀνάπτω, προcυφίcταμαι
ascribed, to be	προcαναθετέον
ashamed, be	αἰcχύνομαι, ἀπαιcχύνομαι
ask in return	ἀπαιτέω
assent	κατάφημι
assistance	βοήθεια
assisting	βοήθεια
assume	ὑπολαμβάνω
assumption	ὑπόληψιc
attack	προcβάλλω
attain	τυγχάνω
attempt	πεῖρα
attention, pay	ἐπιcτρέφομαι, προcέχω
attentive	ἐφεcτηκώc
attuned, must be	ἁρμοcτέον
avaricious	φιλάργυροc
avoid	περίcταμαι, φεύγω
avoided, to be	φευκτόc
aware of, be	ἐπαιcθάνομαι
awareness	αἴcθηcιc
back off	εἴκω
bad	κακόc
bad friend	κακόφιλοc

badly	κακῶς
barbarian language, in a	βαρβαρικῶς
base	μοχθηρός, πονηρός
baseness	μοχθηρία
be	ὑπάρχω
be attached	cυνανάπτομαι
be present	πάρειμι
be there	πρόcειμι
bear, one must	ἀνεκτέον
bear with	φέρω
bearable	ἀνεκτός
befall	παραπίπτω
begin	κατάρχομαι
beginning	ἀρχή
belief	πίcτιc
believe	νομίζω, πιcτεύω
belong	ὑπάρχω
bemused, be	καταναρκάομαι
benefit	ὠφελία
benefit (v.)	ὠφελέω
bereave	cτερέω
best	βέλτιcτα
bestial, be	θηριόομαι
better	βελτίων, κρείττων
birth	γένεcιc
bitter	πικρός
bitterly	πικρῶc
bitterness	πικρότηc
blame	κακιcμός
blame (v.)	κακίζω, μέμφομαι
blameworthy	μεμπτός
boaster	ἀλαζών
body	cῶμα
boldly	τεθαρρηκότωc
book	βυβλίον
bring forward	προcφέρω
bring in	cυμπαραλαμβάνω
bring up	ἐπιφέρομαι
bring up	cυντρέφω
brother	ἀδελφός
burst	διαρρήγνυμαι
calculate, unable to	ἀδιαλόγιcτοc
call	καλέω
call back	μετακαλέω
call (upon)	παρακαλέω
calmly	ἀταράχωc
can	δύναμαι
capacity	ἀφορμή
careful, be	εὐλαβέομαι

caring	κηδεμονικός
carping	μεμψίμοιρος
carried away, be	cυνεκφέρομαι
cast	ἐπιρρ(ε)ίπτω
cast blame	ἐπιμέμφομαι
catch	καταλαμβάνω
cause	αἰτία
cautiously	εὐλαβῶc
cease	λήγω, παύομαι
censure	ψόγοc
censure (v.)	ψέγω
chafe	ἀμύττω
chance (to, upon)	τυγχάνω
change	μεταθεcία
change (v.)	μετατίθεμαι
change (v. trans.)	μετατίθημι
change one's mind	τρέπομαι
changelessness	ἀμεταθεcία
character	διάθεcιc, ἕξιc, ἦθος, τρόπος
character, attached to	φιλότροπος
charge	ἐπιφώνηcιc
charge (v.)	ἐγκαλέω
charlatan	γόηc
chatter	θρυλλόc
cheer, good	εὐφροcύνη
cheerful	εὐήμεροc
cheerful, be	εὐφρονέω
cheerfully	ἱλαρῶc
chide	κακολογέω
child	παῖc
choice	αἵρεcιc
choose	αἱρέομαι, προαιρέομαι
circumscribe	περιέχω
cite	ἐπιφωνέω
clean	καθαρόc
cleansed, be	παρακαθαρεύω
clear	φανερόc
clear, make	διαcαφέω
clearly	διατρανῶc
clothed, be	περιβάλλομαι
clyster	κλυcτήρ
colt	πῶλοc
colt-tamer	πωλοδάμνηc
combine	κεράννυμι
come	βαδίζω, ἥκω
come on	προcεπέρχομαι
come together	cυνεμπίπτω
comic poet	κωμῳδογράφοc
common trait	κοινότηc

daintiness	κομψεία
dare	τολμάω
dawdle	ἐγχρονίζω
dearest	φίλτατος
declare	προφέρω
deed	ἔργον
deem	τίθεμαι
deem worthy	καταξιόω
deep	βαθύς
defend	φυλάττω
defend oneself	ἀπολογέομαι
defense, say in one's	ἀπολογίζομαι
deficiently	ἐλλειπόντως
deflate	κολούω
deliberative	cυμβουλευτικός
delight	γλυκύτης
demonstrate	περιδεικνύω
denial	ἀπόφαcιc
depend on	ἐναπερείδομαι
deprive	ἀποστερέω
depth	βάθος
deserving of	ἄξιοc
desire	ἐπιθυμία
desire (v.)	ἐπιθυμέω, ὀρέγομαι
desist	μεθίcταμαι
desperate	ἀπογνώcιμοc
despise	καταφρονέω
despised, must be	καταφρονητέον
detect	φωράω
deteriorate	μειόομαι
determine	περιγράφω
devoted, be	προcπάcχω
die	ἀποθνήcκω
differ	διαφέρω
difference	διαφορά
different, be	διαφέρω
difficult	χαλεπός
difficulty	δύcκολον
dine together	cυναριcτάω, cυνδείπνω
disappointed, be	παρελπίζω
discern	διαγινώcκω
disciple	μαθητήc
disclose	μηνύω
discover	εὑρίcκω
discredited, be	διαβάλλομαι
discussion, worthy of	ἀξιόλογοc
disdain	ὑπεροράω
disease	νόcημα, νόcοc
disgrace	ἀδοξία

dishearten	ἀθυμόω
dishonor	ἀτιμία
dislike	ἀηδία
disobedience	ἀπειθία
disobey	ἀπειθέω
disparaging	διασυρτικός
dispassionately	ἀπαθῶς
dispose	ἐξοικονομέω
disposed, be	διάκειμαι, διατίθημαι
disposition	διάθεσις
disregard	παρίημι
distinction, without	ἀδιαλήπτως
distinctly	διειλημμένως
distinguish	διαλαμβάνω
distort	διαστρέφω
distrust	ἀπιστέω
disturb	κινέω
diverge	παραλάττω
divert	ἀποδιαστρέφω
do	πράττω
doctor	ἰατρός
dog, little	κυνίδιον
doubt	διστάζω
draw	ἀνάγομαι
draw away	ἀποσπάω
drink	πίνω
eagerness	προθυμία
earlier	πρότερον
easily, more	ῥᾷον
effective	δραστική
effortlessly	ἀμοχθεί
eminent, be	διαπρέπω
employ	χράομαι
empty	κενεός, κενός
enchant	κατεπᾴδω
encompass	συνέχω
encounter	ἐντυγχάνω, τυγχάνω
encourage	διακελεύομαι
end up	ἐκτελέω
endure	τολμάω, ὑπομένω, φέρω
enmity	ἔχθρα
enraged	θυμόομαι
enroll	συγκαταριθμέω
entice	δελεάζω
entreaty	λιτή
envy	φθόνος
envy (v.)	φθονέω
epitome, by way of an	ἐπιτομικῶς
equal	ἴσος

equally	ἐξ ἴcου
err	ἁμαρτάνω, διαμαρτάνω, ἐξαμαρτάνω
error	ἁμάρτημα, ἁμαρτία, διαμαρτία
error, prone to	ἁμαρτωλόc
escape notice	λανθάνω
establish	καθίcτημι
evil	πονηρόc
evil (n.)	κακόν
evilly	κακῶc
exactly	ἀκριβῶc
examine	διαλέγω, ἐξετάζω
exceedingly	ὑπερβαλλόντωc
exhaustively	ἀνελλιπῶc
exhibit	ἐπιδείκνυμι, παρέχω, προcφέρομαι, ὑποδείκνυμι
exhort	παρακαλέω, προτρέπομαι
expect	κατελπίζω, προcδοκάω
expectation	προcδοκία
experience	πάcχω
explore	ζητέω
expose	ἐλέγχω
external	ἔξωθεν
eye	ὄμμα
failing	ἐλάττωcιc, cφάλμα
failure	διάπτωcιc
false modesty	δυcωπία
fame, indifferent to	ἀφιλόδοξοc
family	οἰκεῖοι
famous	λαμπρόc
fare well	εὐτυχέω
father	πατήρ
fatuity	ἀβελτερία
favorably	εὐνόωc
favoritism, show	καταχαρίζομαι
fear	δέοc, φόβοc
fear (v.)	φοβέομαι
fearless	ἀδεήc
feeling	πάθοc
feign	ἀναπλάττω
fellow-student	cυγκαταcκευαζόμενοc, cυcχολάζων
fine	καλόc
first	πρότερον
fitting	πρόcφοροc
fittingly	δεόντωc
fixed	μόνιμοc
flatter	κολακεύω
flattering	κολακευτικόc
flattery	κολακεία
flinch	πηδάω

flock	ἀγέλη
follow	παρακολουθέω
folly	μανία
fondness	φίλησις
food	τροφή
foolish	ἀνόητος, ἄφρων, μωρός
foolish, be	ἀφρονέω
foolishness	ἀφροσύνη
foreign	ἀλλότριος
foremost	ἄκρος
foresee	προνοέομαι
foresight	πρόνοια
forget	διαλανθάνομαι, ἐπιλανθάνομαι
form	εἶδος
forthrightly	ἀνυποστόλως
fortunate	εὐτυχής
frank, be	παρρησιάζομαι
frank criticism	παρρησία
frank speaker	παρρησιάστης
frankness	παρρησία
frankness, lover of	φιλοπαρρησιάστης
friend	φίλος
friend, bad	κακόφιλος
friend, of a	φιλικός
friend of the bad	φιλόκακος
friend to one's friend	φιλόφιλος
friendly	φίλιος, φιλόφιλος
friendship	φιλία
furious, be	μαίνομαι
gain	προσλαμβάνω
gather together	ἐπαθροίζω
generally	κοινῶς
genre	γένος
gentle	ἤπιος
gently	πραέως
give	δίδωμι
give away	μεταδίδωμι
give over	παραδίδωμι
give up	ἀπαγορεύω, ἀπογινώσκω
give way	χωρέω
gladly	ἡδέως
go	φοιτάω
go greatly beyond	ὑπερβαίνω
go (over)	ἐπέρχομαι
go through	διαγίνομαι
goad	κέντρον
god	θεός
good	ἀγαθός
goodwill	εὔνοια

goodwill, bear	εὐνοέω
graceful	πολυχαρής
graciously	δεξιῶς, πρὸς χάριν
grasp	καταλαμβάνω
gratitude	χάρις
great	μέγας
Greek	ἀχαιός
Greek, in	ἑλληνικῶς
grey	πολιός
grey, turn	πολιόω
groundless	ἀγένητος
grow accustomed	συνεθίζομαι
guard	φυλάττω
guide	ὁδηγός
habits	ἔθος
halt	ἵσταμαι
handle	ἐξεργάζομαι, χράομαι
handling	χειρισμός
happen	παρεμπίπτω, συμβαίνω, ὑποπίπτω
happen by	τυγχάνω
harm	βλάπτω
harmless	ἄλυπος
harsh	δριμύ, σκληρός, τραχύς
hate	μισέω, στυγέω
haughtily	σοβαρῶς
head	κεφαλή
heal	ἀκέομαι, ἰάομαι
healable	ἀκεστικός
hear	ἀκούω
heart	ψυχή
heart, in the	ἐγκάρδιος
heavens	αἰθήρ
heed, pay	ὑπακούω
height, be at its	ἀκμάζω
heighten	ἐπιτείνω
hellebore	ἑλλέβορος
help	βοηθέω
help (oneself to)	συναντιλαμβάνομαι
helper	βοηθός
hide	κρύπτω
hinder	ἀντικρούω
honor	τιμή
honor (v.)	τιμάω
human being	ἄνθρωπος
humble	ταπεινός
humbly	ταπεινῶς
hunter	θηρευτής
hurt	λυπέω, πονέω
hypothesis	θέσις

ignorance	ἄγνοια, ἀμαθία
ignorant, be	ἀγνόω
ignore	καταγνοέω
ill, be	νοσέω
ill will	δύcνοια
illustrious	λαμπρόc
image	εἴδωλον, φαντασία
imitate	μιμέομαι
imitation	ἀπομίμηcιc
impersonal	ἀπρόcωποc
important	κύριοc
impossible	ἀδύνατοc
improper	ἀπρεπήc
impulsive	θραcύc
in accord with one's character	προcχαρακτηρικῶc
in general	καθόλου
in short	cυνελόντι (εἰπεῖν)
inappropriately	ἀνοικείωc
inclined	εὐεπίφοροc
incomparable	ἀcύμβλητοc
incurable	ἀναλθήc, ἀνήκεcτοc
indicate	ἐμφαίνω, ἐπιcημαίνω
indifferent, be	ἀπαθέω
individual character	ἰδιώτηc
individual trait	ἰδίωμα
induce	αἱρέω
infer	cυλλογίζομαι, τεκμαίρομαι
infer from signs	cημειόομαι
inflame further	προcεκκάω
inflict	παρεμβάλλω
inform	φρενόω
ingratiating, be	χαριεντίζομαι
injury	βλάβη
inquire	πυνθάνομαι
inquire further	ἐπιζητέομαι
insinuate oneself	παρυποδύνω
insolence	ἀcέλγεια, ὕβριc
insolent	ὑβριcτικόc
instruct	καταcκευάζω
insubordination	ἀνυποταξία
insult	λοιδορία
insult (v.)	λοιδορέομαι, λοιδορέω
intellect	διάνοια
intelligent	cυνετόc
intelligently	cυνετῶc
intemperate	ἄνετοc
intense	ἀτενήc, ἐπιτεταμένοc
intensify	ἐπιτείνω
intentionally	ἐξεπίτηδεc

interpretation of signs	cημείωcιc
interrogate	ἀνακρίνω
invisible	ἀόρατος
invite	παρακαλέω
involved, be	ἐνέχομαι
irascible	ἀκράχολος, ὀργίλος
irk	νύττω
irony	εἰρωνία
irritable	ἐρεθιcτός
irritate	ἐρεθίζω
irritated, be very	διερεθίζομαι
irritation	ἐρεθιcμός, κνίcμα
jab	καταφορά
jettison	ἀπαντλέω
jointly	κοινῶc
jokes, make	διαπαίζω
judge	νοέω
judge right	καταξιόω
just	δίκαιος
just now	πρώην
keep up	τηρέω, φυλάττω
kind	εἶδος, γένος
kindness	φιλοφροcύνη
king	βαcιλεύς
kinsman	προcήκων
know	γινώcκω, οἶδα, cύνοιδα
know beforehand	πρόοιδα
knowledge	ἱcτορία
labor	πονέω
lad	μειράκιον
large	ἁδρός
later	ὕcτερον
laugh at	ἐπεγγελάω, διαγελάω
laughter	γέλωc
lavish	περιττός
layman	ἰδιώτηc
laziness	ἀργία
learn	καταμανθάνω, πυνθάνομαι
letter	ἐπιcτολή
liable, be	ὀφλιcκάνω
life	βίοc, ζωή
life, way of	δίαιτα
lift up	ἐπαίρω
lightly	ῥᾳδίωc
like	παραπλήcιοc
like (adv.)	παραπλήcιον
like (v.)	φιλέω
likely	εἰκόc
liking	ἡδονή

limit	περιγράφω
listen	ἀκούω
little by little	κατὰ ὀλίγον
live	ζάω
logically	ἐπιλογιστικῶς
long stretch	μακρότης
long-term	πολυχρόνιος
look to	βλέπω, διαβλέπω
look-out, be on the	ἀντιδοκεύω
loss	στέρησις
loss, be at a	ἀπορέω
love	ἀγάπη, ἀγάπησις, στοργή, φιλότης
love (v.)	στέργω, φιλέω
love, be in	ἐράω
lover of frankness	φιλοπαρρησιάστης
maddened, be	θυμόομαι
madness	ἀπόνοια
magnitude	μέγεθος
maintain	ἵσταμαι
make a mistake	διαπίπτω
make claims for	παρέχομαι
make use of	χράομαι
malediction	κατάρα
malign	βλασφημέω
man	ἀνήρ
manage	οἰκονομέω
mark, hit the	κατατυγχάνω
mark, miss the	ἀποτυγχάνω
mark, missing the	ἀστόχως
mean	μέσος
measure	μέτρον
measure out	μετρέω
medicine	ἀκεῖον
meet with	τυγχάνω
memorize	διαλαμβάνω
mention	ὑπόμνησις
merriment	διάχυσις
mete out	μερίζω
mild	βληχρός, πρᾶος
mildly	ἐπιεικῶς
minimal	ἐλάχιστος
mishap	συμφορά
mixed	μεικτός
mock	σκώπτω
mockery	σκῶμμα
moderate	μέτριος
moderately	μετρίως
moderation, in	μετρίως
moment (critical or right)	καιρός

move	κινέω
move on	μεταβαίνω
multitude	πλῆθος
music, make	μουσιάζω
must	χρή
naturally inclined, be	φύω
nature	φύσις
nearby	πέλας
necessarily	ἀναγκαίως
necessary, be	δέον
necessary, it is	χρή
necessity	ἀνάγκη
need	χρεία
need, be in	προσδέομαι
need, in	καταδεήc
need (v.)	δέομαι
neglect	ἀμελέω
new	καινός
nicely	καλῶς
nobility	εὐγένεια
nobly	καλῶς
notice, escape	λανθάνω
obdurate	δυσκίνητος
obey	πειθαρχέω
observe	ἐπιβλέπω, θεωρέω
obstruct	καταποδίζω
obtain	κομίζομαι, τυγχάνω
obvious	δῆλος, φανερός
obvious that	δηλονότι
occasional	σπάνιος
occur	συμπίπτω
offense	λύμη
offensive, be	δυσχεραίνομαι
office	ἔργον
offshoot	ἀπότομος
old	πρεσβύτης
old age	γῆρας
old, grow	γηράσκω
old man	γέρων
one's own	οἰκεῖος
one's own, acknowledge as	οἰκειόω
only	μόνος
operation	διαίρεσις
opinion	οἴησις
opinion, have the	δοξάζω
opportunity	καιρός
oppose	ἀντιτάττομαι
opposed	ἐναντίον
opposite	ἐναντίον

order	κελεύω
orderliness	κόσμος
ought	χρή
outstanding	ἔξοχος
overlook	παροράω
own (one's)	ἴδιος
pained, be	ὀδυνάομαι
painful	ὀδυνηρός
painful, more	ἀλγίων
painfully	περιλύπως
pardon	cυγγνώμη
parent	γονεύς
pass	παρέρχομαι
passion	θυμός, πάθος
passionate for, be	ἐράω
peer	ἡλικιώτης
people	δῆμος
perceive	cυνοράω
perceive in common	cυναιcθάνομαι
perceive (in oneself)	cυναιcθάνομαι
perfect	τέλειος
perfect (v.)	τελειόω
perfection	τελειότης, τέλος
perform	ἐπιτηδέω, πράττω
persistence	προσκαρτέρηcιc
persistently	προσκαρτερητικῶc
person	ἄνθρωπος, πρόcωπον
person-tamer	ἀνθρωποδάμνης
persuade	πείθω
philosopher	φιλόcοφος
philosophy	φιλοcοφία
philosophy, practice	φιλοcοφέω
pique	κνίζω
pity	ἐλέω
place	τόπος
place (v.)	τίθημι
pleasantly, more	ἥδιον
please	ἀρέcκω
pleasing	φίλος
pleasurably	ἡδέως
pleasurably, most	ὑπερηδέως
pleasure	ἡδονή
pleasure, with	ἡδέως
pleasurelessly	ἀηδῶc
plentiful	δαψιλής
point of departure	ἀρχή
point out	δείκνυμι, παραδείκνυμι
polite	ἀcτεῖος
politely	ἀcτείως

politeness	ἀπευφημισμός
politician	δημαγωγός
portray	μιμέομαι
possessed	κατάσχετος
possible	δυνατόν
power	δύναμις
powerful, be	δύναμαι
practically	ἐμπράκτως
practice	ἄγω
practice an art	διαφιλοτεχνέω
praise	αἴνεσις, ἔπαινος
praise (v.)	ἐπαινέω
pray	εὔχομαι
precise, be	ἀκρειβόω
preconceive	προλαμβάνω
predominantly	πλεοναζόντως
preferable	κρείττων
preparation	προκατασκευή
present	δίδωμι, ἐπέχω, παρέχω, προσφέρομαι
pretend	προσποιέομαι, ψεύδομαι
pretense	πλάσμα
pretty much	ἐπιεικῶς
prevent	κωλύω
private	ἰδιωτικός
probe	διακινέω
proceed	ἔρχομαι, προβαίνω
procrastination	ἀναβολή
profit	ὀνίναμαι
prognostication	προσημείωσις
progress	προκοπή
prominent	ὑπερέχων
promptly	προχείρως
prone	εὐεπίφορος
properly	κατὰ τρόπον
propose for consideration	ὑποτίθεμαι
provision	παρασκευή
prudence	φρόνησις
publicly	κοινῶς
puff up	ἐκχαυνόω
puffed up	ἀνατεταμένος
purchase	ὠνέομαι
pure, be	καθαρεύω
purge	κένωμα
purge (v.)	κενόω
purification	κάθαρσις
purify	ἁγνεύω
put	τίθεμαι, τίθημι
put forward	προβάλλω
quality	ποιότης

quickly	ταχέωc
reach	καταντάω
rear	τρέφω
rear the neck	ἀπαυχενίζω
reason	λογιcμόc, λόγοc
reason (cause)	αἰτία, αἴτιον
reason (v.)	λογίζομαι
reason falsely	παραλογίζομαι
reasonable	εὐλόγιcτον, εὔλογοc
reasonable argument	εὐλογία
reasonably	εὐλόγωc
rebuke	ἐπίπληξιc
rebuke (v.)	ἐπιπλήττω
receive	δέχομαι, λαμβάνω
recognition	ἐπίγνωcιc
recognize	γινώcκω, ἐπιγινώcκω, cύνοιδα
recourse	ἀποcτροφή
recover	ἀπαλλάττω
reduce	ἐλλατόω
reform	μεταποιέω
refrain	ἀπέχομαι
rejoice	εὐφραίνω, χαίρω
rejoinder	ἀπάντηcιc
relationship	ἀναλογία
relax	ἀνίημι
relevant	προcών
relieve	κουφίζω
rely	προcαναπαύομαι
remember	μέμνημαι, μνημονεύω
remind	μιμνήcκω, ὑπομιμνήcκω
reminder	ὑπόμνηcιc
remiss, be	ῥαθυμέω
remit	ἐφίημι
renew	ἀνανεόομαι
repeat	καταλέγω
repel	ἀλλοτριόω
report	ἀπαγγέλλω, ἐμφανίζω, προcαναφέρω
reproach	ἐπιτίμηcιc, ἐπιφορά
reproach (v.)	ἐπιτιμάω
reprove	ἐπικόπτω
reputation	δόξα
reputation, be eager for	φιλοδοξέω
reputation, desire for	δοξοκοπία
reputation, fond of	φιλόδοξοc
repute, ill	ἀδοξία
resemblance	ἀναλογία
resist	ἀντέχω, ἀντιτείνω
resolutely	ἀτενῶc
resource	περιουcία

respond (with)	ἀποδίδωμι
restore	ἀναπλάττω
restore fully	διανορθόω
restrain	ἐπέχω
result	περιγίνομαι
resume	ἀναλαμβάνω
return	καταγωγή
return (v.)	ἐπανέρχομαι
reveal	δηλόω, ἐκκαλύπτω, ἐμφαίνω
revelation	ἐπιφάνεια
revere	θαυμάζω
reverence	σεβασμός
revile	ὀνειδίζω
rhythms, expert in	ῥυθμικός
richness	εὐθήνησις
ridicule	ἀνακάκχεσις
ridicule (v.)	κωμῳδέω, προπηλακίζω
ridiculous	καταγέλαστος
right	ὀρθός
rightly	ὀρθῶς
rigidly	παγίως
rise	ἐξανίσταμαι
risked, it must be	παρακινδυνευτέον
ruin, come to	ἀπόλλυμαι
rule	κανών
rule (v.)	ἄρχω
run up	προστροχάζω
said, must be	ῥητέον
sailing	πλοῦς
salvation	σωτηρία
save	σῴζω
savior	σωτήρ
say (future)	ἐρέω
saying	φωνή
scalpel	ζμίλιον
scholar	φιλόλογος
scorn	καθυβρίζω, χλευάζω
scrutinize	περιαθρέω
second	δεύτερος
secret, act in	λαθραιοπραγέω
security	ἀσφάλεια, σωτηρία
see	βλέπω, ὁράω
seek	ἐπιζητέω, ζητέω
seem	δοκέω
seem (the case)	φαίνομαι
seen, be	φαίνομαι
seize	ἐλλαμβάνω
seldom	σπανίως
selectively	ἐλλιπῶς

senseless   ἀγνώμων
sententious   ἀποφθεγματίας
separation   ἀποσπασμός
serious   μέγας, σπουδαῖος
service, do a   εὐεργετέω
set   τίθημι
set forth   διατίθημι, ἐκτίθημι
setting right   ἀπόθεσις
shame   αἰδώς, αἰσχύνη
shameful   αἰσχρός
share   μέρος
share (v.)   μεταδίδωμι
sharp   πικρός
shout at   ἐπικραυγάζω
show   δείκνυμι, ἐκφαίνω, ἐπιδείκνυμι
show off   περιαυτίζομαι
shown, be   φαίνομαι
shrink from, one must   ἀποκνητέον
shun   ἀφίσταμαι
shy   αἰδήμων
shy away   ὑποσπάω
sick   ἀσθενής
sign   σημεῖον
signs, infer from   σημειόομαι
signs, interpretation of   σημείωσις
silence   ἡσυχία
silly   ἄνους
similarity   ὁμοιότης
simile   ὁμοίωσις
simply   ἁπλῶς
sincerely   ἀκεραίως
skilled   σοφός
skillfully   ἐντέχνως
skim   ἀπομάσσω
skin, get under one's   ὑποδύνω
slander   διαβολή
slander (v.)   διαβάλλω
slanderer   διάβολος
slave   οἰκέτης
slight   παραμελέω
slip   παράπτωσις
slip (v.)   πίπτω
slip up   διαπίπτω
sluggish   νωθρός
smack of   προσβάλλω
snappish   κυνώδης
sociability   περιφορά
sociable   κοινός, πότιμος
sociably   περιφερόμενος

solemnly, most	cεμνότατα
son	υἱός
sophistical	coφιcτικός
soul	ψυχή
sound	ὑγιής
sparing, be	ὑποφείδομαι
sparingly	cπανίως
speak	λαλέω
speak badly of	δυcφημέω
speak frankly	ἐπιπαρρηcιάζομαι, παρρηcιάζομαι, παρρηcιάζω
speak out (future)	ἐξερέω
speech	λόγος
spirit	θυμός
spot	χωρίον
stage, bring on	εἰcάγω
stamp	ἐκκόπτω
state	διατίθημι
statement	φάcιc
status	τάγμα
stay	μένω
sting	δηγμός
sting (v.)	δάκνω
stinging	δηκτικός
stop	παύομαι
strained	ἐπιτεταμένος
stress	ἀνάταcιc
strict	ἀκριβής
strictly	ἄκρως
stride	περιπατέω
strip	γυμνόω
strong	ἰcχυρός
strongly	cφόδρα
strut	πομπεύω
student	καταcκευαζόμενος
subject	ὑποτάττω
submit	ὑποφέρω
subordinate	ὑποτάττω
subtle	ποικίλος
subtly	ποικίλως
succeed	ἐφικνέομαι, κατορθόω, τελεcφορέω
success	ἐπιτυχία
sudden	αἰφνίδιος
suffer	ἀλγέω, πάcχω
suffer undeservedly	ἀναξιοπαθέω
suffice	ἀποχράω
suitable	ἴδιος
suitable, be	προcήκω
suitably	προcηκόντως

suited, be	ἐιτήδειος
superiority	ὑπεροχή
supplies	ἐφόδιον
suppose	διαλαμβάνω
surmount	ὑπερβάλλω
surpass	ὑπερέχω
suspect	παρυπονοέω, ὑπονοέω, ὑποπτεύω
swagger	cοβαρότηc
sweetest	γλυκύτατος
swelling	cυνοίδηcιc
sympathetically	cυμπαθῶc
sympathy	cυμπαθία
take	λαμβάνω
take into account	ὑπολέγω
take up	ἀναιρέομαι, ὑπολαμβάνω
talk	λαλέω
talk back	ἀντιλέγω
tame	τιθαcεύω
tame human beings	ἀνθρωποδαμνάω
tame like a colt	πωλοδαμνάω
teach	διδάcκω, καθηγέομαι, παιδεύω
teacher	καθηγητήc, καθηγούμενος
tear	δάκρυον
tell	προcεπεῖπον
ten thousand	μύριοι
tender	ἀπαλόc
tentative, be very	ὑπεροκνέομαι
terrible	δεινόc
terribly	δεινῶc
test	ἐξελέγχω
thankful, be	εὐχαριcτέω
thankfulness	εὐχαριcτία
theoretical	κατὰ πρόβλημα
think	νοέω, οἶμαι, φρονέω
think right	ἀξιόω
think worthy	ἀξιόω
time	χρόνος
today	cήμερον
toil	πόνοc
tolerate	ἀνέχομαι
tone	τόνος
tongue	γλῶcσα
topic	τόπος
totally	καθόλου
touch upon	παρεφάπτομαι
train a chorus	χοροδιδαcκαλέω
transfer	μεταγωγή
transfer (v.)	μετάγω, μετατίθημι, μεταφέρω
transmit	παραδίδωμι

treat	διαλαμβάνω
treat fully	κατεγχειρέω
treat (medically)	θεραπεύω
treat roughly	βιάζω
treatment	ἐπίcτacιc, θεραπεία, θεράπευcιc
trip, make a	πορεύομαι
trip up	cφάλλω
trouble, give	ἐνοχλέω
truly	ὄντωc
truth	ἀλήθεια
truthful	ἀληθινόc
try	πειράομαι
turn away	ἀποτρέπομαι
turn away (trans.)	ἀποτρέπω, ἀποφέρω
turn out	ἀποβαίνω
tyrannically	δεcποτικῶc
unable, be	ἀδυνατέω
unaccepted	ἀπρόcληπτοc
unbeknownst	ἀγνώcτωc
understand	ἐπίcταμαι
understanding	cύνεcιc
undo	λύω
unendurable	ἀφόρητοc
unexamined	ἀνεφόδευτοc
unexpected	παράλογοc .
unfriendly	ἄφιλοc
unhesitatingly	ἀπροφαcίcτωc
unmovable	ἀκίνητοc
unrecognized, be	ἀγνοέομαι
unspoken	ἄρρητοc
untoward	παράδοξοc
untreatable	ἀθεράπευτοc
unworthy	ἀνάξιοc
upbraid	καθάπτομαι
upbringing	ἐκτροφή
upset	χειμάζω
urge on	ἐπείγω
utter	λαλέω
vain	χαῦνοc
vehement	cφοδρόc
vehemently	cφόδρα, cφοδρῶc
very	μεγάλωc
vexed, be	ἄχθομαι
vice	κακία
vigorously	ἐρρωμένωc
virtue	ἀρετή
voluntarily	ἐθελόντηc
vulgar	φαῦλοc
vulgarity	ἀπειροκαλία

wage	ἐπίχειρον
wait for	προσμένω
wandering about	πλανωδῶc
want	cπάνιc
want (v.)	βούλομαι
wanting, be	δέον
war, make	πολεμέω
ward off	ἀμύνομαι
watchfulness	ἐπαγρύπνηcιc
way	δίκη, τρόποc
weak	ἀcθενήc
weaken	μειόομαι
weakness	ἀcθένεια
welcoming (n.)	δεξιά
well	καλῶc
well disposed	φιλόφρων
well-being	εὐτύχημα
wheedling	θωπεία
whip	μαcτιγόω
whole	cύνολοc
winged	πτηνόc
wise	cοφόc, φρόνιμοc
wish	θέλω
withdraw	ἀπάγω
woman	γυνή
word	λόγοc, μῦθοc, φωνή
work, hard	ἔργον
world	κόcμοc
wormwood	ἀψίνθιον
worth	ἀξία
worth (adj.)	ἄξιοc
worthy	ἀξιόπιcτοc
write	γράφω
wrong	ἀδικέω
wrongly	ἀτόπωc
young	νέοc
youngster	νεανίcκοc
youth	νεότηc

INDEX NOMINUM

CPSIA information can be obtained
at www.ICGtesting.com
Printed in the USA
BVOW08s1242050117
472561BV00003B/123/P

9 781589 832923